Corporate Ties

Corporate Ties

Relocation, Recruitment,
and Romance
in the Workplace*

By Ben Woods

*Business gibberish included!

This is a work of fiction. Any references to real people (living or dead), historical events, establishments, organizations, or locations are used solely to lend the fiction an appropriate cultural and historical setting. There is definitely some junk in this book that may seem all too familiar to certain individuals. But let's face it: How many times have you read fiction and wondered if the author was actually stalking you to add flavor for his next novel?

To help debug future versions of this book, please send corrections and comments to info@spumonipress.com.

Website: corporatetiesbook.com

ISBN: 978-0-9827819-0-6

Publisher: Spumoni Press, Baltimore, Maryland
Publisher Website: spumonipress.com

Designed by Brad Samuelson and Ben Woods
Edited by Patrick Coyle and Georgette Beatty

First Edition: September 2011

In the first place, know who you are,
and then adorn yourself appropriately.

- Epictetus

1
The Big News

Wednesday, June 22

This type of email could mean a few things in my line of work. Spam would be the obvious guess, even if on the surface, it appears to have originated from someone inside the company. At least, I assume this lady works here. Her email signature line looks legit, and as I squint at the phone list (printed at roughly 8 percent to fit on a single side), I find her name.

However, spammers could easily fake this email. The problem, though, is there are no links to porn sites or V1@GR@

pitches, no politicians-in-drag attachments, and no Nigerian here's-15-million-dollars-I'm-dying schemes. There's not even a random paragraph of words below the message that spammers use to discombobulate email filters.

And why would a hacker want to fool everyone here into surfacing at the downstairs conference room? Would he be providing coffee and doughnuts during a seminar titled "Your Email, Your Profit"?

No, this email probably means something much worse, like mass firings. That's about as final as you can get — well, unless they are planning to kill us, bury us in the parking lot across the street, and continue to spam our unused email accounts.

Don is packing. He lives in a cubicle diagonal from mine. I peer around the partition and watch him thump books into a cardboard box, which sits on top of another box already full and sealed.

Where did the boxes come from? I don't even think he knows. Did the spammers leave a trail of containers for believability? Don doesn't appear to be concerned with the reason; he just wants to be the first one out the door and beat the traffic in the funnel-shaped parking garage.

After reading the email one last time, it occurs to me that the meeting might be a way to warn us of a terrorist attack. But through my eighth day, I'm not so sure that would be much of a change here.

Let me clarify. There haven't been any weapons involved (to my knowledge), and I haven't had to watch any telecasts that are months old regarding our mission to destroy a religiously oppressive country. Mettle Life Insurance, located in Louisville, Kentucky, is just a blip in the financial world, trying to overthrow the gargantuan pecuniary players in the global market by offering somewhat different products.

Instead of jihads, we sell annuities, from what I understand.

Then again, I haven't actually seen an annuity, let alone a sold one. It's not like I've been to the gift shop yet.

Or maybe people purchase them through the website I'm supposed to be maintaining, but in less than two weeks, I haven't gotten that far yet. Jeff said he was going to train me on a few things, but he's on the phone. He sits across from me, but I can't see him. Our computers face each other, but cubicles separate us. We can't even play footsie.

"Oh, I see," says Jeff to the person on the phone. "Well, I've been calling around to find out what's up. No one up here seems to know. OK, let me know if you find out anything."

He hangs up, possibly with some info about the mysterious email. The good thing is that I don't have to leave my cubicle; Jeff will come over and tell me. To this point, I have noticed that he is the glue that holds our web development team together, delivering messages faster than Western Union and Hermes.

Jeff rolls his seat into my cubicle, spinning two full revolutions, which is good for at least a 9 in the Olympic Swivel Chair competition.

"Raj's not positive, but he thinks something big is going on," Jeff says.

"Big?" I say. "Like what?"

"So big that he apparently doesn't have any details," Jeff says. "No one on his floor does."

"How could no one know?"

"Who knows? Oh well, I guess I'll go think about it a little more on the crapper."

Regardless of what happens, packing does seem like a good idea. At least I don't have much to store; the only thing on my desk, besides my computer, is the corporate handbook, which I use to keep dust from reaching my desk.

I decide to ask Barry for his opinion, because he's been with the company for a fairly long time. I walk over to Barry's cube and notice he is frantically calling people on his phone.

"Well hello there, Jason," Barry says. "Don't ask about the email. I'm not sure what to make of it. So can you sub for volleyball tonight or what?"

Possibly his next call will reveal something important.

"No, no, we're still on for lunch. I'd like to go earlier, I'm already hungry, but I have to go to this stupid meeting at 10. And it's not even 9 right now!"

Not wishing to loiter any longer, I pass by a few other cubes and wander over to Ken's and Diya's areas. They both appear to be working, but they are also both experts at moving windows around on their machines to pretend they are doing something noteworthy.

Ken is talking on the phone at a whisper level, reading and sending new email. Diya, on the other hand, has her head buried in a command line window, perhaps analyzing data. However, I keep my distance because according to Ken, interrupting Diya can cause the systems to crash.

Ken notices me standing between the adjacent cubes, and at the same instant, Jeff returns to propagate the latest news.

"Raj doesn't know anything," Jeff says to Ken, also catching Diya's attention.

"No one on our floor seems to know, either," Ken says.

"Why is he packing?" I say, peering over to Don's area.

"Don is always doing his own thing," Diya says.

I just reached the point where I can remember the names of my team members.

As the new guy, I have no freakin' idea who may actually hold the truth behind the email. Let's face it, though — the spammers and terrorists could make their moves at any time.

During the next hour, numerous other questions enter my mind. Are they firing everyone? Are we moving? Will my position be eliminated? Do you have to move to Nigeria to run a Nigerian spam scheme? My coworkers on the seventh floor continue to mull the responses they have received so far. Most comments point toward something big, and Don continues to stock his boxes. Barry, meanwhile, continues to look for that elusive sixth player for his Wednesday night volleyball team.

I can't help but consider that I am being set up for an

unprovoked catastrophe with the job I began just eight days ago.

"Why would they even hire you to start with if they are going to let you go?" Ken says.

"I don't know. It's a little odd they didn't tell me that when I started," I say. "Surely this isn't something they came up with overnight."

"If they are announcing something today, they've known for a while. But the head honchos at Northern Lineage don't always let everyone know what's happening. A few years ago, they hired a guy specifically for one type of programming, and a week later, they stopped using that program."

"So what happened with that guy?"

"He fell into a vat of lava downstairs," shouts Don from his cube. "Beware of that first left when you go to the basement."

"He was just a contractor," Ken says.

That really doesn't make me feel any better. Not the part about the lava — of course, that scares the shit out of me — but I just spent three-and-a-half months looking for a job, and I'm not ready to start looking again. The people here are nice enough and extraordinarily quirky.

I wander back to Jeff's cube to see if he's ready to head to the meeting in the basement. It's already teetering on 10 a.m. I think he's doing maintenance work, but separating work from play is sometimes difficult with Jeff. He's one of the few people I know who can seemingly get almost as much work accomplished while screwing around as he does actually concentrating.

Barry and Ken also gather outside Jeff's cube, which I found out last week is the official town meeting place. Jeff pushes away from his desk and heads behind us toward the seventh-floor elevator. We descend to the basement, packed like beef jerky in a cardboard box, minus the individual plastic wrapping.

I follow Jeff, Barry, and Ken to the middle rows, although

I'd rather find Diya and sit next to her. Let's face it: She's a female programmer, and she's cute. How often does that appear in a non-virtual world setting? She hasn't appeared yet, but I do find a seat next to the guys. Up front, there are a handful of important-looking people, none of whom I've ever seen.

"Who are these guys?" I ask the others.

"That's Ryan Bender, the president of Mettle," says Jeff, pointing to the man on the left. "And the other guy is Claude Simpson. He's the president of Northern Lineage Financial. This is huge ... I wouldn't have expected him to be here."

The two men seem to be having a jovial time, exchanging short comments and jokes.

"They look like the best of buds," I say.

"When your company makes $100 million a year not doing much of anything, it's easy to joke," Ken says.

The lady on stage introduces herself as Ann. I assume she's the email creator/spammer. She speaks briefly and calls Bender to the podium. Bender glares out to the crowd for a fortnight. He then locks his eyes to the paper in front of him. This is a bad signal to me. I brace for the worst.

"This has been a difficult decision to make, but in the end, we think this will be a huge step up, and the best scenario for Mettle Life Insurance as a whole. We are announcing today that essentially all of the staff based in Louisville will move to Cincinnati and merge forces with the parent company. It will be a challenge, but an exciting challenge that we hope all of you will accept."

Jeff and Ken both have looks of indifference on their faces, yet I can sense their minds are churning. I try to make eye contact with Diya, who is in the back, but she's still looking at Bender, probably hoping for more information. I scan the room for Don, who must have already departed.

Barry, seated to my left, has his head buried in his lap. I go over to console him, but I realize he's just scanning a takeout menu for one of the local Chinese restaurants.

2
Aftershock

Wednesday, June 22 (continued)

My life has become a cross between a low-budget '80s film and a game show. "Hey guys, I'm in charge, and you need to pack your bags for a trip to … your new cubicle, centrally located nowhere near your current location!"

I'm back at my desk, breathing heavily and waiting for everyone else to return from the basement. Standing among what seemed like millions of business people at the meeting was bad enough. I realized they were all staring at me. I thought maybe I had a stain on my shirt, or possibly I had forgotten to remove my clown nose/eye patch combo. When I found both in my pocket, I realized there must be another reason.

As they filed into the cattle-herding elevator, I waited for the punch line. "Hilarious, guys," I was ready to shout. "You really had me going, with the all-hands meeting and everything. You pulled an epic prank on the new guy. You should have seen my face … you really got me good. Guys?"

But I never had the chance. Apparently, this wasn't "The Office" version of "Candid Camera."

"Jason, I'm really sorry for you," said some guy who I assumed was the ringleader of the prank. "When they made the announcement, you were the first person I thought of."

Do I know this guy? I wonder whether he has a crush on me, or whether he just talks to all of the new hires like this. I don't remember ever meeting him, but somehow, he knows my name.

They just kept filing into the cattle herder, so I took the stairs. At least staircases don't move abruptly the minute you start walking up or down them, outside of some mystical wizard world.

I stare at my computer while the others return and gab voraciously about the announcement. I still can't if it's a good thing that my cubicle sits right in the middle of the Mettle universe, as nearly all sounds within 50 feet reverberate off the metal shelving to my right.

I overheard someone saying that most of us will receive acceptance letters for jobs in Cincinnati. Does that include me? I've been here eight days; the programming language of choice (Java) is one I've never used; and I know absolutely nothing about this place's internal financial processes. OK, I do know a little about accessing servers, updating web pages, and using the code repository. And I'm a master at checking the logs.

But if I had to do any of this stuff by myself, I would either crash a server or accidentally remove $54 million in assets from some poor soul's account. And where are all of the funds stored, anyway? I'm still in search of the money vault.

"Jeff, you're meeting with Sally next," says Chris, our supervisor, as everyone hovers around Jeff's cube. Why are people always there? And for what possible reason? I'm starting to suspect that Jeff, when I'm not looking, hands out beer and doughnuts.

As our boss, Chris commands the floor, but it's clear that he's not even sure what to say. He's fairly young (maybe mid-30s), and seems to be a good enough guy, but through my limited time, I've talked with him maybe three times. I assume he stays busy, though I'm still trying to learn everyone's names and not blow up my computer. Perhaps he guards the money vault.

"So newbie, what do you think about all of this?" says Barry, smiling as if he just won a hot dog eating contest. I don't know what Barry's facial responses mean, so I can only wonder whether this is an expression of cleverness or deception. I peg Barry to be a man of many faces, most of which are covered in condiments.

"Who the hell is Sally?" I say.

"She's Chris's boss!" Barry says with a pat (more like a whack!) on my back and a sinister laugh. He reminds me a bit of Batman's primary nemesis, the Joker, although I don't remember the comic book version wearing glasses or the same short-sleeve polo shirt that has gone through the laundry 1,024 times.

Barry would make a decent prototype for today's Java programmer: He's got a full backlog of computer science knowledge, he's white and in his early 40s, and he's never short of confidence when it comes to his capabilities. He even took a math class in college that my mom taught. I theorize he was the type of student who attempted to impress the chicks with his enormous ... knowledge of fractals.

"It doesn't seem like they'll offer me a job," I say. "They could easily just have someone up there and not have to worry about moving me."

"But this isn't going to happen overnight," Barry says. "It will be months before we move. I bet they'll want you to come along."

Barry might be right. It would be sensible to keep me, especially because I'm already here and working. But Northern Lineage could have just waited another two weeks to fill my position. Then again, it took Mettle a month and a half after my interview to offer me the job. The people here seemed cool enough, so I took the position with the idea that after a month or so, I could always start looking again. Or join the circus.

Either way, I should have waited to stop trimming my facial hair, just in case I need to climb back into the bearded woman outfit.

Jeff returns from his meeting with Sally, and like maggots

on a dead rat, other coworkers return to his cube to gossip. He's carrying a folder that contains an acceptance letter, a Northern Lineage mission statement, and quite possibly discount oil change coupons in Cincinnati. Ken jumps in and rifles through the materials.

"This is all you got?" Ken says. "Did they give you a time table about when the move will occur? Did they ask you what your likelihood of moving would be? Did they tell you about your bonus?"

Ken already has begun to theorize his optimal plans for the move. Ken, the half-Japanese metrosexual of the group, is not holding back his inquisitive mind and conniving demeanor today. He's the type of person who would complete thorough research about a decision, analyzing every possible angle to determine the best possible action and feel confident about the choice.

And the next day, he would change his mind.

While Ken looks through the materials to find answers, Jeff picks up the single piece of paper that remains on the left-hand side of his desk.

"It's all covered here," Jeff says. "But I can't let you see this offer sheet. You'll see yours soon enough. We have until August 15 to make a decision ... a decent chunk of time from now. The bonus looks good. They are really bending over backward for us."

Jeff does his fair share of worrying, too. Besides the goatee and the age discrepancy (Ken's 42, while Jeff is 26), the difference between Ken and Jeff is that Jeff makes decisions fast and allows ample time to change if other prospects become more acceptable.

"Come on, Jeff, share the offer sheet with the crowd," Barry growls. But as Barry reaches for the paper in Jeff's hand, Jeff turns his chair away. Of course, that doesn't stop Barry from moving closer and putting Jeff in a headlock. Jeff doesn't seem interested in wrestling, so he pushes Barry away.

Fortunately, with no title belt on the line, Barry's playfulness subsides, and he steps back.

Meanwhile, Don must have heard the commotion and drifts over.

"Isn't this great?" Don beams. "We get to move to Cincinnati!"

"Maybe for you," Ken says. "Why are you so happy?"

"I just got one step of the process out of the way," Don says excitedly. "I'm closing on my house here next week. So I was planning on finding a new place. I guess I'll just have to start looking in a different neighborhood."

For the most part, Don keeps to himself, although he stands out in our circle because he's a few inches taller than the rest of us. Occasionally, he throws himself into whatever conversation is occurring, usually taking a harsh stance on the opposite side of the strongest arguer. He could be an intelligent and effective debater, but much of the time, people just nod as he speaks. Everyone assumes he isn't finished talking. But this time, he is.

Usually Diya ignores Don's diatribes, but for whatever reason today, she joins the party in Jeff's workspace.

"Hey Diya, where have you been?" Barry says.

"I have been working," Diya says. "There is so much to get accomplished, and I don't have time to sit around and discuss the inevitable. Maybe tomorrow will be different."

"Of course tomorrow will be different," says Don, turning away from the crowd. "Tomorrow will be the first full day we know we're going to Cincy!"

"Why is he so happy?" says Diya, staring cautiously at Don as he strolls back to his desk.

"Dude wants to move," Jeff says.

Don seems to be alone in temperament, but I haven't quite mastered a read on Diya yet. She is overtly immersed in her work, and maybe she doesn't think too much about the change of venue with the company. The only thing I really know about her is that she's a crazily attractive Indian woman, which I haven't seen in any previous office job.

Chris appears, trying to slip into the group unnoticed, which is always difficult when you're in charge.

"Jason, you're next up with Sally," says Chris, and then he disappears, back doing whatever he is usually doing.

"Where is this lady's office, anyway?" I ask. No one responds. I'm not sure whether they don't know where the office is, or whether their sullenness about the work predicament is starting to affect their ears. Maybe fun has been outlawed and replaced with mandatory limb amputations.

"I'll show you," Jeff says. The others disband as Jeff and I trek toward the office of this fabled Sally. It isn't difficult to find; she has a corner office, as expected, opposite of our work area. As I approach her door, one employee leaves, looking glum, while another enters gingerly. I notice Chris sitting inside.

"Good luck," Jeff says.

Upon hearing Jeff, the floor secretary tries to start a conversation with him. I wonder why all the people look as if they have been diagnosed with multiple terminal illnesses. I can't imagine people here always look so sad. The first few days seemed like a joyous place; I mean, there weren't carnival rides or orgies spontaneously breaking out, but the place appeared to be harmonious.

Sally's door opens, and the exiting employee doesn't appear too distraught. Chris beckons me to enter.

"Jason, this is Sally," says Chris, flipping through papers I assume will end up in my possession. He hands the papers to Sally.

"Good to meet you," I say, standing to shake Sally's hand. I feel like Socrates trying to strike up a conversation with the guy who eventually gives him the hemlock.

"Sorry we have to meet for the first time under these terms," says Sally. I wonder what "terms" she means; we haven't negotiated terms yet. Maybe I missed the fine print in my job contract, which spells out a list of conditions that I must fulfill, including something to do with a protractor and a baby seal. Am I still under full warranty?

She hands me the folder, but before I can review it, she continues.

"Honestly, if we had known about the move, we probably wouldn't have hired you."

I don't hesitate to respond.

"I'm glad you didn't know," I say, noticing the offer letter that awaits me in the grab bag of material. "Still, I'm fortunate to have this opportunity."

Neither Sally nor Chris has much to say after that. They waltz through the motions of explaining the offer and the August 15 deadline. I'm slightly paying attention, as I'm still stuck on Sally's comment about the whole not-being-hired bit. It's difficult for me to believe a person in that position would not know about the relocation. Then again, I haven't been here long enough to comprehend the organizational communication between Mettle and the mother ship.

I leave the meeting and hurry back to my workstation, but just about everyone has left for the day. It's 4:45, and apparently, the announcement has put enough emotional strain on the employees that they have to leave work early. Jeff is still pounding away on his computer.

"Oh, there you are," Jeff says. "Do you want to stick around and help me with this build?"

The build, Jeff acknowledges, will be an integral part of my job. Because numerous updated code files need to go on the website, we have to take all of the newest ones in the code repository, make copies in various locations to test, and then deploy them to the live server. The build is sort of like a briefcase that contains every single file for the website. Each time there are changes, all the files need to be stuffed into the briefcase and then emptied into the correct directories on the server. I can't tell yet how complex this is, but I doubt I'll be able to offer Jeff much assistance.

"So what happened in the meeting?" Jeff says.

"They are offering me a position in Cincinnati," I say.

"I told you! I think just about everyone got an offer."

Jeff turns back to his computer. "I'll give you a ride home so you don't have to catch the bus."

Awkward silence. And keystrokes.

"Everyone took off in a hurry today," I say, waiting for Jeff to show me the steps in building the website.

"Yeah, it's ghostly in here," Jeff says. "I suspect there will be many more days like this, when people start jumping ship or just not doing anything. Do you have plans for the weekend?"

"I'm just going to visit a friend ... actually, it's a blind date in Cincinnati. Pretty weird timing, especially if I end up moving."

"I have to finish my basement. That sucks ass."

I've overheard Jeff discuss his basement work. Jeff must love all types of building assembly. I wonder if he was the one who started those silly "Under construction" animated graphics on partially completed websites.

"I doubt we do many more website builds before the move," Jeff says. "They probably want to hold off most of the maintenance. Besides, most people won't want to do any work. I mean, it was dead today at 4:30."

"So what do you think Northern Lineage will want us to do in the meantime?" I say.

"At this point, the best thing for us to do will be to lie low and wait to see what happens."

Saturday, June 25

It's tough to think about a major life decision with William Howard Taft staring down at you.

First, the guy is huge. How many former presidents had the nickname "Big Lub"? Second, this isn't a normal U.S. presidential statue, as the plaque that accompanies it highlights

Taft's time as the 10th Chief Justice of the United States.

"Hey, um, Big Lub?" I imagine myself saying. "I know you're busy and all hanging out with the pigeons, but I have a bone to pick with you. I started this job two weeks ago, and they want me to move to that building right over there. I don't live anywhere near here, but gravity seems to be pulling me toward it. Hello, Big Lub, are you listening? Can you at least give me a tip on who has the best chili in town?"

I'm on my blind date. It's really not going that well. The girl is nice enough, maybe the type I would have gone for in college … fun, bubbly, and visibly interested. Instead, I'm talking to a dead president about a major career decision. Shit, I hope she didn't think I called her "Big Lub," or I might end up in the water.

Why am I even here with this girl? I'm in no hurry to find a match in Cincinnati. I have two upcoming dates in Louisville, and I recently met one of my sister's East Coast college friends. But I keep thinking about Diya, although she's not even available, right? We've emailed each other a few times, and I don't know anything about her personal life.

If I think about Diya, does that mean I'm contemplating work or girls or how many toppings I can legitimately add to a single serving of chili?

"You need to do what you feel is right," the girl says, as I wonder if Taft played the piano much before being buried in a piano case.

"I just haven't been at this job long enough to know what 'right' is," I say.

"You will know," the girl says. Is she serious? Or is she trying to turn this into a *Casablanca*-esque ending? It is true that we are just a few miles from the airport. "With these types of things, you always know."

I know close to jack shit about what I will do. But whatever you want to call it — the job hunt, the moving game — it looks as if I'll be playing it again.

3
Getting Cozy
with Coworkers

Monday, June 27

A bad start today … I arrive at work a few minutes late, just after 8:30. It's pretty empty inside, though. Maybe the rain has something to do with it, or maybe today is a financial holiday, something like Fund Your Big Fat Assets Day, and everyone stayed home.

Usually, Barry is the last to arrive in the morning, but he's already here. He plays some role in handling the online transactions, so maybe he has to be here when money comes pouring out of boots and into our system.

"Hey Barry, how was the weekend?" I say.

"Not bad, newbie," Barry says. "I cooked barbecue all day Sunday. Do you like barbecue? I make some mean barbecue … you'll have to come to one of my world-famous parties."

"I will," I say, slowly backpedaling toward my cube. I came to Barry's desk to find something to work on, but I had stumbled into the beginning of a lecture on grilling.

"I went to visit my mom, but I didn't tell her the news yet," Barry continues. "I didn't want to upset her when I don't even know what I'll do."

We all have reasonable notions about moving, and Barry really does not want to go. He has lived in Louisville his entire life and has bounced around between multiple companies. He has been with Mettle the longest — six years — and started just weeks before Ken. Barry lived with his mother for a period before buying his own house a couple of years back, but he's still her primary caretaker, running errands and clearing his schedule, "just in case." At this stage in the moving decision, Barry is pretty much convinced he won't be heading anywhere.

"Barry, you have plenty of time," I say. "We have two months to figure it out. But instead of contemplating that, can you help me find something to work on today?"

"Sure, I have plenty for you to do. Today would be the perfect day to have you work on fixing some of the errors in this batch script on the server. Maybe you can recognize the code and get the scripts to run. You're pretty good at Java, right?"

"I really don't know any of it."

"I see. Why don't you start flipping through this book and I'm sure by lunchtime, you'll figure out what the problem is."

Barry hands me his Java book. Actually, he lifts the book with all of his might and heaves it in my general direction. I take the book and stumble back to my desk, managing to lay it down without experiencing a hernia.

I've always wondered what it would look like to bind a book including every page of an encyclopedia in at least 23 languages, along with a special section for acknowledgments and an unabridged dictionary. I'm quite sure it's heavy enough to tip the scale and automatically win a prize at one of those carnival guess-your-weight games. Because I have nothing else to do, I figure it can't hurt to start thumbing through the book, assuming I can lift enough pages to safely make it past the table of contents.

I had just sifted through the first couple of paragraphs of the preface when I notice something out of the corner of my eye. I glance quickly to see Diya gliding past. I stand from my cube and watch Diya walk away from me and into her cube.

Jeff waves his hand in front of my face; apparently, I was stuck in a motionless gaze.

"Dude, if you're going to stare at Diya, you should at least be able to see her," Jeff says. "Unless you can see through cube partitions."

"What?" I say. "I wasn't staring, I was … just opening my handbook and … "

"Why else would you be looking in that direction? She's hot. If you wanted to look out the window, you could walk over to Don's or Barry's cubes. That would be a lot easier."

Jeff is quick to notice my strong appreciation for beautiful women, perhaps because he shares the same admiration. And when a man is faced with the conquest of a beautiful woman, there's only one thing to do: imitate Sean Connery.

Who knew the greatest womanizer of all time would spend his geriatric years as the mentor and spiritual guide to two lost IT employees? In fact, moments ago, Connery lent me his wisdom as I sent an email to Jeff with the subject line "Pleashhheesse send me the fileshhh."

Jeff reads the email, giggles, and pounds his desk.

"Damnit boy, we have quite a meshhh on our hands this morning," Jeff says.

Some people would say the Connery impersonations are ridiculous, and while Jeff and I would like to think we've mastered the accent, we both know the truth: You can never really master the master.

I head back to my desk and again rifle through the Java book. Jeff begins his daily quest to parse his email. Sorting weekend spam on a Monday morning isn't an easy task. Luckily for me, hardly anyone knows my email address. Or the fact that I work here.

"Did you get the basement finished?" Ken says, just before I do. I walk back over to see Jeff's reaction. His head is planted on his desk.

"Are you kidding? Not even close," Jeff says. "I need help with pretty much everything. I want to start the drywall soon, but I'm still unsure about the plumbing items."

"I can help you one weekend with the drywall, assuming Mary lets me," Ken says. "How soon do you think it will be?"

"I'd like to have it finished sometime during my lifetime! At least now I can key off the August 15 date as the time I need to finish it. It's too bad I won't get to enjoy it for very long."

"Who says you have to move?" I say, also waving hello to Ken.

"At this point, it seems like a no-brainer," says Jeff. "The deal is too good to pass up. I think we're in about as good of a situation as we could be."

I nod, although I don't completely agree. Then again, I don't disagree. I haven't reviewed all the material yet. I had hoped to find balloons and noisemakers in my goodie bag. Instead, I found was a page that said I would receive an $8,000 bonus and moving expenses plus other amenities if I moved.

Sweet! That's enough to purchase a helium tank, too!

I've been here only a short time, but Mettle is giving me the benefits of a seasoned employee. I can't complain. I've also been impressed with the organization and presentation of the material, which includes handouts about the parent company, living in Cincinnati, Q&A about benefits, and a link to a website devoted solely to the move. I plan to check out all of it later this week.

I assume, however, that Jeff and Ken are already in the preliminary steps of discussing with their wives the best plan of action. Even though Ken is the elder, he hardly looks the part. His youthful nature probably comes from a myriad of things: his Japanese heritage, his delay of marriage until his late 30s, and his zeal for eating healthily and watching his weight. He has a lovely wife, two young sons, and a sizable house just over the river in Indiana. If Mettle were to make a poster of a happy-looking family, Ken's could be in front of the camera.

The prospect of moving seems exciting to Ken, if for nothing else as an opportunity to enhance his computing skills, for this job … or the next. While both he and his wife, Mary, have family in Louisville, moving won't create too many obstacles regarding personal matters. Mary is a stay-at-home mom, and as long as Ken is able to keep the same flexible schedule with the company, everything will likely work out.

On the other hand, Jeff has been married for just two years. He is from Memphis and has been with Mettle exactly five years. Jeff and Laura, his wife, don't have any children, and she works as a physical therapist just down the road from where I live. Besides Don, Jeff is the most gung-ho about moving. He is also interested in learning new business skills from the parent company, but he is just biding time until he is able to pursue his dream: graphic design school in California. He reasons that a couple of years of working and saving money will allow him to do just that. Until that time, he is using every spare minute to produce possible portfolio pieces.

"Instead of working on the basement exclusively this weekend, I did more 3-D rendering," Jeff says as Ken and I lurch closer to his screen. "I think with this new software I'm using, I'll be able to do the texture layering for these 3-D scenes."

Jeff shows the images to Ken, but before I can move closer to check Jeff's monitor, Barry storms over and nudges Jeff's chair.

"So, you've been playing on your computer instead of getting your fat ass in gear to finish the basement, eh?" says a grinning Barry. It is important to mention that Jeff is not grossly overweight, nor is Barry toned like Arnold Schwarzenegger during his heyday. I'm starting to find that Barry's puzzling asides are relatively normal.

Everyone continues to gaze at Jeff's monitor and ignore Barry, which gives Barry the notion that he should continue.

"Has anyone turned in their offer letter yet?" Barry asks.

"I wouldn't be surprised if Don has," Ken says. "The guy just sold his house ... his cousins live in Dayton. I don't think there's much thought to it."

"What about you, Diya, are you going to Cincinnati?" shouts Barry, who expects her to respond from 30 feet and three partition walls away. She doesn't answer, but no doubt hears Barry's booming voice. I decide to sneak over to Diya's cube. At least it gives me the opportunity to stare at her.

"Sorry about Barry yelling like a madman over there," I begin, trying not to disturb her, as it appears she's again doing something ridiculously important.

"That's OK, Jason, I'm used to it by now," Diya says. "How was your weekend?"

"It wasn't too bad. I went to Cincinnati to meet up with a friend ... actually it was sort of a date."

"Oh really?" Diya says. "Was she nice? Did you like her? Did you have a good time?"

"The date was OK. She's just really young, and our lives don't seem to mesh very well at this stage."

"Well, if you move to Cincinnati, you will already have a girlfriend there!"

"Yeah, maybe I should try to pick up girlfriends in every city, in case the company moves somewhere else!"

Well, that wasn't a very good pickup line. Then again, does it really matter? All I know about Diya at this point is she's 29 (a few months older than me) and from India, and she has been with the company for two years. It seems logical that she would move to Cincinnati, only because her job seems to be an integral one. Instead of prying, I sense it is time to maneuver back to my cube and find something else to do.

But there still isn't anything for me to do — at least, nothing I can do on my own. I thought Barry was going to start me with fixing scripts that need debugging, but he's immersed in something else. I think about asking Jeff if I can do some of his work, but he's on the phone, maybe talking to someone in the building, or maybe trying to find the right materials to build a water slide and Olympic-size pool for his basement.

Switching between skimming the Java book and eavesdropping on Jeff doesn't quench my need to do something. Surely there is work to be done; both Jeff and Barry are supposed to continue the training process so I can build the annuity website files and work on the updates. There's also a rumor that I'll be working on reorganizing the intranet (Mettle's internal website). I hate being at work with nothing to do.

Since the announcement last Wednesday, my thoughts have been consumed by the relocation decision. Before that, during my first seven days here, I had remained solidly unattached to Mettle and my coworkers. I had grandiose ideas about starting a job in such rich surroundings, with people from all walks of life, various ethnicities, religions, office chair sitting habits, etc. But as an outsider, I assumed I could keep my distance while I decided if this was the best place for me.

And now, on the eleventh day at my new place of business, I've made a sudden realization. Mettle is the place I need to be. It is just the close-knit, thought-provoking atmosphere I have been craving since I left my last job.

Then again, it would be nice to have some freakin' work to do.

It was difficult to assess how I would fit in at the beginning, but that is not an issue anymore. Belonging to a team of web developers is great — until the team no longer exists. And while I jumped into an optimal situation with the team here, the clock is already ticking on how long this will continue. August 15 seems like a decade away from today. Jeff visits my cube to give me the latest about the move to Cincinnati.

"It looks like there's a chance I might be switching teams," Jeff whispers. "Raj just told me he's pretty certain most of the people down in creative services won't be moving, so they'll need someone to do the graphics."

Raj, a good guy and not a lying sack of shit, oversees the e-commerce graphic design work on the fifth floor. He's familiar enough with Jeff's goals and looking to expand the competency of his group. Jeff isn't a programmer by trade, but then again, his current position doesn't necessitate a hard-core programmer like Barry. Jeff's best opportunity would include more design work and less monotonous code building.

"So when will you know if you switch departments?" I say.

"It won't be soon," Jeff says. "It's more like something that could happen eventually."

"Will that affect the number of people we have up here?"

"In the long run, perhaps. At first, Northern Lineage won't meddle too much in what we are doing. They'll have to learn our processes before they get too involved. The way Raj talks, there is going to be some restructuring within Mettle before the actual move. But who knows if that will even happen."

"Do we know anything that will actually happen?"

"In reality, I guess the only thing I know is that the company is moving to Cincy."

Jeff heads back to his cube. So much for the web team staying intact. It's tough to figure out if you're in the right place if everyone around you is moving. Maybe they can just throw us all in a centrifuge and separate the employees into designers, programmers, and liquids.

Before I turn another page in the Java book, I notice that Diya responded to my earlier email. I had written her minutes before she arrived this morning. I think I remember asking her to dinner.

So Jason...I had to leave on Friday because of my MBA class. I think I will be free over the weekend but I am not sure yet because a friend's sister is visiting and she wanted me to come home for dinner sometime this week... Let me have your number so that I can call u or u can have my cell number. So how is ur day going so far? I am very tired and I need a break...

Through all the craziness here, I managed to score a date with the hottest girl in the building. Despite not receiving any balloons today, the answer to Diya's question is simple: My day is fabulous.

4
Propaganda

Wednesday, June 29

I listen in disbelief as representatives from a Realty company in Cincinnati answer questions from Mettle employees regarding relocation. The reps from Community Choice Realtors seem to be avoiding unveiling any useful information, instead opting to change the subject and/or ignore the question altogether.

"Could you tell us how property taxes differ in northern Kentucky and in Ohio?" someone from the crowd asks.

"Well, we know they work differently," the woman rep says.

"Oh yes, they are different," the man chimes in. Both of them nod their heads.

"Yep, it's crazy how they are different," the woman says. Then they both pause and await the next question.

Maybe they think this is supposed to be a comedy routine, and they are just trying to find the best time to work in the juggling-four-chainsaws-on-a-unicycle segment. Now might be appropriate, but someone else raises a hand.

"Does the city have a good snow removal plan in place?" asks someone else in the crowd.

"They do usually remove the snow, if it snows," the man says. "I guess it's pretty much like any other city with snow removal."

I think of all the snowplows they use in Florida.

25

The show, a grand finale of "relo info" sessions, continues through more bizarre and worthless exchanges between the Community Choice people and Mettle employees. Since Tuesday, our parent company has been pumping us full of details through large and small informational get-togethers. At least the others gave me insight as to what to expect if I do move.

First, there was our weekly team meeting late Tuesday afternoon.

"I'm trying to get all of the information to you guys as quickly as I can," Chris said. "Right now, they are telling us things sporadically, but they want us to wait until they have all the results."

"Results?" said Barry, starting to jump a bit out of his chair. "I'll give you results!"

We waited for Barry's punch line, but he was too fidgety to give it. Barry continued to bob gleefully in his chair without saying a word, like a child on the mechanical horse in front of the grocery store. I wondered if I should fetch a cowboy hat that's probably in one of his desk drawers.

"So are they going to start firing people?" Ken said. "That's something we should at least know now."

"From what I've heard, no one is being let go," Chris said.

"Yeah, Northern Lineage can't just drop someone because they don't know enough yet about Mettle processes," Jeff said.

"But they'll send people down to learn it," Don said. "It's just like an alien invasion."

I wanted him to expand on this theory, but Chris cut in.

"There are a couple of things I can tell you now," Chris said. "First, everyone will have an opportunity to take a business day trip to Cincinnati to see the offices and meet with your new coworkers. You can sign up for a trip after we finish. Second, people will be down from Northern Lineage tomorrow and Thursday to go over various items with you regarding the move. There are a handful of meetings planned, so you should be receiving invitations in your inbox before you leave this evening. Also, Marshall MacDougal will be meeting with each of you individually to see if he can answer any of your questions."

I looked at the others to gauge their emotions about this news. As usual, everyone's eyes looked more glazed than a Krispy Kreme doughnut. I was all for receiving more information about this craziness, and even I knew Marshall MacDougal. He's the VP of technology for the parent company, and he was at Mettle on the day of the announcement. From what I had heard, he's a go-getter, and I was curious as to how he would respond to our individual questions and requests.

Besides the always-wiggling Barry, everyone sat motionless as Chris continued his spiel to the peons. I have to admit, I feel bad for our boss. He has a wife and two kids with another on the way. This is not a good time for him to pack up and ship out, but it doesn't appear he has much of a choice. Furthermore, Barry and Jeff mentioned the other day that some of the middle managers could be expendable to Northern Lineage. The relocation is an obvious way to cut expenses. Assuming that Chris moves, and he's one of the first ones to say so, he is almost guaranteed to survive.

"If no one has anything else, then I guess we're finished," said Chris nonchalantly. Barry immediately jumped from his seat and exited.

"Do you have any clue what any of the meetings are about tomorrow?" I said as everyone else left.

"They'll be overviews of the company's dealings," Chris said. "Actually, it says the first one will deal with annuities."

"That should be interesting," I said, "considering I'm supposed to be programming annuity stuff, and I know nothing about them."

"I think you'll find it interesting," Chris said. "The annuity business is quite bizarre, if you haven't already figured that out yet."

This morning, I learned a little about why Northern Lineage

needs something larger than a single money vault. Jeff, Ken, and I again headed to the downstairs conference room as Anita Williams, the chief financial officer of Northern Lineage, exhibited a fascinating PowerPoint presentation to a fairly crowded Mettle audience.

The slide show turned out to be much more than a bunch of 10-point Helvetica words sliding across a bright yellow and paisley background. As a Fortune 500 company, Northern Lineage is currently one of the top mutual life and health insurers in the United States. Last year, the company ranked in the top five among both insurers and total profits per assets. And while the company is privately held, it is one of just a handful of companies that hold an AAA rating.

It sounded good, but it really meant nothing to me. Then the dollar-figure slide show portion began. The company profited more than $20 billion six years ago and $35 billion last year, which came to nearly a 10 percent compound annual growth rate. Altogether, the company now serves approximately half a million customers. Two weeks ago, the company purchased Indiana Life, based in Indianapolis. It appeared that Northern Lineage was still in expansion mode.

I continued to review the slides and listen to Anita, wondering what the others in the room were making of the presentation. Did anyone have any clue what goes on at headquarters? Jeff had made a comment that corporate pretty much did its own thing and left the Louisville office alone. That was made evident when I saw a slide saying the Mettle brand will remain. What was the point in offering multiple, perhaps identical, products through what will soon be the same company?

After the presentation, Jeff, Ken, and I grabbed lunch, and then we returned to our battle stations on the seventh floor. There was another meeting scheduled at 2, which gave us time to check email (of course, I had none) and plan additional work for later in the day. I noticed Don and Barry speaking to a man I didn't recognize, so I decided to be nosy. As I approached

Barry's cube, I overheard enough of the conversation to know that the man must be Stephen Payne. He used to work in IT at Mettle but moved to Cincinnati two years ago. He is still our point of contact on most server issues, because the actual hardware sits in a climate-controlled room at Northern Lineage. I wonderd if the server had to sit through all of these meetings when it was relocated.

"The working hours are pretty flexible," Stephen said. "As long as you are there for the core hours, from 9-3, you can work pretty much whenever. I leave my house at 8:30, and it takes me 30 minutes to get there, but I'm always out by 4:45. Of course, I occasionally have things to work on over the weekend, but it's usually not very much."

Jeff and Ken also approached the small congregation at Barry's cube.

"How's the cafeteria?" said Barry. It was amazing how Barry never missed a chance to bring up food.

"It's pretty good overall," Stephen said. "It's your typical cafeteria. They offer a couple of different main dishes, a bunch of sides, box lunches if you can't get away from your desk."

"Not bad, and much better than Mettle!" Barry said. "I still haven't found the cafeteria here."

"What about the dress?" Ken said.

"You want to wear a dress to work?" said Barry, turning to expect a high five after spouting another vacuous comment.

"As long as you wear a decent shirt, dress pants, and a tie, you'll be all right," Stephen said. "I had to buy new clothes when I first moved up here. It took awhile to get used to, but now, it doesn't bother me at all."

"You have to wear a tie every day?" Barry said.

"Pretty much," Stephen said. "Well, on dress-down days, you don't."

"Oh, so you can wear jeans?" Ken said.

"No, you have to wear the same stuff ... you just don't have to wear a tie," Stephen said. "Well guys, it looks like it's about time for the meeting. See you in a few minutes."

I always thought dress-down days meant business casual, but according to *Dress Casually for Success ... for Men*, there are various levels of casualness, from traditional (polo shirt and khakis), dress traditional (oxford shirt and khakis), contemporary (jeans and shirt), and dress contemporary (black slacks and black shirt).[1] The book apparently leaves off vegetarian casual (salad and khakis), which is popular among herbivores, and causal casual, which involves wearing nothing until you are told to dress casually.

At Mettle, the normal dress code is a shirt with a collar and khakis. The thought of wearing a dress shirt, slacks, and a tie every day, however, seemed unbearable for us.

"I'm not too interested in wearing a tie every day," Barry said.

"You don't have to wear one every day," Don said. "They have dress-down days!"

"Of course ... dress-down days," Barry said. "I can't wait."

We tried to catch up with Diya, who was already headed to the elevator, but she was the last one in yet another sardine-packed ride downstairs to the large conference room. Our ride, consisting of myself, Jeff, Barry, Ken, Don, and two IT guys, was much more comfortable.

Ann Singleton, the same woman who sent that fateful urgent email regarding the relocation announcement, was again on the stage. This time, she was a pseudo talk-show host, asking questions to the Northern Lineage panel of experts: Stephen, Boris Granger, and Mike Mann. Ann finished a quick introduction and began to ask questions to the panel:

Ann: Why did you move?

Boris: I was briefly in the human resources department in Louisville, but I wanted to get into the other side of things, the more technical side in Cincinnati.

Stephen: Northern Lineage seemed like a stable place, and

I received a pretty nice package to move.

Mike: I needed to redefine my focus and myself. I saw a lot of growth potential in moving, so I reviewed it and realized that could be just the thing to re-energize my career.

Ann: Were there any surprises from the move?

Boris: The cafeteria is really good. Hardly anyone goes out to lunch.

Stephen: When I was in Louisville, I was always under the impression that Northern Lineage was a big, stagnant company, stuck in the '60s. Even the decor seemed outdated. But once I moved up there, I was amazed at how quickly I bonded with everyone.

Mike: Most of the time, when you're stuck in a big company, there's a sense of depersonalization. But the atmosphere has never felt like that. Everyone is nice, and there is a lot of camaraderie.

Ann: How do you feel about the professional dress?

Mike: Personally, I don't care for professional dress. But it kind of grows on you after a while.

Stephen: I've always believed that how you dress is how you feel.

Boris: It's really a non-issue with me.

Ann: Name a negative of your job or the move.

Brett: At the job level, honestly nothing comes to mind.

Stephen: The thing that was the hardest was making the initial decision to move. Since I did that, my wife and I are 100 percent happy that we made the choice.

Mike: Any move is going to be stressful. It's difficult because people don't stay in touch. But in the end, I'm glad this was the outcome.

Ann: How does the company treat its associates?

Boris: It's pretty cool because they have various events, like associate appreciation week and discount days. It really makes you feel like you belong to a family.

Stephen: They do a lot of things that just don't have to be done.

Mike: I've found it remarkable the amount of time people have stayed with Northern Lineage. Just recently, someone had a 20th anniversary, and he was just 100th in line in Information Services.

I jotted down as much as I could. I planned to compare some of these things with impressions from my team ... people who have been around long enough to give their own reactions. One conclusion was evident: Northern Lineage had chosen the panelists wisely. The trio appeared confident in its answers, and the Mettle audience seemed interested. The three guys had given responses that, for the most part, could be trusted by former cohorts.

As an outsider, I felt as if some of this was Northern Lineage propaganda, making it appear that the only choice was to move. At one point, I could have sworn that Ann plugged the robot-like Mike Mann into a wall outlet.

Regardless, Northern Lineage was serious about giving Mettle employees all of the information they could handle. I appreciated that, but I also realized my appointment with Marshall MacDougal was just five minutes away. Ann closed with a handful of questions from the crowd, and just as we were dismissed, I scurried to catch the first elevator.

Back on the seventh floor, I found Marshall, who was in an office just beside Sally's. I told him what I did at Mettle (at least, what I had done during my 13-day tenure) and my previous experience. Then he asked me what I wanted to know. I was curious how he ended up in his current position.

"I bounced around a couple of places before coming to Northern Lineage 10 years ago," Marshall said. "I came here for three reasons. First, it's a very strong financial company. When I worked at one of the large telecom companies, they had grandiose ideas, but they could never complete what they started. Second, there is a strong CEO-level commitment to technology across the board, from mainframe to distributing. Finally, the employees at Northern Lineage are good people, and all things are possible, including data mining, target marketing, etc.

"That telecom company had good vision in a lot of areas, but they just couldn't execute. Good companies focus on execution and grow conservatively. There are a lot of smart people at Northern Lineage."

"Do you think we'll run into many conflicts with the technologies we use down here and what you use up there?" I said.

"We're in the process of moving a lot of our stuff from Visual Basic to .NET," Marshall said. "And of course, you guys use Java down here, and we don't use Java much. But this isn't a matter of choosing between Java and .NET — you can't have just one. Our web services need to interact with both. Our application developers do a tremendous job, and the quality of work is high. I'm also looking forward to Project Giza, but that is sort of under wraps for now."

I thought I would try to catch Marshall off guard by asking a somewhat negative question.

"So far, I've heard a bunch of reasons why I should go to Cincinnati," I said. "Can you give me a reason why I shouldn't go?"

"I can think of three reasons not to go," Marshall said. "If you want to work only for a software company, you might be out of place, because we're doing much more than just software. Or, if you're into consulting, and you build maybe 10 to 12 websites a year, without any maintenance, that's not Northern Lineage either. We are constantly improving on what we build internally, for the end user. The other reason not to go would be if you wanted to work in a really large shop, because again, that's not what it's about."

Marshall was about as convincing as a soaking-wet meteo-rologist shilling ponchos. And his assurances made the earlier meetings seem even more tantalizing. I liked that Northern Lineage is not trying to take over the world. Companies that grow too fast also wither fast as well. Another thing that struck me from Marshall's responses was the importance of exploring emerging technologies and not being pigeonholed as one spe-cific type of development company. When comprehensively de-scribing the company's departments, he mentioned that another possibility was moving around to work on different projects.

I was also interested in this aforementioned Project Giza. I wondered if that relates to the great Egyptian pyramid by the same name, though I've never seen a pharaoh wear a tie.

After the meeting, I returned to my desk. Jeff was still in the office, but he mentioned that Barry and a few others had gone to a nearby Mexican restaurant to hang out before the evening meeting with the Cincinnati Realtors. He was planning to go meet them as soon as Laura, his wife, called.

Minutes later, we were inside the restaurant, which I would later learn doesn't always keep a 183-degree temperature for its patrons. The air conditioner was busted, but that didn't stop the Mettle clan from taking up most of the seating.

When I envision an outing involving a large group of peo-ple from a typical place of business, one word comes to mind: borrrrrrrrr-ing. At one table, people usually sit around and try to one-up one another with stories about their children, and at the other table, the discussion involves trying to decipher the entire current state of world affairs or the rationale behind why reality TV shows still exist. This can be stimulating for longer than 42 minutes, but without an unlimited supply of Ping-Pong and/or alcohol, the partygoers mellow by 9:30 and begin spew-ing every possible reason to leave early, including the old the-apocalypse-begins-tomorrow-and-I-can't-find-my-can-opener excuse.

However, the Mettle employees seemed anything but typical when describing an outside-of-work experience. Most of the people I've come in contact with here like to have fun with their coworkers, in a weird best friend/family-like way. And when people do talk about their children, they somehow don't annoy the people listening.

The restaurant emptied just before 7, and we walked back to even more food and drink in the basement meeting room. We had forgotten they were serving sandwiches. I grabbed a cookie and a Sprite and took a seat for the day's final meeting.

And now, unfortunately, the slapstick show still hasn't ended. At least we received handheld back massagers, which were sitting on our seats when we arrived. The freebies didn't have much to do with relocating to Cincinnati, but then again, neither did most of the answers that the Community Choice representatives had given.

Someone in the back asks the reps if they know anything regarding the difference between sale prices for houses with or without finished basements. Jeff immediately hones in on the answer.

"Off the top of my head, I'm unaware of a distinct difference between houses with finished and unfinished basements," the woman says.

"I think it just comes down to a matter of square footage," the man says. "The more square footage, the more likely the house will sell for more."

"The reason I'm asking," the man in the crowd remarks, "is because here, there are different rules for what is classified as a finished basement. Maybe it's worth more if there's an exit, or if there is some type of escape, unlike basements with extremely small windows."

The Realtors look at each other with puzzled expressions.

"We will have to get back to you on that," the woman says. "We can get additional information you need. Just leave your questions with Ann in HR, and we would be happy to discuss options one-on-one with you."

Jeff looks disappointed, but at least the Community Choice reps did an admirable job of dancing around a solution. Maybe we expected too much out of this meeting; everyone has different needs when finding a new residence, and especially under these circumstances, it can be even more cumbersome to find the appropriate place.

Raj, who is sitting directly behind me, and Jeff spend the final 10 minutes cracking jokes. Jeff told me at dinner that Raj's wife is transferring within her company to a Cincinnati office, meaning that Raj is already in. Jeff has talked highly of Raj and says he's one of the people who knows what's going on at Mettle. I believe Jeff, even though I usually don't like to blindly presuppose someone's credentials.

The audience finally gives up asking questions, and we walk to the parking garage.

"I guess we're going to have to find our own information," I say.

"I suspect once we have an actual Realtor to work with, they'll have answers for us," Jeff says. "Northern Lineage wants us to move up there, so they won't just sit on their hands with the housing crap."

"You would think so," I say. "They're going to have a hard time getting us to move without having a place to live."

"There's an obvious answer for that," says Barry, heading to a different parking garage. "They want you to live at work. Do you think they would be going to all of this trouble if that's not what they wanted?"

5
Green Card

Thursday, June 30

I begin my morning with a trip to Diya's cube. As she turns to face me, it looks as if she has been crying.

"I hope I'm not bothering you," I say.

"No ... I'm just debugging another server issue," Diya says.

"Are you OK?" I say, walking into her cube and sitting down in an extra chair.

"I'll be OK," Diya says unconvincingly.

"If you want to talk, I have a few minutes. Actually, I have plenty of minutes, because no one else is here yet, and I'm not positive what I should be doing. Barry's not even here to make fun of me."

Diya smiles for an instant, but then she turns back to face her screen.

"It's my green card," Diya says. "I have to start the process over because of the move."

I don't understand at all, so she explains some of the specifics.

If you think the government takes advantage of you, try coming from a different country and not being loaded with money or married to a hot-bodied citizen (at least, one without a Sean Connery accent). It used to be a snap to become part of the world's melting pot. And even though more than a million people each year become legal U.S. citizens, immigrating has become an increasingly difficult matter.

For Diya to start working at Mettle, the company had to sponsor her with a two-year work visa. By utilizing a work visa, Diya could stay in the country instead of returning to India. That window of time was supposed to allow her the opportunity to apply for and receive her United States Permanent Resident Card, better known as a green card. It's not green (although the original I-151 form, the precursor to the current I-551, was), but at least it gives immigrants some status within the country.

The problem, Diya says, is because the company is moving to Cincinnati and out of the state of Kentucky, her current green card application will be voided. Because she applied through Mettle for the green card, and the process occurs via the state program, there is no chance of carrying it over to Ohio. On top of that, her work visa will expire sometime early next year, and she does not have the ability to renew. This, of course, means that without a green card, she will have no choice but to move back to India.

I begin to understand her situation, but I can't see why it is so difficult for her to remain here in the U.S., especially if she has a good overall track record and will be working.

"That is not how it works," Diya says. "A company has to sponsor your work visa, and then for the green card, the company has to petition immigration services again. It's all tied to the company, and most companies won't sponsor you because it's just going to cost them more money."

As usual, it all comes down to money. Here's a girl who's brilliant, who apparently likes living in the States and is a great asset to the company. But because of the system and a backlog of immigrants from many nations to obtain a green card, she's stuck. And it's not as if she can bring in a note to the United States Citizen and Immigration Services office and say that her company is moving, or that the dog ate her visa. She has to move to the back of the line, which, if everyone were to actually line up, would stretch from Washington, D.C., to somewhere just barely past Jupiter.

I am curious why she came to America in the first place, how long she has been here, how her relationships have been. I'm not sure which is more unnerving: staring at a computer screen that's filled with intriguing but foreign programming, or staring at Diya, who is intriguing in her own right. Both come with the option of pursuing, but neither will allow much time.

Luckily, I have already taken my first step toward alleviating my fear of rejection. Diya committed to doing something with me after work hours. I suspect she may use this opportunity to attempt to reschedule, with things seemingly unraveling for her.

"Are we still on for tomorrow night?" I say, assuming that maybe another day will work better for her.

"Yes, definitely," Diya says. "We could meet for dinner near my place, if that would be OK?"

"Sure, that sounds good. I should be getting back to my cube and doing some work because I don't want to have to stay late tonight."

"All right. But can I ask you a question first?"

"I suppose."

"Are you the type of guy who would be interested in moving to India?"

"India could be a cool place," I say. "And I do like to travel."

Diya smiles, and I head back to my cube.

I'm still not positive Diya is even available, yet she just indicated that there is an outside shot she may kidnap me, stuff me in her luggage, and haul me back to India. Maybe it was small talk, or maybe her comment was just a cultural thing. I am distinctly aware that this entire visa/green card issue can be resolved by a quick trip to a courthouse with an American citizen. A marriage certificate will pretty much validate her residence here.

I feel a little dirty picturing Diya and me on our

honeymoon, though it would solve her problem. Of course, there's the other side of this: me. Following through with a marriage license at the present time would be fairly insane.

Instead of dwelling on wedding bells, I return to my desk and start looking for things to do. There is another meeting coming up, but I need something to stay occupied for at least 30 minutes. I pick up the Java megabook, flip through chapters 3 and 4 and try to keep my anxiousness of the impending date Friday with Diya in the background.

Friday, July 1

We again find ourselves sitting through another fabulous PowerPoint presentation meeting. I'm falling asleep just telling you about it. Watching slides of textual information is similar to the fourth or fifth hour into one of those obnoxious endurance stunts, whether it's being sealed in a coffin, stuck in a block of ice, or submerged in water for a week or more.

For the first hour or two of the performance, there's an ecstatic crowd, and the adrenaline is pumping. And as the hours progress, especially near the end of the attempt, the ability to concentrate and sustain control over the body is mind-boggling. But during the middle hours, nothing is happening. The crowd has moved on and won't return until the stunt gets juicy.

At the present time, the buried-alive option is tantalizing. This meeting is about as mundane as it can get, but at least it won't be followed by exhaustion and malnourishment.

The meeting is described as a Northern Lineage benefits overview, which is always incredibly riveting. Combine that with the fact that I barely know anything about my current benefits, and I'd almost rather be submerged in water for the remainder of the day.

I somewhat listen to the slide reader, Ann Singleton, who has probably given enough presentations during the past week to receive her PowerPoint merit badge. The first few slides show how the benefits will impact associates leaving the company. Most of this information revolves around the COBRA package, which is just barely less expensive than the national debt for monthly services. The life insurance coverage will end 31 days after the separation date; short- and long-term disability will end immediately upon the last day of employment; and the 401(k) funds can be paid out or rolled over, depending on the current account status. I find it mildly intriguing that, as a company that sells life insurance and annuities, Northern Lineage won't take a longer opportunity to attempt to sell its products to parting employees.

Then again, the company probably realizes that the associates leaving aren't going to fork over millions of dollars, so there's not as much of an incentive to haggle.

Before Ann continues, presumably to outline benefits for those staying with the company, she allows people who have made up their minds to leave the meeting. A handful of people exit as we continue to estimate how many are in and how many are out. There are 234 employees at Mettle. Our group has come to a relative consensus that 40 to 60 percent will move, although most agree the high end will be nearly impossible to attain.

As Ann flips to the next slide, we see the two benefits that will be different: health insurance and the retirement plan.

I assume the health insurance plan will be vaguely the same as the current one. The biggest difference I notice is that the Northern Lineage Hospital Network must be used for full benefits. While every major hospital in Cincinnati and northern Kentucky is listed, there are some minor grumblings concerning Louisville hospitals not being listed.

Then the retirement information appears. One reason people stay with this company for 342 years is that it's tough to walk away from a great retirement package. Of course, this isn't the norm everywhere; a 2004 Bureau of Labor Statistics study noted that the percentage of workers employed for 10 years or more at the same company has dropped 3 to 4 percentage points since 1998.[2]

According to the sample calculations, with early retirement (age 55) and 20-plus years of servitude, an associate can reasonably receive $1,500 a month. If I stay with Northern Lineage that long, I will be close to that range, although Jeff will earn a bit more, since he's younger and has been with the company close to five years. To be eligible at all for the pension plan, you have to stay at least five years; if you don't, you lose any of the retirement funds that could await you.

There are some other terms mentioned — a pre-retirement death benefit and a deferred annuity benefit are among the slew of supposed benefits — that I glaze over. The others listen intently, except Barry, who is undoubtedly debating internally where to eat lunch. I'm content to return to my desk, eat lunch, play around on my computer for the rest of the day, and daydream about tonight's date with Diya.

***

I'm not convinced yet that this is a real date, but I definitely want it to be. I walk from the parking lot and sit on a stone ledge outside. I don't see Diya's vehicle, although I can't vividly remember what it looks like. I know I've seen her in the parking garage at least once. I assume that the minute she pulls in, I will remember.

My memory doesn't fail me. The door swings open from the blue TrailBlazer, which on a normal day can be seen from at least three miles away. It's one of those SUVs that gets close to 4.25 miles per gallon and would probably crumple if it were in an accident with a tricycle. I catch up with Diya as she starts to walk inside the Thai restaurant.

"I thought maybe you were going to stand me up," I say as the hostess takes us to our seat.

"No, I would not do that," Diya says. "A friend called just as I was leaving my apartment. He asked me where I was going, and I told him I was meeting you for dinner. He said that I hadn't told him I was going on a date."

"Ah, he's probably just jealous. He probably thought he would have dinner with you tonight."

"I don't think he's jealous at all. He likes my dog more than me."

"Your dog?"

"Yeah, he'll call and ask to speak to her. And he always asks how she's doing. I think he is my friend just to be friends with the dog."

I laugh. Not that there's anything wrong with calling someone to talk to the dog. I wonder whether the guy really likes the dog, or whether she's just a little naïve to think this. Or possibly she's just making a joke about the whole thing ... the most likely reason. It's always difficult when you meet someone to know how humorous the person is. Diya acts introverted around me 80 percent of the time, but she can also come up with a smart-ass comment at a moment's notice. While Barry can be a straightforward clown, Diya can be more subtle but just as effective at telling jokes. I wonder if my lack of distinguishing between funny and serious will get me in trouble in the future.

The restaurant is dimly lit and can pass for a romantic hideaway or an entrance to a coal mine. Diya requests that I select something without beef or pork so she can try it. She's Hindu, which forbids her from eating the aforementioned foods. I have always been curious about the mystical relationship Hindus have with cows. Because of all the things cows can give (milk in particular), they are considered a symbol of selflessness and abundance. So if cows are selfless, why does Hinduism not condone using them for meat and leather?

Maybe I'm just biased because members of my family raise cattle. It's not that I have anything against bovines — they're just not the most brilliant animals. I'm certain cows would finish mammal *Jeopardy!* with negative money. I have always been intrigued by the religious connections in India that allow cattle to roam free, unharmed, unbranded, and uneaten. Honestly, I'm not trying to make fun of Hinduism; I'm just trying to understand it. My dating future depends on it.

"Do you believe in Santa Cow?" I regretfully ask.

She scowls at me, so I switch subjects.

"So, um, how did you end up in Louisville?" I say.

"When I first came to the United States, I lived in New Jersey for a couple of years and worked as a database admin there," she says. "Then I moved to Colorado for a year and came here after that."

I think back to our earlier conversation in the day and how she has a two-year work visa. This morning, I assumed she started in America with Mettle.

"Wait a minute ... you've been over here longer than I thought," I say. "Haven't you been here long enough to gain citizenship? Or have you been on work visas the entire time? That's at least five years now."

"It's a little more complicated than that," Diya says. She has the same sullen look on her face that she had this morning.

"I was engaged, but he broke it off at the last minute," Diya says. "I didn't know if others at work had told you this yet, so I thought I should tell you before you found out from someone else."

I feel somewhat indifferent about this information. It had not crossed my mind that she could have been married before. Regardless, I'm on a date with an amazingly beautiful girl, so unless the next thing she tells me is that she's really a guy, well...

"My fiancé was already in the U.S. when I came to New Jersey. We planned to get married over here, and I moved with him to Colorado for his job. He sent in all of the information for both of us for the green card process, which is a normal procedure. Then we moved to Louisville. But as soon as we moved here, he started seeing another woman. Then he left ...

he wouldn't contact me back, so I had to reapply for the green card. There was no choice. That's one of the reasons why I don't want to have to apply again with this move to Cincinnati. I've been through this already."

"So you moved to Colorado to be with him, and then he just left?"

"Yes, he just left. It was ... "

She trails off and tilts her head down. I start to say something, but our food arrives. We both smile at the waitress.

"I'm really sorry for bringing this up," I say. "I didn't mean to get so personal."

"It's OK," Diya says. "I don't mind telling you this, really. You should know it. It's just that ... you're the first American guy I've been on a date with. I feel really comfortable around you."

"I don't know if I'll be able to help you much, but it's good to talk about things and let them out."

"You are right. I haven't told very many people about this because I still don't understand it. I don't know what happened."

"What do you mean you don't know? You don't know why he left?"

"No ... I really don't know. He never told me."

"How could he never tell you? How did you find out?"

"From a mutual friend. We had a little fight, and he decided to return to India for a while to visit his family. When he first came back, I thought everything was fine, but I guess it wasn't. He ended up getting a separate apartment, saying he just needed some time to figure it out. I thought that was a good thing, but he never talked to me. After a couple of months, there was a knock at the door, and this guy told me about the other girl. What could I do? He lived in the same apartment complex, just down the road from me."

"But didn't he tell you later?"

"He wouldn't answer the phone. I tried to talk to him at his apartment, and he wouldn't come out. I even went to his parents' house in India, and they wouldn't talk to me."

"And you still don't know? It has been, what, two years? Where is he?"

"He lives in Louisville still. I see him sometimes. I think his mom found a different girl for him to marry."

At this point, I have to ask the obvious.

"Your marriage ... was it arranged?"

"Yes ... but his mom never liked me. We met four times before we were married. He was a nice man, but it just didn't work out. To my friends and family back at home, it looks like my fault."

"Your fault?"

"Yes … in India, if there's a relationship issue, it's always the woman's fault."

So it's Diya's fault that her fiancé's mother found a new woman for her son to marry? And the guy left a gorgeous woman for no reason? Holy cow! I avoid cultural embarrassment by muttering this interjection under my breath.

Apparently in India, marriage works like this: parents of two families arrange a lifetime between their children. And it is up to the woman to adjust to whatever the man and his parents wish. But this isn't applicable for an Indian woman with a job and just a small dose of independence. Unfortunately, there are still numerous people in the homeland stuck on the Old World standards.

I have to be honest: Arranged marriages intrigue me. But I don't understand how she can feel guilty, because he never explained why they split up.

Considering the topics, we have an enjoyable meal, most likely due to the excellent cuisine at the Thai restaurant. All things considered, this can lead somewhere, perhaps back to my place for a nightcap … but then I snap out of it. I'm not putting any moves on her. Not after the story she just told. I mention that my sister has a volleyball game tonight, so we drive over to it.

"So Jason, what is a date to you?" says Diya after we arrive at the nearby sand volleyball courts.

"My definition may differ from other people's," I say. "You may want to ask someone else."

"No, I want to know your definition."

"I guess a date would be a meeting between two unattached people who are at least remotely interested in each other's company."

"But does there have to be something physical between people on a date?"

"I don't think so ... why do you ask?"

"I just thought all American guys wanted something to be physical on a first date."

"There are guys who would expect that. But there are many who don't. There are many different types of dates, and types of guys and girls. There are a lot of American girls who would expect that on a first date, too."

"There are Indian girls who are like that as well ... maybe that's why they come to America."

Afterward, we hang out with my sister and her teammates briefly. I introduce her to various people, saying she is my "friend," which will surely lead to more questions (especially from my sister) in the future. We then start back to the restaurant, where Diya left her vehicle. On the return, I'm curious about her other dating escapades.

"Just recently I was talking to a guy in California," Diya says. "He lived near my brother, in Sacramento. I talked to him on the phone a couple of times and went to visit him. But when I went there, he went off to play cricket."

"Did he know you were coming to visit?" I say.

"Yes! But he wanted me to go by his schedule. And I just sat at his place, waiting for him to come home. Finally, I left and went back to my brother's. That was ridiculous."

"I know cricket is the national sport of India, but does it

always take precedent over a lovely lady?"

She pinches me and laughs. I take that as a good sign. On the return trip, we pass a local jewelry shop.

"Look Jason, we should stop to pick out some diamond earrings for me!" Diya says.

This seems like a strange comment, although we've already touched on the physical nature of relationships ... why not discuss the material side of things?

"It appears that they're closed," I say, with a sigh of relief.

We make it back to Diya's TrailBlazer. An evening like this, we decide subconsciously, is best savored before analyzing what occurs next. As coworkers, we have plenty of issues already with the relocation process. As friends, we still need to discover how to assist each other in making work-related decisions. But as lovers, coming from totally different backgrounds, under rather opposite circumstances ... that's something that will remain unknown for the moment.

Tuesday, July 5

I barely notice the two men and one woman, wearing suits, in the elevator this morning. I initially reason they are going to another floor, for another company, but they press the "5," which is a Mettle floor. Maybe Northern Lineage sent fashion coordinators to properly dress everyone before the move?

I think about it for six seconds, then my mind goes back to Diya. Since Friday's date, we have talked on the phone every day. We have discussed work, but our conversations normally center on our daily activities, family members, and silly/interesting stories. Yeah, it sounds like a burgeoning friendship to me, too.

The time we have spent together has been a welcome change from many girls I've dated in the past. Maybe it's because she's older than me, and more mature, or maybe it's because she's much more intelligent than former female friends. I have dated girls of numerous ethnicities, yet Diya and I so far seem to have a fair amount in common.

Despite the good vibes, there is still something not quite right about the whole thing, and this is where it comes back to work. I have had pretty bad experiences in the past with dating girls from the office, so part of me says that I should stay away from this friendship. With the turmoil at Mettle, and everyone packing their bags to head to Cincinnati or bust, forging a long-lasting relationship would be much more than a consolation prize. I still don't see Diya and me as a couple, but I could probably warm up to the idea if I were standing close to her.

Instead, I find myself snuggling with Jeff at his desk.

I want to tell Jeff something about Diya, maybe commenting (in a Sean Connery voice, obviously) that things are about to get hot and heavy. But she was adamant about not discussing "us" with people at work. It may be strenuous to hide something from Jeff, as close as we have become, but I will try to keep my word.

Jeff hangs up the phone and belts out a strange sigh.

"I can't believe this is happening," Jeff says.

"Don't tell me ... Northern Lineage will be making every Mettle employee wear two ties?" I say. Jeff smirks as if what I said is the dumbest joke in modern history.

"That was Raj on the phone," Jeff says. "Apparently, Sally found out about the conversation Raj and I had about moving teams. She's pissed because she thinks we went around her."

"I thought the move was just speculation," I say. "Why would it matter?"

"I have no clue," Jeff says. "They just told us we were freakin' moving to Cincinnati, and now she's going to get mad because I want to switch departments?"

"Don't get hostile. There's nothing they can do to you."

"Sure they can. They can make my life a living hell."

"What's that supposed to mean?"

"You'll figure it out sooner or later."

I haven't witnessed anything too terrible at Mettle, although

Northern Lineage could be another story. I hadn't seen this emotion from Jeff yet. He seems to be the one happy-go-lucky person who, no matter how bad it looks, would still be able to find time to make jokes. But he's so pissed right now that he can't even play on his computer. He looks a little lost, like a boy whose parents decide to ride a roller coaster while he wanders off into the nearby woods, looking for his favorite theme park character.

"So what are you going do now?" I say, slowly moving back to my cube.

"I just don't want to be stuck doing something I hate," Jeff says.

"Hate" hasn't even entered my vocabulary at this point. My job is cool, I feel as if I belong, and I just had a date with an awesome girl who's a coworker. If hating your job has an opposite, this is it.

Cincinnati isn't that far away, either. A future with the company and the people here isn't out of the question.

But there's something, however minor, that doesn't sit right.

"Why would you hate this?" I say.

"If they are worried about me switching departments, that shows me I don't have a say in my job," Jeff says. "If I'm not happy here, why would I want to stay?"

"Why would people stay if they aren't happy?" I say.

"That's an easy answer. Once you're in for so long, you don't want to leave. It doesn't make sense. You have to stay."

I wonder what the time limit is on having to stay with the company. I don't want to be the guy trapped in the 9-to-5 job, eating the same minestrone soup and stale breadsticks from the cafeteria every day.

Diamonds earrings are forever, not my job at Northern Lineage.

6
Dress for Suck-sess

Tuesday, July 5 (continued)

The history of the modern suit began in the 17th century, when Charles II announced specific formal attire to be worn by the English Court.[3] By the mid-1800s, gentlemen had various coat styles (frock coat, morning coat, tailcoat, waistcoat, dinner jacket) from which to choose, and these begat the earliest suits (the lounge suit and later, the sack suit).[4]

Americans continued tradition, but the switch to ready-made clothes (as opposed to handmade or tailor-made) in the late 19th century allowed stylish men to purchase a variety of suits at affordable prices (author Charles Cist even declared Cincinnati to be the country's largest ready-made clothing market in the late 1850s).[5] During this time period, as tailors tried to salvage their businesses and larger clothing manufacturers tried to beat one another with the best deals, advertising became "a symbolic code of common reference for a broad spectrum of Americans."[6]

No man was safe anymore from being called unkempt in public without wearing a suit because that's what men were wearing in all of the newspaper and magazine ads. It's a good thing the Internet wasn't around then, or we'd have an entire YouTube video library of Charlie Chaplin look-alikes.

Studies have shown that having a formal dress code can benefit work productivity and boost professional image.[7] But wait! Other studies have shown that allowing people to wear what they want to wear to work can benefit work productivity and gives a sense of freedom.[8] This means that if you want to maximize your employees' performance, you should do one of two things: Either focus on their actual work capabilities or make them change wardrobes every hour.

As I complete a few intranet maintenance requests, I think back to the suited individuals I saw earlier on the elevator. If my experience in the workplace has taught me anything, it's to be wary of the suits. Sure, the president probably wears one, along with few other important people in the organization. But what's the purpose of dressing up on a daily basis? Do they have something to prove to others with their attire?

I never wanted to get into the business world because I'm uninterested in wearing a tie every day. I somewhat understand the need to if you are meeting with outside clients. You know, so both parties can be completely miserable and choking to death while settling a deal.

It has become trendy for many businesses to become lax with the dress code and to adopt casual attire, although each company usually has different rules. This is be a good time to review Mettle's dress code, so I pull out the orientation binder.

Monday-Friday: Business casual
Men: a shirt with a collar and dress slacks
Women: a reasonable length skirt or pants with a
respectable top or an informal dress
Items considered unacceptable:
* jeans (any color)
* tennis shoes
* T-shirts or sweatshirts
* jogging suits
* leggings (or other stretchy, tight-fitting slacks)
* microskirts and miniskirts
* halter/tank tops
* tattered or torn clothing
* flip-flops
* sandals
* Capri pants or any pants that are not full length

The biggest complaint I have is the shirt-with-collar deal, just because I have a fair amount of decent shirts without one. I also heard a rumor that some Fridays are Hawaiian shirt days, minus the lei and coconut bra.

Most of the males in the office wear a basic polo shirt and khakis to work. Don will occasionally don a white button-down shirt. The women wear a variety of things, including many tops that don't even have collars. I've seen Diya wear Indian-style clothing on occasion. There is little conformity, which most people seem to find appealing. Wearing a uniform isn't always bad because you don't have to worry too much about how to dress each day. It's the difference between a creative, pleasant atmosphere and one where you would probably prefer to be bludgeoned to death with a plunger.

It's past 10, but the office is pretty quiet, largely due to meetings with the parent company. I have a difficult time completing my intranet tasks because I always find interesting tidbits of information as I surf. Today, I find a web component that allows internal users to search a list of suspected terrorists. In a financial institution, it's probably important to make sure you aren't selling annuities to evil world masterminds. I wonder if suicide bombers receive a break on the death benefit portion of the life insurance form.

Jeff is still on the phone, still mulling his options about the move to the e-commerce team. How would the move benefit him? Our group works closely with that team in building additional functionality for the main website, which is used by customer service reps, brokers, and clients to essentially move money in and out of various funds. New funds appear all of the time, however, and each set of funds has its own set of rules regarding how it can be handled. With any website, it's necessary to design the structure so that it looks nice but simple enough to be used by anyone.

Jeff prefers to be a larger part of the graphic design concept, not just be handed a specification and be told, "This is how it's going to look, so do it!" As a web designer, you have to know what is feasible and what can't be accomplished. If you tell an authority that you can do something, you'd better damn well know how to do it. Lately, Jeff has run into roadblocks with the e-commerce team because its members are unfamiliar with how things work on the web. Most of the designers primarily work in print, a different beast altogether. Jeff would be a key asset to the team, with his vast knowledge of both design and functionality issues.

While Jeff races past my cube, carrying a notebook, I hear Don next door, talking on the phone. It sounds as if he's trying to sell something, maybe life insurance, to the person on the other end.

"Good afternoon Angela, how are you today?" Don says. "I was given your name by Northern Lineage to check with you about relocation information ... Yes, I just recently sold my house, and we will be looking to move pretty soon ... What's that? ... Probably within a month or two. We want to get up there in time to get our kids in school at the beginning of the school year ... We're mostly familiar with the area, but we will be using a Realtor ... thank you so much Angela, I appreciate your help."

I walk over to hear how Don's move is going so far.

"Well, I guess you can call me a company man now!" says Don, wearing his recently typical white button-down shirt. "I've even decided to dress the part now — well, except I'm not going to wear a tie unless I absolutely have to."

"Who was on the phone?" I say.

"I guess it was someone at Northern Lineage; I'm not really sure anymore. I've talked to so many people that I've lost track. I talked to Marshall earlier, and our Realtor here in Louisville, and Chris, and ... "

"Why do you have to talk to all of these people right now?"

"I probably don't have to talk to all of them right now. But I might as well get it taken care of, since I don't have much work to do."

There is a distinct difference in the work performed within our team. Although there is some overlap, Don, Diya, Ken, and Nitya, who is the team leader, handle the database administrator duties. I'm still uncertain as to how they divide projects.

Barry, Jeff, and I take care of site fixes and database interaction. We also have two additional team members: Debbie and Reshmi, who are also Java programmers. We all work together, to a certain extent, but we have our specialties, theoretically. If only we had superpowers like throwing fire or talking to aquatic animals, we could probably complete our jobs a lot faster. At the very least, we could use a utility belt or two.

"Are you going to move?" says Don, looking over his list of numbers for more people to call.

"I don't know," I say. "I'm still weighing my options."

"Well if you do, and you get a premium bid for your house, make sure you get it down in writing. That will help when you take care of the monetary items with Northern Lineage."

"Thanks," I say as I start to back out of Don's cube. "I'll keep that in mind."

I'm not sure what a premium bid is anyway, and I haven't even thought about selling my house. Maybe I'm further away from moving than I thought.

There's some commotion outside Barry's cube, which is on the other side of Don's. I walk around the partition and find Sam, one of the IT guys, and Ken staring over Barry's shoulder at the computer.

"Yeah, I just saw it on the website; it's on the front page of *Business First*," says Sam, referring to Louisville's business newspaper. "I couldn't believe it, but the timing is impeccable."

Barry types the website address, and the story Sam mentioned appears: Waveland Healthcare has announced it is adding 1,100 jobs during the next year to its Louisville offices. Presumably, many of these new jobs will be computer-related, which instantly gives anyone at Mettle who is uninterested in moving a place to work.

"I guess it's time for me to send over my résumé!" Barry says. "Well, maybe I should update it first."

"It's a place in Louisville, that's for sure," Ken says. "But I've heard few good things about working there."

"I can tell you more, if you'd like to hear some," says Don as he enters the conversation while still sitting at his desk.

"Did you work there?" I say.

"Yes ... and there were plenty of reasons to leave," Don says. "I think they always have a lot of jobs because they have a tendency to chase people away. Would anyone like to learn the words to UC's fight song?"

Don continues to wave a sheet of paper that contains the lyrics to the University of Cincinnati's fight song. Why, I'm not really sure, but unless there's a passage devoted to choosing allegiances in the corporate world, they're not going to be too helpful at the moment. I know virtually nothing about Waveland, and I know only two week's worth of Mettle business, but I'm pretty positive that these two companies aren't similar. Waveland is in the class of large shops, by Marshall's definition, while Mettle has a much smaller workforce. Even Northern Lineage is smaller than Waveland. At this point, Don's word in voting Waveland off the island is good enough for me ... although I suppose it can't hurt to investigate the available positions.

Back at my desk, I silently agree with Barry that updating résumés is a good idea. Having just found this job, and being sick of looking for jobs, I really don't want to do it. But I also have no urge to move. The preview trip to Cincinnati is next week, so surely that will answer many questions, including the one about why the hell I would want to stick with a company where I haven't yet hit the 80-hour mark.

Jeff hurries back to his desk, signs into his computer, and then walks into my cube.

"I think this is under control now," says Jeff, ceremonially wiping his forehead.

"What's under control, the move to e-commerce?" I say. "When do you go?"

"Maybe never. I was in Sally's office, and she had Raj on speakerphone. He told her that he had discussed with me the possibility of moving, but there were no promises for anything."

"And?"

"She seemed content with that. I suppose she thought I was moving down to the fifth floor later today or something."

"So are you upset you aren't going to switch teams?"

"The way she talked, the teams would be completely different in Cincinnati anyway. I don't think they want to change anything until we get up there."

If Northern Lineage doesn't know much about our current processes in the first place, why would they care if we changed something? For instance, Mettle just hired me ... isn't that a pretty big change from two weeks ago? Obviously, there is still a lot to learn about the corporate culture here.

"If you can't switch teams, will that affect your decision to move to Cincinnati?" I say.

"Not right now," Jeff says. "There's still a lot to determine. I'll probably base my decision more on the people there, not just where I'm going to be. If they are cool dudes, it's worth checking out. Besides, the bonus money is looking better and better all of the time. Laura is ready to quit her job and work elsewhere, so this is pretty good timing, from her standpoint."

Personally, I'd be a bit peeved if members of upper management disagreed over allowing me to do what I want to do. But Jeff doesn't appear to be too traumatized. At least they didn't make him stand on the corner outside to sell our least successful retirement fund.

For much of the afternoon, I attempt to learn more Java by looking through the monstrosity of a book I have on my desk. I also start looking into Jeff's project, called Annuity Profit Plus, or APP by the Secret Society of Mutual Funders. So far, all I've learned is that this web application will enable users to generate annuity quotes on the fly. I suppose that's a good thing, as long as people know what the hell they are doing.

As I'm sitting in my cube, trying not to fall asleep, Jeff comes over and scares the shit out of me.

"Buddy!" he says as I almost fall out of my chair. "Do you think you can help me on this Annuity Profit Plus thing?"

"What do you want me to do?" I say. "I'm still trying to figure out what an annuity is."

"Well, keep looking at it, but don't stare at it like you do at Diya."

"Whoa, what?"

"You heard me. So are you going to ask her out or what?"

I didn't want to give Jeff too much information, but I don't want to be the lying-sack-of-shit guy. I figured there was no harm in stating the bare minimum.

"We went out a few nights ago," I say. "But she said she'd prefer if we didn't talk about it too much at work."

"That doesn't surprise me," Jeff says. "There are a lot of guys here who thinks she's fine, and they've been trying to get with her for a while now. She's made it clear to them she dates only Indian guys, so that would throw a bit of a wrench into her excuse."

"Unless I am Indian."

"Yesssshhhh, you have a point there, lad."

We continue our lame Sean Connery impersonations until there's a knock at my cube.

Now, I've never had a knock at my cube, as there is no door. But after hearing a knock, I see a man and a woman, both in business attire. Both awaiting our attention. I'm not sure why, but the impression that leaps into my head is that of a brother-sister singing duo. I imagine them singing hits like "Suits Are Sweet" and "We Put the Biz in Showbiz." It's their giddy, over-caffeinated facial expressions that resemble a '70s family singing group.

"Hi, I'm Mindy Green, and this is Marty Valentine," the woman says. Jeff and I shake their hands; I assume they won't decapitate us with razor-sharp cufflinks.

"We're down from Northern Lineage to meet with people, primarily in your department," Marty says. "We'll be overseeing this department once you guys move up to Cincinnati."

"It's great to meet you both," Jeff says. "I'm Jeff, and this is Jason."

"Yes, Chris mentioned you just a few minutes ago," Mindy says. She then looks to me. "This is only your third week?"

"Actually, it's my second," I say. "But I can't wait to hit the 100-hour mark!"

The twins laugh at the comment, while Jeff laughs at me. Old joke, new crowd.

"How was the drive down?" Jeff says.

"It was better today than yesterday," Marty says. "We didn't know until the last minute we were coming, so we got stuck in traffic up in Cincy. Today was a bit more relaxing. There are a few more people who are going to be coming down here the next couple of weeks, so they might have a shuttle."

"I may try the shuttle," Mindy says, "but I'd prefer to drive on my own. That way, I can head out whenever I want and be back at a decent time."

Then I realize that Marty said they would be "overseeing" our department. Does that make them our bosses? Are they Chris's boss? Do they manage together, or is one higher than the other? Are they married? And how are their album sales going, especially with their new hit single "Trapped in Organizational Hell"?

We chat for a few moments. Marty and Mindy actually seem fairly normal, despite their attire.

"Those people are our new bosses?" I say after they leave.

"I think ... possibly," Jeff says. "What did you think?"

"They seem like ... normal bosses, I guess."

"Yeah, they could be OK."

"Or they could turn into demons."

"Or, more likely, they work with the demons. Even if Northern Lineage is evil, our superiors wouldn't be at the bottom depths of hell."

"True. But if it really is an inferno, working your way to the top might mean digging deeper to the bottom."

7
Transfer of Knowledge

Wednesday, July 6

I think more people would job hunt if they could do it with a bow and arrow. Instead, finding a job usually comes far below the following options:

• Dressing up to go to work every day
• Watching the story of heterosexuals in the fashion industry, called _Pinking Shears Are for Straight Guys, Too_!
• Tap-dancing on molten lava
• Doing all of the above at the same time
• Being shot with a bow and arrow

Unfortunately, finding a job is a necessity in our current way of life, and it's difficult to escape. In fact, the only way I've found to avoid it is to have a job. That way, I don't have to look for another, although occasionally I do, because I can always use the money for a new pair of pinking shears.

What's frustrating, however, is that having a job doesn't mean keeping it forever. You may be an exceptional employee. Maybe you offer your coffee, expertise, and body to the boss on a regular basis. While that might keep your position (or a few of them, depending on stamina) there are still no certainties in the workplace. OK, there is one certainty: If you're not screwing someone, you're going to get screwed yourself.

After attempting to find the right job for almost 256 years, I ended up as a programmer for a life insurance company. After seven days, I had already met a fair share of fun, interesting, and entertaining people.

Then on the eighth day, I met everyone else. We all sat in the basement conference room and learned that our jobs were moving to Cincinnati.

The actual work during the first two weeks may have sounded boring. Well, it was. Approximately half the time, Jeff and I looked for Sean Connery sound bites online, just to perfect our accents. Project tasks in the financial world are mundane. There's a greater chance of winning the Out-of-the-Box Thinker Award for a given week than performing a task for most companies.

I suspect this isn't too different than any other company that proclaims to give its employees life "choices." It's sort of like going on the game show *Let's Make a Deal*, winning a lifetime supply of underarm hair, and having the opportunity to trade it in for what's inside the offensive smelling worn-out tennis shoe behind door number 2.

Our options are clear. We can move to Cincinnati and continue to work for a company that has been doing things the same way for roughly 800 years (they have the sundial to prove it). Or, we can stay in Louisville and find a different job, amongst a myriad of barracuda-acting work seekers, in a town where computer jobs aren't standing on corners and looking for the first trick to walk by.

I suppose it could be worse. Not only does the parent company want us to believe we are going to work in Disney World (where we get to hang out with Mickey Mouse and sleep with Snow White and Cinderella), but the company is also going to pay us quite nicely to do so. The best part is that the only real work we have to do is properly knot our ties every morning. We've already signed the waiver to give our souls to the company.

But it's worth it, because there's frozen yogurt every day in the cafeteria.

I didn't see the entire schedule for the week, but at last

count, there are roughly 34,104,497 meetings set for each day. I know this because Ken is supposed to be in three meetings at 8 a.m., while Barry and Jeff have two apiece. Maybe Northern Lineage is jumping the gun a bit on parallel universe web conferencing, or perhaps we should be using stunt doubles. Either way, I'm stuck at my desk, trying to figure out the Annuity Profit Plus program that Jeff built.

I overhear others talking about what is occurring at these meetings. It is something Northern Lineage calls the Transfer of Knowledge. When I say it eight times really fast, I envision two things. First, I picture *The Fellowship of the Ring*, trying to arbitrate the meaning of life, liberty, and pursuit of annuities. But Barry, not Frodo, would be expected to carry the burden of annuities to the promised land of Cincinnati.

After this picture fades away, I see Barry sitting in one chair and a monkey, wearing a tie, in the other. The mad scientist slowly places the lampshade hats on both heads and straps down the arms and legs of Barry and the monkey. With a sinister laugh, the scientist flips the switch, and soon thereafter, a constant electrical stream of knowledge can be seen in the air, passing from Barry to the monkey. After a successful exchange, the scientist unlatches both parties, only to find that the monkey now has a sudden craving for Chinese food.

Either way, with Barry at the helm, Northern Lineage appears to be in good hands, at least from the standpoint of fund transfers. Again, I have no idea if this is true, but judging by Barry's remarks, he is damn proud of his work.

"They were blown away with the information we gave them!" Barry says to me at my desk.

"But Barry, I don't think they were expecting you to talk about your first sexual experience," says Jeff, trailing behind.

Barry and Jeff's banter continues as I notice Ken creeping around the corner of my cube.

"Hey guys, how did the meeting go?" Ken says.

"It was great!" Barry says, slamming his fist down on my

desk, frighteningly close to my keyboard and fingers. "They had no idea we have all of these processes running smoothly. There were a lot of blank stares in the room."

"I'm wondering if I'm getting ready to head into the same thing," Ken says. "I'm supposed to explain the customer relationship management system in a few minutes to the Northern Lineage people. There's another meeting scheduled for the afternoon, but I doubt I'll make it ... I'll probably still be in this one."

"We're done for the day," Jeff says. "That's a good thing, so I can get back to Annuity Profit Plus, the only project that appears to be continuing through this mess."

"So what about tomorrow?" Ken says. "Is everyone going to Cincinnati?"

Jeff, Barry, and I look at each other with similar blank stares, and we realize that tomorrow is the day of our Cincinnati tour. We're closing in on the midway point of our decision ... they sealed the deal close to a month ago, and August 15 looms a little over a month away.

"I'm going on the trip," Jeff says. "If I don't get a good vibe going up there, and things aren't as they've told us they would be, then I won't have a problem saying no. If they really want us to relocate, they should be willing to cater to our needs."

"I second that," Barry says. "Even though I doubt I'll go, it would be nice to find out what the atmosphere is like. I've been up there for small trips, but not in this capacity."

"I'm interested in checking out the cafeteria," I say. "And definitely our team. If I don't like the team, I don't think I'll be making an extra effort to move."

"Yeah, but don't forget that we use different technology than they do," Jeff says. "We're doing essentially the same thing, but we're using Java, while they use .NET. I doubt there will be much crossover at first. I wonder if any of their people will even come in contact with ours."

"Someone up there is going to have to know the system I manage," Ken says. "Because the other people here who know it aren't going. Anyway, I'd better run; I'm already three minutes late."

"I'll walk with you; I need to visit the boys' room," Jeff says.

"And I need to complete this maintenance request," says Barry as he leaves.

My work area is empty. I guess that means I should continue working on the Annuity Profit Plus calculator. I have learned little so far about the application. Apparently, the system will allow users to generate their own annuity quotes. It seems like a neat idea, because people can play with the term lengths and various other options to find the plan that fits their style.

I'm unsure just how long Jeff has been working on the program. The screens (what the public user actually sees) seem intact. I've given a cursory glance at the backend code, and there's a lot to it. From what Jeff says, however, there's still a ton of crap that has to be completed. I remember hearing that the first deadline on the entire product was July 1. Judging by that milestone, I'm assuming that there are just a few touch-up items that need to be accomplished, and then it will be ready to run.

So far today, I have been working on JavaScript validation. I just have to make sure that people enter allowable data into the system. For instance, a user can't enter February 31 for the birthday field. If this happens, the system that receives the data will not know how to handle it. Then, when the daily server process attempts to pick up the data for yet another system, it could become unstable. If that system becomes unstable, all of the daily processes may be thrown awry. And if the domino effect continues, multiple events could take place, from a nuclear holocaust to aliens hosting a talk show to discuss how to properly wear the Brooks Brothers No. 1 tie and an ascot on back-to-back business days.

Maybe I've built up the importance of Javascript validation a bit too much, but what else am I supposed to do? I still haven't been at this job for a month. I'm not an indispensable cog in the Mettle world.

Jeff still hasn't returned from the bathroom. I check the time on the computer and realize that it has been nearly an hour since he left with Ken. As I'm wondering if the plunger has attacked Jeff again, Barry peeks in.

"Where is Jeff?" Barry says. "I thought we were going to lunch, and it's almost 1 now."

"He hasn't been at his desk," I say. "Maybe he went without you."

"That turd! Well, if you see him, tell him that I'm meeting a friend at T.G.I. Friday's. Talk to you later."

Barry takes off toward the elevator, and I see Diya walking toward her cube with lunch.

I haven't thought much about Diya today. Instead, I've been working, and trying to figure out if that's really worth it. If the work itself is not stimulating, then I'm not really interested in it. I'm still on the fringe of the APP project, but if I push for more, I should get a feel for the company's expectations.

Other than that, I'm still unaware of Diya's feelings about me, our date, and our current relationship status. I can't decide if "dating" Diya is the right thing to do in the first place. Besides, her life is hectic enough at work. Diya has work poured on her with a sweatshop ladle. I really don't want to bother her with relationship stuff, too.

"Have you eaten yet?" says Diya. She looks much more awake and happy today.

"No, not yet," I say. "I just brought peanut butter for lunch."

"You should come eat at my cube."

"OK, give me a couple of minutes and I'll join you."

I make my way to Diya's cube, carrying two peanut butter sandwiches, a small bag of wheat crackers, a banana, and my glass of water. Diya has her food sitting next to the keyboard, but she is still working. I don't know whether I should sit in the chair next to her desk, sit on the windowsill a few feet away, or just stand back a bit.

"Don't you ever take a break?" I say.

"Not today," Diya says. "There is too much stuff going on here. Have a seat. Would you like to try this?"

Diya points to a delicious-smelling concoction that is sitting in a Tupperware container. It sort of looks like a home-style roast, with potatoes, carrots, and onions, only it smells completely different. She also has soft taco-like shells to eat with the dish.

"I like trying different food," I say. "But I should finish my food first. Are you excited about the trip tomorrow?"

I'm uncertain if Diya is paying attention to me any longer, because she is once again engaging her computer screen in a staring contest.

"The trip will be ... interesting," Diya says. "But the trip doesn't mean much to me. As it stands, I have to move anyway because of the green card."

"But that might change," I say. "There have to be other options, right?"

Diya shrugs, and I'm not sure what to say. I want to help Diya, and there must be some role I can play in the solution.

I taste the food, and it's delicious. It is fairly spicy, with a lot of red pepper, but I'm not breathing fire. I take a drink of water and unpeel a banana. As I examine Diya's screen full of white code on black text, Tom Nelson wanders nearby. Nelson (for whatever reason, the guy goes by his last name, possibly due to other Toms in the building) works on a different programming team and sits on the other side of me, which makes it strange that he is traveling near Diya's cube. He glances out the window, then over at me and then at Diya.

"Whoa! What's going on here?" says Nelson. He really hasn't talked to me much since I started working at Mettle, so

I'm not quite sure how to respond.

"We're eating lunch," I say. "What are you doing?"

"Oh, I finally just got out of a three-hour meeting," Nelson says. "Transfer of Knowledge equals gobs and gobs of meetings."

"Maybe it is a good time to be the new guy," I say. "Since I don't know anything, I don't have to go to the meetings. I just wish I had a little more work to do."

Nelson scans Diya's cube like a private investigator and heads back to his desk. I say something to Diya, but she is already back to her routine and doesn't hear me.

Back at my desk, I continue the excitement of trying to figure out what dates are valid for the annuity program. I notice on the notes Jeff gave me that there are a variety of allowable dates, depending on the user's choices. I'm closer to finally grasping the program's purpose, but there are still items I really don't understand. I jot down a few of these when I notice Jeff hurriedly walking past my cube. Chris is right behind him, walking nearly as fast. I wander over to Jeff's cube, but the second I arrive, Chris heads back past my cube, toward his office.

"We're going to have a quick web team meeting to go over the ... meetings," Jeff says.

Barry shoots out of his cube, across the hall.

"What meetings would these be?" Barry says.

"Just ... all of these meetings that are going on," Jeff says. "The Transfer of Knowledge and such. We just got out of one of them and ... "

"What meeting were you in?" Barry says. "I thought you were done for the day?"

"Yeah, I thought so too," Jeff says. "I was coming back from the bathroom, and Chris said to come with him. I didn't have a notebook or pen or anything, and they were asking questions."

"Who's 'they'?" Barry says.

"People from Northern Lineage," Jeff says. "The lady we met the other day, Mindy, was in the there ... and a bunch of other people I didn't recognize."

"Why didn't I know about this meeting?" Barry says. "Maybe I should have gone."

"I don't know, man," Jeff says. "I didn't even know about it. Anyway, we're supposed to head over to Chris's office for a brief update."

As Jeff rounds up everyone else for the meeting, I watch a tinge of anger build on Barry's face.

"I know these systems better than Jeff, so if someone is going to go to these meetings, it should be me," Barry says.

"I wouldn't worry too much about it," I say. "It was probably a worthless meeting, like most of them."

"You're probably right," Barry says. "I just think there's something going on ... like they're trying to push me out."

"Can they really do that?" I say. "It seems like you know a lot of stuff they don't."

In the IT realm, one reason people never train each other is simple: job security. If I'm the only person who knows how to do Task X, then how can they get rid of me? What these people fail to realize, however, is that some people who have this philosophy are the same people who are reluctant to learn new things. So, over time, the older systems are replaced with new ones, and at some point, Task X is phased out.

In the meantime, there's always room for a good trainer, because those people make the company more efficient. Assuming that Barry's earlier seminar on the current system was stellar, there's no doubt they'd want him along for the bus ride to the Queen City.

We gather in Chris's office. We wait for Chris to speak, but he's checking his email. I look around, wondering if someone else is going to talk. I reason that perhaps those who have gone to the Transfer of Knowledge meetings have been equipped with microchips and are actually communicating with the mothership. Maybe the reception is better in Chris's office.

"Sorry, I'm just reading an email here from Anita Williams, one of the senior VPs," Chris says. "She's given me a list of meetings for tomorrow, Friday, next week ... "

"None of us will be here tomorrow," Ken says. "We're going on the Cincinnati tour."

"I'm not going," Don says. "Unless they are furnishing a U-Haul for all of my stuff. I'll stay back and man the office. And no, I'm not going to any meetings, either."

"I forgot about the trip tomorrow," Chris says. "Luckily, the agenda tomorrow is light. However, there are a few next week. We just need a body at each."

"Are these meetings specifically about our systems, like the one this morning?" Barry says. "I should go see if they have questions."

"It's not really that big of a deal," Chris says. "It's a meet-and-greet thing. They want to know the contacts in each area. There is a meeting about fund transfers, so you'll be at that one, Barry. There's one about the intranet, Jeff, so keep an eye out for that. The others, it doesn't really matter to me."

Some people think it's soooo exciting to have a meeting. Yuck. A pointless meeting was the top answer on the board in a 2004 Microsoft study regarding productivity in small businesses.[9] In other psychological research, it was found that those people who like meetings typically don't like to finish the job, whereas employees who hated meetings were better workers and more focused.[10] Of course, the studies never mentioned companies that had meetings to talk about how much they hated meetings. Or those other small businesses that always made sure there were drinks and strippers at their meetings, so that it would never been considered a wasted effort.

As for Barry, with his days as a stripper almost behind him, meetings weren't always high on his list of priorities. In this case, it was more of a challenge, or a threat to his usefulness with Mettle.

"Why would Jeff go to any of these meetings?" Barry quietly says to me as we leave Chris's office. "I can understand the intranet one, but I built a bunch of the functionality. I should be the one to explain it."

"Just chill out, man," I say. "There seem to be plenty of meetings to go around!"

Barry and I are conversing just outside Barry's cube when Jeff tries to join in the conversation. Barry spins the other way and doesn't acknowledge Jeff. Instead, he sighs and sits at his computer.

"Look, I'm not trying to steal your thunder," Jeff says. "If you want to go to them, by all means, go to the meetings!"

"It's not just that," Jeff says. "I think Chris is shunning me intentionally, to get rid of me."

"That's crazy," Jeff says. "They can't get rid of you ... yet!"

"All I can say is that I'm not going to have the annuity system topple during my tenure here," Barry says.

With that, we decide it's best for us to go back to our cubes, and maybe even get some work accomplished. It's almost the end of the day, but I still would like to figure out these questions regarding Annuity Profit Plus. Jeff says he'll come to my cube after he checks his email.

But less than two minutes later, Jeff's phone rings. Again, I'm stuck reviewing the same code. The problem now is that I've seen the code so many times that it's starting to look funny, like if you type the same word too many times in a row.

"That was my Realtor," says Jeff as he stands in my cube.

"How did you get a Realtor?" I say. "That sounds like a personal problem."

"I'm guessing Northern Lineage started assigning Realtors to people who are going on the weekend trips," Jeff says. "Since mine is this weekend, she wanted to introduce herself and go over a couple of things."

The weekend trip is one of the most impressive things Northern Lineage has offered for the moving experience.

Basically, you get to take a weekend trip to Cincinnati. They put you up in a hotel Friday night and feed you, and then Saturday, you spend the majority of the day checking out housing in your requested areas. On top of that, the company is anteing up a $100 per diem for Saturday meals. I had yet to sign up because I really don't think I need a Realtor. A lot of people in my situation would go ahead and use the company for the trip. I'm sure I could even find a date for a night at the hotel, but I just don't think it's worth what would ensue the next day: A knock-out, drag-down battle with someone telling you to purchase not just one ridiculously priced home, but possibly several.

If I need someone screaming at me to buy something obnoxious, I just flip to one of the home shopping channels. And I turn up the volume.

For someone like Jeff, however, who has a wife and at least a notion of having a family, looking for a house during this process makes sense. Besides, the company is paying for the move, so why not take advantage of the niceties the parent company offers? That is, assuming you can handle the drawbacks of not totally making the decision to move just yet.

"The lady acted a little ... rushed on the phone," Jeff continues. "She wanted to know if I had decided to move yet. I said that I'm pretty sure, but ... and she cut me off. It's like she wants to work with me only if I'm definitely moving."

"They don't want to waste time if you aren't moving at all," I say. "And I really don't want to be pressured into buying a house somewhere I don't plan to live for very long."

"I'm in as much as I can be right now. Then again, tomorrow could play a huge factor in all of that. If I go up there, and they treat us like outsiders, then I'll just cancel this trip."

"Even if they aren't interested in Mettle employees, surely they can act nice for one day."

"Yeah, but it would be comforting to know that they are genuine. That will probably be enough for me to sign my life over to them ... for at least a couple more years."

8
Let's See the New Place

Thursday, July 7

Every job has a defining moment.

But with every job, it's not so easy to see that moment at the time it occurs. A typical moment is not like Peyton Manning winning a Super Bowl, Louis Pasteur discovering penicillin, or Keanu Reeves uttering his first epic "Whoa" in *Bill and Ted's Excellent Adventure.*

Most of the time, something specific occurs that makes you realize that you want to be at your job. Maybe it's as simple as receiving a compliment from upper management. Maybe it's a project on which you're allowed to call the shots, the first at this particular company. Or maybe it's realizing that the work you've put in for the past month or so is finally coming to fruition.

There are so many possibilities of defining moments, and these types of things give us all understanding as to why we do what we do. When you start a job, you hope you're in the right place. After a few weeks of adjustments, you reason that it's not so bad, minus all of the dropped passes by some third-string wide receiver. You reason that with a little more time, and more petri dishes, you have a shot at doing something unfathomable. And, with a little luck, you might even be able to, you know, philosophize with So-crates.

I had set the alarm for 6:32 a.m., an hour earlier than usual, because I didn't want to be late for a potential defining moment. The bus was supposed to leave for Cincinnati right at 8, so I figured I should get there a little early. Finally, I have the opportunity to see what Northern Lineage represents. The other team members going on the trip — Jeff, Ken, Barry, Diya, Chris, Debbie, and Reshmi — have been to the headquarters before. But I've never been inside the buildings ... just window shopping during my previous blind date.

My clock now shows 7:13, and I mention this because I'm in the process of properly knotting my tie. People who know me realize that dressing up is not on top of my list of things to do. I wore a tie for four years during high school, so it's not as if I'm unwilling to do so. My major rift with the slinky silk accessory is that it's uncomfortable. I'll tolerate it for important events, and taking a trip to my potential new place of business is an important event.

This is my newest defining moment.

The parking garage is rather barren at 7:40 a.m., almost an hour earlier than I normally arrive. I park on the third floor (I usually park on the sixth) and walk across the street, where a charter bus sits in front of the Mettle building. There are a handful of people waiting for the ride, although no one else from my team has appeared. At 7:50, we begin to board the bus. As I find a seat, I see Ken, Chris, and Jeff outside. The bus fills rapidly, and everyone is wearing nice attire. As for me, I'm wearing a gray button-down shirt and khakis. I notice that almost every guy is wearing suit-style pants, or at least black dress slacks.

Barry jumps on the bus, sits down across from me, and immediately comments on my clothing.

"Hey newbie, you're supposed to dress up for this!" says Barry, looking as if he is waiting for a hug from Jeff, his bus-riding seat-sharer.

"This is all I have," I say. "I'm not going to buy more clothes just to take a trip to Cincinnati. If they don't like me because of my clothes, maybe I don't want to work there in the first place."

It's not that I intentionally want to start a skirmish over the dress code ... I'm fully within it. But I just plopped down money for a zillion polo shirts about a month ago, and I didn't think it was necessary to pick up additional pants at that time. Unfortunately, I don't have a suit that fits, although I did wear the one from high school just three years ago. I seemed to do OK in job interviews with what I had already, and I already have this job ... so I can save my money for something more useful, like frozen yogurt.

And if I do end up moving, I doubt I'll complete my wardrobe in the same fashion (no pun intended) as outlined in John T. Molloy's *New Dress for Success*. He recommends owning 27 dress shirts, which includes a mix of solid white broadcloth and oxford cloth; blue pencil-striped, broadcloth, end-on-end weaves, oxford cloth, and pinstriped; and a handful of pale yellow, pastels, and random patterns.[11] Oh, and we must not forget, "One dressy solid white broadcloth, to be kept in a plastic bag, clean, ironed, and always ready for emergencies."[12] What sort of emergency could happen ... like putting a clothing store out of business by buying every shirt it carries?

We pull into the parking area for what I assume is the Northern Lineage main hub. We evacuate the bus and head inside a large, white, two-story building. We enter a large room that contains six tables with letters on them. I see Diya, Ken, and a few other people from our floor at a table near the front, so I find a seat there.

In the back of the room, people are lining up and filling their plates with goodies. Even though I have already eaten breakfast, I'm still hungry. I pick up a small bowl of mixed fruit, a pineapple muffin, a cookie, and a carton of orange juice. Back at my seat, I notice a folder of information, with the corresponding letter at the top of it: "A." In the back of the room, right behind the food spread, there's a fairly large banner that reads "Welcome Mettle Employees."

I flip through the papers and find an interesting sheet labeled "Northern Lineage Fun Facts." Here's a sample of the items:

• Northern Lineage was founded in 1863, and most people don't realize that Abraham Lincoln scrawled the Gettysburg Address on NL letterhead.

• The founders of Northern Lineage were Bill "Moonlight" Northern and Pops Lineage, both of whom became journeymen for the Cincinnati Red Stockings baseball team in the 1870s.

• While people "Panicked" in 1893, Northern and Lineage invested in the B&O Railroad, mainly because it had the best snack cart of all the railroads.

• During the '30s, Northern Lineage produced a radio drama called *As the Money Clip Turns* to compete with soap operas, only to see a substantial drop in new policies.

• In 1985, Northern Lineage attempted to delve into the movie-making business, creating *Financedance*, a sequel to the 1983 musical romance *Flashdance*.

• The entire Northern Lineage team placed its name in the *Guinness World Book of Records* in 1997 by sending a single email that announced new mutual fund offerings to 1.4 million individuals.

I laugh in disbelief at these "facts," then I notice at the bottom of the page that many NL employees add random Fun Facts to their email address signatures. Is there anything better than a ridiculous email signature? As long as I can combine it with text to save the environment and prevent people from printing emails, I will be all set.

A man with a nametag of "Roy Perkins" and a suit that says "$$$$$" speaks to us while we are still munching on snacks. He seems overly excited to see the Mettle turnout.

Then something happens that no one expects. Roy introduces Mr. Northern Lineage himself, Claude Simpson. Yes, this is the same Claude Simpson who is in charge of this permanent commute from Louisville to Cincinnati. He's the same one who stood next to Mettle president Ryan Bender down in the basement the day we found out about the move. He's the definition of dapper today. I couldn't even hold a top hat to him.

"I'm honored to see such a crowd partake in the tour we have lined up for you today," Simpson says. "Many of you may not believe it, but the Northern Lineage family needs you. Life insurance is a growing business. For example, the three largest banks in the world hold more than $4 trillion, while the entire life insurance industry has $3.6 trillion. We are making strides to compete with a range of financial options, and not just life insurance and annuities.

"By adding the Mettle team, we are continuing to grow exponentially. You'll find that a number of Northern Lineage employees have been here for a large portion of their lives. There's a reason for that: They enjoy what they are doing. They enjoy being part of the Northern Lineage family. Not only that, but I've heard time and time again that the hardest job to get in Cincinnati is with us. If you decide to move, which I hope you will, you will have the opportunity to be a part of something extraordinary. You'll be a huge part of Project Giza. Don't hesitate to ask anyone here a question about the company, the city, or anything else. We've brought you here because we want you to be a part of our family. Have a great day!"

Simpson leaves the stage to a smattering of applause. Even if the man weren't wearing a tie, I would still admit that his sale pitch was so great it looked effortless. It sounded as if it were rehearsed and given numerous times, but at the same time, it seemed as if he were talking to us each individually. The skeptic in me has a hard time believing the all-for-one-and-one-for-all speech in general, let alone from someone who has enough money to buy a small country.

Then again, I still haven't met a lying sack of shit with this company.

As emcee Roy talks again, we review the remaining folder contents. There's nothing too remarkable, except for the large silver Northern Lineage pen, tucked inside a felt holding case. Roy tells us that we have been assigned a host by the letters on our table. Our next move will be determined by the fact that we're one of two "A" tables.

While we wait, Barry motions to Jeff and Ken.

"What is Project Giza?" Barry says.

"I heard it was some big thing Northern Lineage is putting together to cut costs throughout the company," Ken says. "They're trying to get rid of old systems, upgrade newer ones, even trying to figure out how to save money on electricity."

"Someone said they are going to grow vegetables on the roof," Jeff says.

"Maybe I'll be the head gardener!" Barry says.

Our group meets in the front with Ronald Hastings (we are all wearing nametags now), and he gives a brief history of this particular building, which used to be either an elementary school or whorehouse (I couldn't hear the entire story). Ronald starts to take us on the first-floor tour, but two other suit wearers stop him. No one else says much, except for Barry whispering secrets to Ken. Reading their body language, they are apparently discussing the intricacies of notched and peaked lapels.

Ronald leads us down the hallway to the educational rooms. He points out the "fishbowls," which are the university-style cubicles where employees take online classes and tests. We find it barely enthralling, and we're ready to check out the gym, which is in the basement. Ronald eagerly takes us to the elevator. He swipes his access card across the scanner to start the elevator.

I don't think we're moving. He swipes it again, but still, nothing happens. Ken tries to hold back his laughter. Ronald is a bit flustered, and he hits a few buttons and swipes again. Finally, the elevator begins to move downward. It opens, and we finally step out into the famous Northern Lineage gym.

There's no one here. This is to be expected, of course, as

we're reminded that the gym is open only from 6 to 8 a.m. and from 5 to 7 p.m. The gym looks ridiculously clean ... so clean that I wonder if anyone even uses it. There's a nice workout room, including weight machines, free weights, bicycles, and ellipticals; a fitness room; a basketball court; and locker rooms with whirlpools and saunas.

As Ronald continues the tour, we discover that the gym contains all of the amenities you would find at a normal fitness facility. Sort of. In the workout room, there are perhaps 20 or so machines, including some that look dated. The basketball court resembles a grade school gym, probably because it once was. The 3-point line runs out before it reaches the end line, and there are beams that block a regular-arcing shot at the top of the key. The locker rooms have showers, but soap is not furnished.

We gather awkwardly in the men's locker room right next to the whirlpool. It's as if we're the Northern Lineage Olympic swim team, minus the swim caps. The smell of chlorine is so intense that a few blocks away, the bacteria in the Ohio River is dying. The cleanliness of the locker room is impeccable. "One of the cleanest in Cincinnati," Ronald says. I'm scared to put my hand in the whirlpool, just in case the acidity levels haven't been tested recently.

As we follow in almost complete silence, Ronald takes us back to the first floor, but not before we end up stuck in the elevator on the third floor for a brief time. We head outside to take a look at a new 30-story building being erected across the street, which apparently is slated to open by the end of the year. We then make our way across the block to one of the other main Northern Lineage buildings.

We climb three floors on a metal spiral staircase that unfortunately does not include a fire pole. When we reach the top, the speckled green floor tiles remind me of a '50s doctor's office. We notice another "Welcome Mettle Employees" sign, this one in a hallway.

Now we stop in a rather strange room, packed with books, a man reading a newspaper, and gift shop paraphernalia. I scan the shelved books, noting that most appear to be riddled with financial documentation from the late 19th century. Closer to the gift shop area, there's a display with a handful of paperbacks. This looks more like a museum than a library.

"This is Associate Resources," the woman behind the counter says. Unlike everyone else we've met today, she's not wearing a nametag or a tie. "We provide numerous services to help employees with their day-to-day activities. Some of these services include dry cleaning, shoe repair, and film development. We also offer discount tickets for many local attractions, movies, car rental, hotels, computers, cellphones, and so forth.

"Our company store contains items like greeting cards, stamps, film, bus passes, and gift certificates, so you don't have to make another trip after work. We are able to save associates both time and money in picking up these items.

"The library contains approximately 4,000 books on business and leisure topics, plus newspapers and magazines. Additionally, this is the place where you can place an order for holiday pies. If no one has told you about it yet, the cafeteria makes a variety of delicious pies during the holiday months. Here's a brochure with all of the items."

A holiday pie does sound pretty good about now, but we still have a few more stops before lunch. I step back into the hallway with Jeff, while Barry asks the lady a question.

"This place reminds me of school," I say. "We had this stuff in our dorm. Since when did work turn into school?"

"It probably just feels this way because you don't work here right now," Jeff says.

"I don't know ... the whole campus connotation bothers me a bit. They can take care of everything you need right here, so why would you need to go anywhere else?"

"That's not a school. That sounds more like a cult."

The others exit, and we proceed down the hallway to

Health Services. We meet the on-call nurse and find out they offer numerous screenings, Weight Watchers, and smoking cessation programs. Before we leave, the nurse hands us a wad of neon-colored writing pens to disperse.

Our next stop is the seventh floor, so we make our way back to the metal staircase and find ourselves at a place called Client Connections. This time, not only do they have a "Welcome Mettle Employees" sign hanging, but paintings and drawings of fish and oceans wallpaper the main room. I feel like the bearded ship captain that's usually anchored to an aquarium floor, swaying back and forth to avoid a paper cut.

The CC is the call center, and besides the underwater feeling, there's not much to it. Because it's almost noon, we assume the trip will continue to the cafeteria. However, as we're waiting for Ronald to direct us to the grub, we review pictures that are located on the bulletin board. Barry scrutinizes one particular photo, which shows two young women throwing bagged objects toward a piece of wood.

"What is going on in this picture?" Barry says.

"They are playing cornhole," Ronald says. "Do you know what that is?"

Ronald sees that there are blank stares all around.

"Some people call it beanbag toss. It's sort of like horseshoes," Ronald says. "The game was invented in Cincinnati, and it's really popular all over town. This is a picture from our company picnic, and we had a little competition."

We pretend to care, but in all actuality, we're hungry. Ronald senses an uprising and hauls us to the cafeteria.

Unfortunately, we don't eat right away. Instead, we take a trip through the backside of the cafeteria. There's no chlorine smell, but it's as immaculate as the whirlpool. The workers are preparing today's lunch, and Ronald reminds us that Northern Lineage takes its cafeteria procedures seriously. So much so, he says, that the city often cites this cafeteria as an example for other regional locations to follow.

Again, our group is impressed, but when you're hungry and you're standing next to lavish utensils and hundreds of pounds of flour and sugar, it's hard to care too much. At least, until you can at least sample a tasty treat.

Lunch is the new defining moment of the day.

There are multiple lines to choose from, including salad, deli sandwiches, hot food, kosher, and dessert. I wander, pick up a salad, and wait for fajitas, which apparently is one of the specialties.

Jeff and I fill our plates at the same pace, and we notice that there's a section roped off in the back for the Mettle riftraft. There are a couple of familiar-looking people in the area, including Ken and Barry, who are already seated. They are speaking to someone I've never seen before. We walk over to join them.

The rice is pretty good. The fajitas, well, they are a step below the level of great. Then again it's a "free" lunch, according to the sign near the entrance.

"So why do you think 'free' is in quotes?" I say. "Is it not really free?"

"Of course it's not really free," Barry says. "You have to hand over your life before you can eat in here."

"The food's not bad," Jeff says. "Still, it's typical cafeteria food."

"Did you see the frozen yogurt machines are off?" Ken says. "I thought they always have yogurt."

"It looks like they have some sort of spice cake instead," I say. "I'll try it, but I really wanted frozen yogurt."

When your favorite food is ice cream, it's disappointing to find out that the frozen yogurt machines are off. I was told Northern Lineage had it in the cafeteria every day. Apparently, it's every day except when visitors are here.

Diya, Debbie, and Reshmi make it to the table. Another guy who is following them sits down across from me, next to Jeff.

"Hi, I'm Grant," the new guy says. "Mindy wanted me to

bring you to our work area, after you finish eating."

I'm pretty sure I remember Grant coming down to Mettle at some point. Yesterday, Chris confirmed that Mindy would be our boss, and Marty was her boss, not the elder sibling in a hit music group.

We assume that Grant is Mindy's right-hand man. He stays and eats with us, and through small talk, he seems cool enough to sit at the "cool" table. Jeff and I take a trip to grab a little more soft drink and a section of spice cake, which turns out to be above-average pineapple cake.

We notice a TV room right beside the cafeteria. All of a sudden, we step into the room — and a different era. There are several rows of waiting room chairs that all point to a big screen. There are three older women watching the news, sitting in chairs that have to be at least 40 years old. They are not talking; I'm not positive they are even awake. I'm pretty sure they are alive, however, as I see one of them lean from the left side to the right.

"I think they are cafeteria workers taking a break," I say.

"Maybe they're waiting to pick up holiday pies," Jeff says.

"For what holiday ... Christmas of 1954?"

Grant joins us in the entrance of the TV room and motions that it's time to go. Diya, however, is still eating, but Grant says that she will meet with a different team. Because the web team and database administrators won't be working side by side in Cincinnati, she's waiting with Chris for another Northern Lineage tour guide. We exit the cafeteria and start on our way to encounter the team.

But before we can do this, Barry has made a simple request to Grant, unbeknownst to the group. Barry wants to see the server room, and more importantly, where our current running servers are located. Luckily, they are in the same building as the cafeteria, so we climb a couple of flights of stairs and rummage through the residence of just about every Northern Lineage server.

After a little searching, Grant and Barry find the Mettle servers. They have been in Cincinnati for more than two years, when Northern Lineage already knew this move would be coming. I can guarantee you that Northern Lineage didn't woo the servers by showing them the cafeteria and gym.

Computers are amazingly loyal machines. That is, as long as users don't screw up their input, or as long as they aren't overworked. Computers follow directions well ... even if you tell them to delete all of their files.

Barry is tempted to caress "his" servers. Judging by the look on his face, he's having a good time, possibly warming up to the idea of moving to Cincinnati.

This is Barry's defining moment.

The rest of us are more interested in meeting the rest of the team. Grant leads us outside, down the road, and into yet another building. This one contains a doughnut shop in the lobby and even has a revolving door at the entrance. That's almost enough to make me want to move.

It's been awhile since that first wooden revolving door was installed in 1899 at Rector's, a restaurant on Times Square in Manhattan.[13] Although moving from Louisville to Cincinnati wouldn't necessarily constitute as a revolving door, it's safe to assume that there would be plenty of position gyrations in the coming months.

Finally, it's time to meet the rest of our team ... or, at least the others who work for Mindy. The main office has a window, but the window doesn't give a glimpse of outside. Instead, you can see the first-floor coffee shop.

The cubicles are set up differently, as groups of twos share workspaces. At Mettle, 5- to 6-foot gray dividers separate everyone. Here, the gray dividers exist, but there are not dividers between every individual. No one seems to be particular about which way is best, but we all agree that the desks in the call center would be nonfunctional. There, the desks are arranged in a four-leaf clover design, and the dividers do not exist.

Theoretically, if you had long arms, you could reach around and slap someone on the head.

Then again, maybe that is needed in some parts of Northern Lineage.

One of the lead programmers speaks briefly about using .NET and attempting to redesign their existing website functions. He has printed out a few website screens and taped them on his wall. Upon taking a closer look at the printouts and his screen, I notice that it looks uncannily similar to Annuity Profit Plus. I gather that Jeff sees the same thing when he looks over at me, gawks at the wall, and rolls his eyes.

Barry, Debbie, and the developer discuss some of the differences between .NET and Java, but the majority of us have had enough. It's after 2, and the bus will be leaving shortly. The team seems quiet and nice. Mindy talks briefly about the systems, but it's so general that I wonder how much she really knows about them.

Grant leads us back downstairs, out the revolving door (wheeee!), and back to the bus. As we line up, emcee Roy is handing out pretzels, and sitting next to him is a blue tub with iced drinks. I pull out a Sprite, grab a bag of pretzels, and head to the back of the bus. I save a seat for Diya because I haven't had a chance to talk to her today.

Just about everyone on the bus, including Barry, is in chipper spirits. If Northern Lineage wanted this trip to make a bold statement about why we should move our lives to Cincinnati, it worked. As Jeff mentioned, the campus feeling does sort of grow on you after a while.

As we walked to the bus, I asked Grant about the apartment complexes downtown and if there were any close to work. He pointed to two buildings right across the street, one of which Northern Lineage owns. Grant assured me that he could help find that type of information next week.

As I sit on the bus and stare at the apartment buildings, then over to the park where William Howard Taft oversees birds flocking for fast food scraps, I ponder that maybe this isn't such a bad gig after all. Why not move here, live right across the street from the office, and work in a true technological environment?

Diya, one of the last people to board our departing bus, takes the seat next to me.

"What did you think of the trip?" I say to Diya.

"The other DBAs were really nice," Diya says. "It's a different atmosphere here, but I'll get used to it."

"So you are definitely moving?"

"I have no choice. With the green card situation, I have to come up here for now. After that, they might even send me back to India, who knows."

"Well, you never know what will happen. Before I came up here today, I was leaning toward not going. But after seeing what's available ... this will be tough to pass up."

Diya bats her eyes.

"I doubt any of you will go," she says.

"What do you mean?" I say.

"You, Jeff, Barry, Ken ... I don't think any of you are going to go. That's just the way I feel about it."

"I don't even know if I will go. How do you know that I won't go?"

"I don't know for certain, but that's just how I feel."

I'm not sure why she thinks none of us are going. She has a reason to believe Barry won't be going, and maybe me, but Ken and Jeff seem like locks to go.

"I think you should just sit back and see what happens with everything," I say to her. "There's still more than a month to go before we have to turn in the forms. I can't speak for everyone, but my options are completely open."

There's no point in explaining this in more detail to Diya, not necessarily because she doesn't believe me, but because she's asleep. I hope she's dreaming of a happy ending to the relocation. The rest of us could use our own defining moment.

9
Afterglow

Friday, July 8

In the old days, if you existed in the corporate world as a bottom feeder, you knew exactly what you would be doing each day: the same damn thing you did the day before.

Northern Lineage is full of lifers who carry out their precise functions during a daily routine reminiscent of a sci-fi robot. But at the same time, the newer, hipper breed at the company seems to have more flexibility with a work schedule.

Scholar Tim Hall originally equated this type of employee as having a protean career.[14] The term comes from the sea god Proteus, who had the ability to change forms at a moment's notice. Being versatile allows an employee not only to escape boredom but also have the opportunity to do something different every day. Then again, it's too bad that Proteus can't summon schools of fish out of the Ohio River to move Cincinnati a little closer to Louisville, therefore halting the relocation process.

Our Mettle team doesn't necessarily have anything new happening today. But after yesterday's trip, we have a different perspective about the situation. Morale is at an all-time high. Northern Lineage did an impressive job of setting the stage for our arrival. The people were as welcoming as a grandmother with a pile of baked goods on her kitchen table. Of course, it's easy to be like that for one day; what happens when the cookies and pies and the *esprit de corps* disappear?

I unlock my computer and continue work on the Annuity Profit Plus date validation. Just as I finally determine the line of code that needed debugging, Jeff steps into my cube.

"So ... are you any closer to deciding what to do?" says Jeff, seemingly unsure if he really wants to ask that question in the first place.

"They put on a great show," I say. "And I think it's within the realm of possibility that I'll go. But between moving, giving up the house I just bought, leaving my family ... too many factors are telling me to stay."

"The trip confirmed the way I have been feeling since the start, that I will go. I just don't have the portfolio ready yet to get into the 3-D graphics world yet. I still want to go to L.A. and go to school out there. I think with Northern Lineage, I can bide my time and work on other things. It's a comfort zone."

"And you don't have to look for jobs, if you already have one. But is it worth moving just for that?"

Ken arrives in my cube.

"If it were just me, it might be easier to pursue something else," Jeff says. "But Laura is talking about changing jobs, too. She's from Louisville, but Cincinnati really isn't that far away. If I want to move, I think she'll be supportive of me. What about you, Ken?"

Ken is a bit surprised to be called on and takes a moment to react.

"It was better than expected," Ken says. "I knew they were going to try to woo us, but I had a pretty good feeling about the place. I wouldn't say it's like Mettle, not by a long shot, but it's definitely a place where I could see myself working a little longer. That leads me to my next question ... "

Ken takes a step closer to Jeff and me and leans in slightly, as if he were going to tell us the final resting place of Jimmy Hoffa.

"What do you guys think about buying a condo together?" Ken says. "That way, we can still keep our places here, and we can always move back. I'm not so sure I want to move Mary and the kids right away, so that might be a perfect solution, just the three of us."

Jeff and I look at each other and ponder the possibilities.

"I'm not sure I can afford to do something like that," I say. "I just bought my house a few months ago. If I move, I'll have to get rid of it."

"And Laura would be moving too," Jeff says.

"I'm just throwing the idea out there," Ken says. "Or maybe we could just get an apartment together or something. At least at first, I'm planning on coming back down here every weekend to be with my family. And if I really can't stand it up there, I don't want to have to make a huge investment."

"Yeah, I would rather rent up there or stay with someone before selling my house," I say. "Didn't they say they had temporary housing available?"

"I bet they do, at least for a certain amount of time," Jeff says. "Living together might not be so bad. We'll have to think about it more."

"Yeah, it's just an idea," Ken says. "But if some of us are definitely moving, yet not quite sure how long we're going to be there, it makes sense to go in on it together. Just keep it in the back of your mind as you're making the decision. I have a meeting to run to, so I'll catch up with you later."

Ken is off, and Jeff and I continue the conversation.

"So you're pretty confident about the team up there and everything?" I say.

"I guess so, but we're still going to be working separate from them," Jeff says. "So it's not really a team atmosphere. As long as a couple of us go ... and if Barry goes, we'll be set. But that's doubtful."

I don't want to sound negative, but I'm curious to know what Jeff thinks about our potential new boss.

"What about Mindy?" I say. "There's something that just didn't seem right."

"She seems nice," Jeff says. "Remember, it was just one day."

"I know, but it didn't seem like she knew what was going on, really. There just weren't that many details."

"I don't think there were supposed to be that many details. They want to keep it simple for now. The details are coming later, with the completion of the knowledge transfer."

"Ah, of course, the knowledge transfer. I can't wait to wear the metal helmet so they can suck my brain as well. Oh wait, I don't know anything."

Jeff chuckles for an instant, then motions that he should return to his cube and work. I also turn back toward my machine, but before I start anything, I check my email for the link to the relocation website.

Little did I know that I was in the process of unveiling another impressive, not to mention critical, item in the relocation ordeal.

For starters, the site actually looks pretty decent. The home page contains a couple of upcoming events, the recent questions asked (that are also listed in the question-and-answer section), recent news items, and an email link to ask questions. A quick scan of the Q&A page shows a fair amount of interesting information, including some items that I haven't even thought about just yet.

Q: What conditions do I have to satisfy to receive my severance benefit?
A: In order to receive your severance benefit, including any Mettle bonus this year that is paid, you need to remain employed with Mettle through the date your position is no longer needed. Each associate will receive an estimated separation date for his/her position if choosing not to move to Cincinnati. That separation date will be only an approximation. We will give you at least 30 days notice of a firm separation date as we move through the transition period.

We will have a great deal of work during the transition period to service our customers, reach our
sales goals, integrate web-enabled methodologies,
and transform mission-critical paradigms to Cincinnati. Therefore, it will be important that Mettle
associates are fully engaged in their functions,
producing high-quality work, embracing ubiquitous
platforms, and supporting their peers. In order to
receive severance pay, an associate must be in good
standing. Do you think we'd just let you sit around
and do nothing? ;)

This is consistent with the information I've been told. The ones who have already solidified their decision to stay must convince prospective employers a need to stay at Mettle until their respective separation dates if they plan to earn the severance benefit. I suspect many people are stuck in a quagmire to determine when they should even begin to look for jobs because there have been few signs of ending dates. At least they'll give us a 30-day notice.

The severance package is a pretty sweet deal. However, not having a job for too long after that would be detrimental for someone who has a family to support. Assuming that Northern Lineage is honest about the end dates, and the managers can work with their employees regarding separation, it's feasible that this might not be a big issue. Of course, that's assuming a lot for a company that has to provide for almost 300 individuals in a unique manner.

**Q: If I accept a position in Cincinnati and later
change my mind, what is the impact on severance?**
A: We ask Mettle associates to be certain of their
decision to join us in Cincinnati. Picture Regis
Philbin on the other side of the sheet of paper.
"Is that your final answer?" If, at a later point in
time, you decide not to go forward with the relocation, you won't be eligible for severance or any
Mettle performance bonus. We'd love to just give
all of our money away, but that hurts the company
profits. ;)

Of course, when you accept any job, the employer wants you to be "certain" you plan to stay with the company. Even if you don't sign a contract, it's presumed you'll stay with the company for ... a while. But how long do you have to stay to receive the entire bonus? I've heard rumors that we will have to pay back a certain percentage of the bonus, or possibly even all of it, depending on how long we work there. I expect that when these time segments become clearer, people will be circling dates on their calendars for when they'll be able to come out from behind bars.

And speaking of bars ...

Q: What is the policy regarding a spouse that may come by the office?
A: Given the confidential nature of the information that our associates are working with, we ask that any individuals visiting the workplace have their visit scheduled in advance and approved by the manager of the area. If your mom is baking cookies, though, make sure she brings enough for everyone. ;)

Northern Lineage must have removed the security cages while we visited yesterday. I also don't seem to remember seeing any of those little vending machines where you can pop in a quarter, turn the dial, and receive a handful of pellets to feed the caged programmers. Maybe they were being cleaned.

Also, what's the deal with the cute comments and emoticons at the end of each answer? Is this supposed to make me more inclined to relocate?

Although I pretty much know the answer to the next one, I have to read it again:

Q: What is the dress code in the home office?
A: We maintain professional dress in the home office. Management associates are expected to wear suits. Male associates who are not in management are expected to wear dress pants, a dress shirt, and a tie. Female associates who are not in manage-

```
ment are expected to wear a dress, dress slacks, or
a skirt, with a dress sweater or blouse. Associ-
ates who work in areas that require heavier physi-
cal work are provided uniforms. Sorry, there are no
clown positions available at this time. ;)
```

There are no pictures of the uniforms provided, either! The last item I find particularly interesting:

```
Q: After the August 15th deadline, will there be a
list published showing those people relocating and/
or those not?
A: The Mettle Transition website is capturing the
names of individuals who are relocating to Cin-
cinnati and have indicated their approval to have
their names published. We will continue to update
this site with new information as it becomes avail-
able to us. We will not be compiling and publish-
ing a list of names of individuals who are not
relocating to Cincinnati. If you need a full list
of employees, there's always the directory on the
intranet … ;)
```

At the very least, we can start attaching scarlet letters on the individuals who are relocating, assuming they will be prepared for the public scorning.

All in all, the answers do not surprise me. With an updated site chocked full of relevant material, there's little guesswork involved in the intricacies of the move.

It's past lunchtime, but no one appears to be around at first glance. I grab my peanut butter sandwich, Chex Mix, banana, and water and check quickly to see if Diya is in her cube. She is having lunch with Reshmi, so I pull up a chair and hope that I'm invited to eat.

"Hello Jason," Diya says. "Would you like to try this? It is chicken with chickpeas, but it's not too spicy."

"Yeah, you should try it," Reshmi says. "It's really good, and Diya made it all by herself!"

I oblige and take that as an invitation.

"Anything exciting going on in your world today?" I say

while attempting to cool down the portion of food Diya has handed to me in naan.

"No, just catching up with what I missed yesterday," Diya says. "I should be surprised at the number of emails people sent, but this always seems to happen when I'm away for a day."

I have yet to see a moment at Diya's desk when she's not working. Even while eating, she's still working on something, whether it's checking database queries or class work. I found out recently that she is taking classes to earn a business degree, and her homework sits to the right of her keyboard.

The steam continues to rise from her food, but Diya becomes almost oblivious to it ... and me as well. I almost finish my entire lunch before she says anything.

"Are you busy today?" says Diya, as I almost drop my banana peel.

"Not really," I say. "I'm supposed to be working on date validation stuff for Annuity Profit Plus, but it's hard to concentrate, with the talk of moving."

"I know," Diya says. "That's why I'm glad I sit in the back. I have a window view plus people don't bother me too much. Then again, it's always more quiet when Barry's not around. Where is he today?"

"Beats me. I haven't gone out of my way to look for him, either. What are you doing over the weekend? Do you want to do something?"

"I might have time, but I have a lot of homework for my class. You should just give me a call Saturday afternoon, and we can figure something out."

"OK. Good luck getting your work finished."

With Diya already immersed in her work again, I don't know if she heard me, but I am not too concerned. There's so much going on in her life that I'm surprised she's surviving. Saturday, I will try to pull her from the dregs of work, and if she accepts, at least I know I'm worth fitting into her busy schedule. I'm not pleased with our current relationship circumstances, but I don't have much of a choice. Sort of like my choice in this entire relocation process.

I begin the jaunt back to my cube when Barry arrives. He appears to be just a small notch below exuberant, which usually occurs either after he proves his code works or after he polishes off the baby-back ribs at T.G.I. Friday's. There's no barbecue sauce on his mouth, so I assume it's the former.

"Hey buddy!" says Barry, and I take a step back to make sure I'm not slapped too hard. He whacks me in the back anyway.

"Hey Barry," I say. "Where have you been all day?"

"I've been dominating at the meetings," Barry says. "They have so many questions, and I have a lot of answers, but not quite all of them."

Barry meanders around his desk and thumbs through a couple of binders located on a shelf in his cube.

"This is exactly what I need!" Barry says. "This contains all of the notes I created for our system. Man, these are out of date. I have more work to do before they throw me out on the street."

"I doubt they are going to just throw you out," I say.

"Yeah, but it's fun to pretend. Besides, they can't, because I'm the only one who knows most of this stuff. By the way, I think we need a sub Wednesday at volleyball. Can you play?"

I had planned to ask what he knows that others don't and if he would tell me, so that I could kill him and be the only person who knows the information. Instead, Barry catches me off guard, as he's prone to do, with the volleyball question.

"Sure, I should be able to play," I say. "What time is the match?"

"We play at 8:15," Barry says. "You might be a full-time player because our other guy is still hurt."

"That's cool," I say. "I've been looking to find a new team anyway."

"A lot of people here at Mettle play. I've been trying to get a team together with Nelson and some others, but no luck so far. Everyone else is already on a team. Maybe we can do it next season."

"I didn't realize volleyball was so big here, but that's awesome."

Tom Nelson must have overheard us because he is approaching Barry's cube now.

"So are you playing with Barry?" Nelson says. "We are in his league, so I'll probably see you out there."

"Nelson's on the *good* team, though," Barry says. "We are near the bottom right now, but I think we would be a lot better with a consistent showing. We've had different players every week."

We chat a bit more about volleyball, which at this juncture is probably the highlight of my day. As a noble gesture, Barry, who stands about 5'7", initiates a bit of trash talking with Nelson, who is roughly 6'4". If you base it solely on height, this is similar to one of the Three Little Pigs trying to tell the giant cyclops that his eye is missing.

I gingerly step out of that conversation and head back to my desk. I've managed to salt away almost the entire day, so I should attempt to do something with this date validation. There are a fair amount of things I need to test. For instance, a user can't select November 31 or February 30. But to make matters worse, the annuities are supposed to allow people in certain age groups, either older than 85 or 69½. So I also have to build code to check ages, which isn't always the simplest thing in various programming languages. At this rate, I'll probably also need the system to send out e-cards for users' half birthdays ... but how will I choose the background color and song for each one?

I make a decent amount of headway before I hear a whisper from behind me. I ignore it first and then realize it's Nelson, whose cubicle is just behind mine.

"Did you see the part on the relo website about how many hours we would have to work a week?"

"No, I must have missed that one."

"Oh, well then I'll send it to you."

I check my email and reveal what Nelson had found:

Q: Mettle employees work 37.5 hours per week. There is an unwritten expectation that the management staff work additional hours. It has been rumored that Northern Lineage management is required to work 50 hours minimum. Is this accurate?

A: Business needs and personal drive are the prevailing determinants of hours worked. Exempt associates are expected to work whatever hours are necessary to complete their jobs in a quality and timely manner. We find that our associates are very committed to fulfilling the mission of their jobs, and hours worked is not an issue for them. For different levels of exempt associates, typical hours worked may vary. Estimated average hours by level are listed below:

* Entry-level management and technical/professional positions - 45 hours per week.
* Mid-level management (directors) and technical/professionals at pay grade 33 and above - 50 hours per week.
* Officers - 55 hours per week.
* Clowns - 10-80 hours per week, depending on the number of petals on water-shooting flower. ;)

"This is crazy!" Nelson says. "We aren't getting a pay raise, and they expect us to work eight hours a week more?"

It's true that our current pay is based on a 37.5-hour workweek. It does seem a bit excessive to load that many hours without other compensation.

"Not only that, but the cost of living is higher in Cincinnati," Nelson says. "They're saying it isn't, but I've lived there before."

"Do you think this will affect people's decision to move?" I say. "Eight hours extra is a pretty big chunk of your life."

"So far, from the dealings I've had with Northern Lineage, they aren't taking away any time from your life. That's because work is your life, unlike Mettle. If anything, that should deter people who want to have a personal life from going to Cincinnati."

I'm not jumping to any conclusions, but Nelson has a good point. Do people want to choose work or life? I'm looking for a workplace that allows both. Normally, it's tough to decipher the workload without even being there. And for that matter, how would the workload be even more in Cincinnati than in Louisville? I thought we would be doing roughly the same thing, at least for an extended period of time. While Northern Lineage has provided a great deal of information and literature, the company still hasn't told me what I have to give in return. If it's my best in a work environment, I can handle that. But if it's a piece of my individuality and personal freedom ... that would be hard to relinquish, if not impossible.

10
Quandary

Maybe I'm just paranoid, but everyone appears to be giving me a look.

I can't really explain this look, but I'll try. It's the look that your mom gave you when you tried to go out in public without combing your hair. It's a look that says, "Maybe you think things are OK, but I see you, and there's something off, and it's not just your hair."

I'm guessing that I see this look because of a simple problem: *Ich habe einen Bärenhunger*. For you non-Germans out there, that means I'm as hungry as a bear. Fortunately for me, I'm standing outside one of my favorite places to eat: Olive Garden. Not only is the food decent, but they also supply you with an endless amount of salad (full of croutons, black olives, and red onions) and Italian bread. I'm salivating just thinking about it.

I'm not standing here by myself. Diya suggested Olive Garden; she lives right down the road from the restaurant, here in the east end of Louisville. First, I stopped at the O.G. to put my name on the list, and the attendant handed me one of those automatic beepers, so you know when your table is ready. Because it is dinnertime, and the amount of people who converge on this place is approximately equivalent to a Super Bowl attendance record, I decided to pick up Diya after adding our name.

As we wait to be beckoned by the buzzer, I notice a couple of subtle yet noticeable looks from patrons waiting outside the O.G. It dawns on me that perhaps the folks have never seen a Caucasian man and an Indian woman together before. In this part of town, white people probably outnumber all other races 10-to-1. While there are sectors of Hispanic, Asian, African-American, and Indian people in Louisville's east end ... well, they don't always mix. A quick glance around the parking lot and nearby food joints confirms this.

I don't dwell on this too much, however, because a bright light is flashing in my hand. Inside, we have a seat in a cozy booth and await the bottomless bowl of salad.

"So, I have to ask you ... why are you always ridiculously busy at work?" I say.

"Sometimes, it's just my schoolwork," Diya says. "This week has been busier than usual. With the move going on, it's difficult to get everything accomplished. Ken, Nitya, and Reshmi are always coming over to talk about relocation too. And on top of that, I try to get everything done so that I can get to my dance class on Thursdays."

"Dance class?"

"Yes, I teach dance to young girls ... it's a traditional Indian-style dance. One of the best teachers in India is coming to Louisville soon, so we are putting together a production. I'm going to dance as well. Will you come to the performance?"

"Sure!" I eagerly answer. "I'd like to learn more about the dances and your culture."

"Do you like dancing?"

"Well, yeah, I do, but I like to learn about other types of things too, you know."

"You may like some Indian movies, because there is a lot of dancing in most of the films. Maybe we can watch one tonight or something."

I really hadn't come up with any plans after dinner, but if Diya wants to invite me back to her place, I'm not going to argue. I'm still in awe of her and the many things I don't know about her culture. I try to listen intently as she explains some of the movies she has at home, but I lose focus because her beauty overtakes me.

That, and the salad bowl is empty.

Diya and I also chat about the relocation dilemma. She is still stuck on moving, due to the green card fiasco. At this point, the only thing I can do is listen and reassure her that things will work out, and that she has plenty of friends in the States who will help her out.

After dinner, we end up back at Diya's place.

"Which movie do you want to watch?" Diya asks. She opens the door to her dimly lit apartment and points me to the living room.

"Anything is fine by me," I say. "I don't think I've ever seen any Indian movies before."

"Great, I'll play one of my newest favorites!"

The name of the movie is *Main Hoon Na*. The story line is decent and somewhat complex: A man is hired by a government official to keep a close eye on his daughter, who is attending a local high school. The man, however, is in his 40s, so he's ridiculed by a number of the students (how often do you see 40-year-olds passing as high school students?). But he proves worthy enough to befriend the girl and her boyfriend. Later in the movie, we find out that the girl's boyfriend is actually the hired man's brother, and together, they fight the "bad guys."

While the plot does keep the movie interesting for more than three hours, it's the dancing and music numbers that keep it lively. The color shown throughout is magnificently intertwined with a number of dance numbers. In some ways, the movie reminds me of *Grease* and *Charlie and the Chocolate Factory*. Like *Grease*, the cast includes dynamite attractive actors and actresses, but the sexuality is nearly always downplayed. Diya explains that unlike American movies, there are many things (like kissing) that can't be shown in an Indian movie. On the flip side, there are a few Bollywood-style dancing scenes where the girls, including the government official's gorgeous daughter, are scantily clad.

Another striking thing about the flick is the clothing worn by the younger generation. They almost exclusively wear American-style clothing, which, as Diya explains, is a hot commodity in India. However, while it's definitely an American style thing, it's a couple of years behind the current style in the States. For instance, the girl's boyfriend somewhat resembles Bruce Springsteen, complete with the denim getup and bandanna in his back pocket. The other actors and actresses remind me of punk rock videos of the early '90s. Diya says this movie came out just two years ago.

I ask what section this movie is in at the video store, and she claims she rented it from the Indian restaurant. I stay interested in the movie developments, and I have more questions about whether the subtitles are doing justice to the real meaning of the film. But I realize I won't have any additional answers tonight. Diya has fallen asleep again, this time with her head in my lap.

Monday, July 11

I must be late to work because there's already a powwow going on in Jeff's cube. I hear the voices of Jeff, Ken, and Chris, so I unlock my computer and stroll over. They are discussing their weekend trip up to see the big city of Cincinnati and find a place to live. I hear the names "Cool Springs" and "Richwood," which I assume are small cities in northern Kentucky, outside of Cincy. Ken, appearing mildly dejected overall about the trip, hears his phone ringing and heads back to his cube. Chris discusses a couple of minor maintenance jobs on one of our websites and then returns to his office.

"Was the weekend trip worth it?" I say.

"Yeah ... at least you get a nice dinner and a night at the hotel!" Jeff says. "No really, there was pretty good information.

Claude Simpson spoke with us Friday night after dinner. They had a guy come in and talk about the school systems. There were some other important Northern Lineage people there that we mingled with. Saturday, we took a bus trip through the city, downtown and then over to northern Kentucky. In the afternoon, we finally met with the Realtor. It didn't seem like we did much, but I was exhausted by the time we got home Saturday night."

"Did the trip make a dent on your decision?"

"It didn't change anything from Thursday's trip up there. We are about 90 percent sure we're going. Laura was a little scared to move, but this past weekend eased her mind a bit. It sucks we have to move out so far for the sake of pricing. But the neighborhood in Richwood is cool. It even has a community pool ... Laura really likes that. Pool party, anyone?"

"Yessshh, Richhhhhwood ... it just sort of rolls off your tongue."

It's tough to envision a pool party without a gaggle of Bond girls, wandering around in skimpy bikinis, wondering what cuisine will be served that day at the Northern Lineage cafeteria. Besides looking as svelte as the next employee, Sean Connery would seem rather awkward stuck in a cube at a financial company.

I exit Jeff's cube and walk to Ken's and Diya's cubes, along the back wall. I want to talk to Diya because I haven't spoken to her since our date on Saturday. Now, she's on the phone with what seems to be a work-related issue, so I visit Ken instead. He's on JobImp.com.

"I updated my résumé on there last week," I say. "I've already had a couple of calls and emails, but nothing too exciting ... yet."

"I've found a handful of decent opportunities," Ken says. "And a friend of mine has been looking for me, too. I'm just really torn now with what I want to do. Moving to Northern Lineage might end up as the best opportunity."

"Would you be doing the same thing that you do with Mettle?"

Ken shrugs.

"That's the thing," Ken says. "I'm tired of working on this particular system. I don't know what you know about it, but it's just an application that interfaces with some of the sales activities within the company. At the moment, I'm the expert, and no one else really knows it. If I go to Northern Lineage, I want to learn new things. I'd really like to learn Oracle. If I could get up there and get involved in other things, I could go anywhere. Or, if they'll work with me and allow me to grow with the new technology, then maybe I'll retire there. So far, though, it just looks like I'll be pigeonholed into using this same thing."

"So you want to find a position where you could learn the cutting-edge stuff, and not just a daily routine?" I say.

"I've been laid off a couple of times from jobs. In fact, before I started working here, I thought about going back to Japan and getting into the music business. Or maybe technical writing, since I've done that in the past. There are many different arenas I wouldn't mind diving into ... I just don't want to be stuck in one."

"You should follow your passion."

"True, but it changes when you have a wife and kids. I love to play the guitar. Sometimes, I come home at night and just play for a bit. It's a great way to clear my mind. The other night, I was playing, and my 4-year-old came in the room. He started to say something, but then he stopped. I said, 'What's up?' and he said, 'I can tell you later; I won't bother you.' That really bothered me ... I feel like I'm being selfish, but I also need time to relax."

"Maybe you can get him interested in playing the guitar, and you can do it together."

"Yeah, I've thought about that. But I also want to do some screenwriting. I just bounce around a lot of ideas ... there are a lot of things I want to do."

Ken wants to have some control over his life. It's clear to me that part of his dilemma, though, is that he's not always sure what he wants. If his wants keep changing, he'll never be able to do what he wants. I think he needs to narrow down his options, or at least take care of things he wants to do, one at a time.

Maybe I should consider this same advice, because I still don't have a complete grasp on what I want out of all of this, either.

"Hey, have you looked at the relocation website yet?" Ken says. "There's a bunch of good stuff on there, and answers to things they haven't really told us in the meetings. Apparently, we have a full year to take advantage of housing closing costs. At least I don't feel quite as rushed to sell the one down here immediately."

"That is pretty good," I say. "I don't think I'll sell mine right away, so that's a nice out if I do decide to come back."

"Are you going for sure?"

"Oh, no, but I'm definitely considering it. I'm still trying to gather as much information as I can. I need to check all of the options before deciding."

I turn for a moment to see that Diya is now standing in the separation space between her cube and Ken's.

"You're not fooling anyone," Diya says. "I know you're not going."

"How would you know that if I don't even know that?" I say.

She doesn't respond and walks away. Ken shrugs. I return to my desk.

I check my mail, and Jeff has forwarded me work to do. I also notice an email from Grant at Northern Lineage. He responded to my apartment hunt questions with a few leads and an apartment finder website. The continual display of cooperation from Northern Lineage — both from a company stand-point and from potential coworkers — is lending to my attitude of believing that relocating may be the solution after all. It's one thing to say you are going to help employees with the decision, but it's another to have individuals offer servitude on a consistent basis. I continue to have tons of questions, but every time an uncertainty appears, there's an answer within minutes.

I ponder this as I continue my assignment, and during a quick break for lunch (simple again: peanut butter sandwiches and Chex Mix), I peruse my personal email account. I open a message from Katrina Henderson, a recruiter whom a family friend mentioned a few days ago. She has set up a lunch between the three of us for Wednesday. While I contemplate the move, I have to look out for my best interests in town. From what little I've heard, Katrina is the type of person who can play Concentration blindfolded with companies and job seekers. I'm curious to find out just how she can help me, and she has already provided me with tips concerning my résumé, cover letter, and other factors.

Katrina wants me to put together a wish list pertaining to what I want in a new job. She lists a bunch of questions that cover everything from workplace environment to company size to dress code requirements. I consider working on this after finishing lunch, but I find a few more maintenance requests to handle. And just as I finish those, Barry comes strolling into my workspace.

"Hey newbie!" Barry says.

Regardless of the situation, Barry remains impressively animated. I envision that he would approach me the same way if he told me "I just won a million dollars!" as he would "I just broke my neck skydiving!"

"I'm doing all right," I say. "I'm getting stuff done, I guess."

"Don't worry about all of the work," Barry says. "We're moving, all of the projects have been stopped, and you have plenty of time."

"Yeah, but I don't like being bored."

"Speaking of work, I have good news about the job hunting fun! I'm meeting with a recruiter tomorrow. He has a couple of jobs he thinks might work for me. Some are Java, and one is more of a back-end Unix position. But hey, I can't be picky right now, can I?"

"You can't if you're not moving."

Barry looks outside of my cube and steps closer.

"Honestly, I'll admit something to you," says Barry in a hushed tone. I think it's the first time I've ever heard him talk at a lower decibel level. "I'm pretty certain I'll be staying. With my mom here, the deal would have to be too good ... and the job market in town would have to dry up completely."

Barry isn't telling me anything I don't already know, or anything that everyone else doesn't know, for that matter. I do appreciate the notion that he feels comfortable enough to confide in me, even though we met just a few weeks ago.

"I'm not saying you should go or not go," I say. "As long as you're open to what will work best, then by all means, investigate. I am meeting with a recruiter later this week. I'm not expecting much, though."

"What's the problem?" Barry says.

"The recruiter was supposed to help me before, but there weren't any leads. I think she's geared toward higher-paying tech jobs, but I could be wrong. I hope I'm wrong."

"At least you'll get your name and résumé out there. That's half the battle. Oh well, I need to contact that recruiter before the day is through. You are still playing volleyball Wednesday, right?"

"Oh yeah, I wouldn't miss it."

Barry retreats to his desk, and I can't believe it's already 4 p.m. Just going back and forth between working, attempting to work, and consuming the relocation process information makes the day go by faster than Superman flying counterclockwise around the earth to turn back time.

I notice Jeff is back at his desk, and as I enter his cube, I find Ken sitting on Jeff's desk. They both stop talking and look at me. I'm interested to hear what they were talking about, so I stay mute, but they remain silent long enough for me to try on multiple sets of cufflinks, if I had any.

Finally, Ken breaks the quietness.

"We were just talking about the condo idea again," Ken says. "Mary gave me the go-ahead over the weekend, but I don't think Jeff is going for it."

"It's not that I'm totally out, but my wife is coming with me!" Jeff says. "So it won't just be a guys' place."

"Hey, I don't mind, I like your wife, just as long as there's room in the bed for me!" Ken says in a stoic manner.

"I'm looking at apartments," I say. "Grant is helping me look for a place in town. If I go, I want to be able to walk to work. I'm not going to drive hours just to get downtown."

"For house living, I don't think there's a way around that," Jeff says. "I'm supposed to talk to our Realtor sometime this week and let her know our level of interest. She doesn't seem to be as pushy now as she was before ... probably because she knows she will make some money off us."

"I'm still talking to our Realtor, but I'm trying to avoid it," Ken says. "We have a year for the closing cost offer. I may just wait until the last minute."

Ken still wins the award for being the hardest to read. Most signs point toward him hopping on the bus to Cincinnati, but a small doubt still lingers from his words. It's almost as if he's expecting a bit more from Northern Lineage before making a full-fledged effort to move.

"The biggest problem I have with the ordeal is the contract we could be potentially signing," I say. "What is stopping them from changing the deal?"

"How could they change the deal?" Jeff says. "It's in writing."

"True, it is in writing, but most of the items are still somewhat vague," I say. "The bonus stuff is in there, but the moving help, paying for closing costs, etc. ... I'm not saying they would renege, but what's stopping them?"

"They're not going to go back on it all," Jeff says. "There are too many people they have promised things to. They can't just give one person one thing and leave another person out in the cold."

"It all comes down to how the deal works for each individual," Ken says. "For some people, it's going to be an offer they can't refuse. For others, like the majority of us on this floor, it's still somewhat up in the air. And still for others, the deal will suck. So hopefully people will be smart enough and look at the entire situation."

Ken heads back to his desk, Jeff returns to his work, and I go back to my cube. Ken is right about one thing: Everyone's deal is unique, at least, when you consider it from each person's perspective.

For one individual (Don), you have a cut-and-dry answer: a definite "yes." He was already moving before they even made the announcement. And Chris is pretty close to a "yes" as well, but he seems to be going as a company man. Then on the other side (Barry), you have a fairly resounding "no." For someone who has been in Louisville essentially his entire life, it doesn't make sense to pick up and leave.

The rest of us don't have blatant conclusions. Diya is telling herself she has to go, but it's somewhat uncertain as to just how the green card stuff will work. Jeff is closer to going than not going, but he has said repeatedly that his plans with the company are short term at best. Ken shifts frequently and overall doesn't seem to fit with the scheme of things at Northern Lineage. I don't have a good enough grasp on Nitya, Debbie, and Reshmi, but I'm pretty certain they won't all be moving.

I truthfully can't make my decision in a bubble. The others have that privilege, although they recurrently agree that they hope everyone goes. If no one goes, I can't go either ... I don't know enough about the systems. At the same time, I've already forged much closer relationships with my coworkers than I could have possibly imagined. Besides, I wouldn't mind moving, even if I just finally returned to Louisville anyway.

While moving is always a hassle, not moving could cost me job experience, excellent friendships, and a potential date/girlfriend/something more. And let's face it: Who can resist being part of an ever-changing story like this one? The Queen City could be calling ... or maybe that's just my stomach.

11
Team Players

Tuesday, July 12

Today is my 21st day of work, whatever that is worth.

The organizational restructuring hits high gear this morning as we meet with Mindy, our new superior. Most of the team is here: Chris, Nitya, Diya, and Don are not included. I'm starting to understand how this is going to work in Cincinnati. Chris will be in charge of both DBA teams, and Mindy will be over both web teams. Mettle will still be its own brand, separate from Northern Lineage, and will sell distinct products. So the arrangement of just the web/database side of things will be this:

	Northern Lineage	**Mettle**
Chris	NL team	Nitya, Diya, Don
Mindy	Grant et al	Jeff, Debbie, Reshmi, Ken, Barry, and me

Of course, the Mettle database administrators will still have to support the Mettle web dev team, even though we probably won't be sitting footsteps away, as we are now.

While we're still trying to grasp the configuration, Mindy is more concerned with a different type of architecture: the Mettle server setup. After 30 minutes or so, the team creates an award-winning diagram (kindergarten division) that incorporates all of the main servers: development, staging, and production, as well as the email server, code repository, and library. It's just that when you draw a diagram with four Sharpie colors, and have to remap channels between servers more than six times, it's not going to be pretty, even if the paper you are using is roughly the size of the Netherlands.

Mindy appoints Grant the task of turning the Van Gogh into an easy-to-read floor plan. Grant doesn't talk much, unless it's at Mindy's command. During this meeting, the only sound coming from Grant's space has been meticulous note writing and drawing.

Grant's attire also differs from the rest of us. He's wearing a white dress shirt, slacks, and a skinny dark tie. Of course, Mindy is playing the part too, wearing a business suit. The rest of us get by with our collared shirts and khakis.

After the meeting, I'm back at my desk to do work. Today's lesson involves reviewing Jeff's Java code and trying to determine how to work on server-side date validation. If that doesn't make any sense to you, you aren't alone. I comprehend Jeff's pages from a logic standpoint. But I'm eons behind in the Java syntax category. Fortunately, I still have the behemoth Java programming book, which is sitting next to my computer and holding up the building's eighth, ninth, and tenth floors. I've decided that I have a better chance of finding examples online than I do accidentally turning to the right page.

"How's the validating going?" says Jeff as he strolls into my cube.

"Um, it's OK," I say. "I'm learning a lot, that's for sure."

"Yessshhh boy, you have a lot to learn," Jeff says.

Just then, Mindy appears behind Jeff, although he doesn't notice right away.

"Will you guys be able to meet for a brief period tomorrow as well?" says Mindy, startling Jeff. "Grant and I will compile these notes tonight, and we just want to make sure that we have everything down right."

"Sure!" Jeff says.

"And if it's OK with him, it's OK with me," I say. "Mindy,

I do have a quick question for you. How long have you known about the move?"

Mindy shrugs.

"We knew it was going to happen, but we didn't think it was going to occur this soon," Mindy says. "There's a lot going on right now, with the new building being built, the teams shuffling, and now this. I don't know when would be a better time, but if I were going to pick the worst time, it would be now."

"Will we be in the new building?" Jeff says.

"Yep, we're going in there as planned," Mindy says. "It's supposed to be completed October 17. I can tell you that they are still a long way from having any part of it completed!"

I notice my cellphone ringing, and Jeff and Mindy take their conversation outside my cube.

"Hello, is this Jason Harris?"

"Yes, who is this?"

"Hi, my name is Dan Watts, and I'm with Tech Strategy Consultants here in Louisville. I noticed your résumé on JobImp.com, and I think I have just the position for you."

I'm not sure why, but it always seems as if job recruiters have the perfect job sitting around for you. I envision a pile of papers, with a single job printed on each. Then, as the recruiter aimlessly wanders around JobImp's website, the pile of job papers forms a small tsunami, with the perfect job appearing in proximity to the recruiter's right hand.

"I see that you have a variety of experience, and I think this position will suit you well," Dan continues. "The company needs a Java and Unix expert, which you have on your résumé."

"I wouldn't go so far as to say that I'm an expert in either field, though," I say.

"That's OK. You have a bunch of the other qualifications they are looking for, so I expect they'll want to take a look."

As I'm sitting at my desk, I check my email and notice that Dan has already sent me the job description. The position calls

for someone with at least three years of Java programming
and five years of Unix administration. I quickly count on my
fingers four years of limited Unix experience. I'm not close to
qualifying on the Java programming experience.

"I'm looking at my email right now," I say. "This position
looks interesting, but I'm not exactly sure how interested I am.
Maybe I can get back to you at a later time?"

"Sure, that's fine," Dan says. "They are looking to hire
someone fairly quickly, so the sooner you let me know, the better."

"That's no problem, Dan. Thanks again for the lead."

At least it's a possible job. I just made my résumé live on
JobImp.com and a few other job placement websites this past
weekend, so that was a fast turnaround. Of course, I'm sure to
start receiving emails about careers in the modeling world, or
possibly the work-from-home-and-make-six-figures variety.
It's not so much that I mind a headhunter sending me positions;
what really irritates me is when you send an email back and say
you aren't interested in any jobs, and the recruiter translates
that to meaning "he's not interested now, so I'll send him a
new job next week." Of course, that goes hand in hand with the
recruiters who think that saying buzzwords proves an understanding of the technology world. Maybe they think you can
accurately perform a job interview over the phone with aid of
the web-based Bullshit Generator.

Judging from the swiftness at which my JobImp résumé
was summoned from the depths of recruiting torment, surely
there will be other possibilities before the Aug. 15 decision.
Besides, even if I couldn't care less about a Java position, there
are other people in the office who may be interested.

Barry and Ken appear just outside of my cubicle.

"So newbie, you were talking to a recruiter?" Barry says.

"Yeah ... why were you listening to my conversation?"
I say. Not that I really care that much, but it seems strange
that they would be lurking near my desk when the fun and

excitement take place pretty much everywhere else in the building.

"Barry has a knack at eavesdropping," Ken says. "And I have a knack for knowing when Barry is listening to conversations. So does the job sound good?"

"Not really," I say. "It's a Java/Unix position. It seems like an intermediate-level job, which obviously I'm nowhere near. But maybe others will be interested."

"I doubt they would pay me what I make here," Barry says. "I have over 10 years in Java and more than that in Unix."

"It's out of my realm," Ken says. "But you shouldn't just automatically assume you're not qualified. Let them make that decision."

"I don't know if I even want to do Java, much less whether or not I can do it," I say.

"You'll be fine," Barry says. "You can learn on the job, just like you are doing here. That's awesome you already got a call."

"You'll have recruiters lining up outside your cubicle in no time!" Ken says.

I notice that I need a refill on water, so I head for the break room. Before I can go anywhere, Diya joins the covey of Mettle employees at my cube's entrance.

"Jason got a call from a recruiter!" Barry eagerly shouts. That prompts Tom Nelson, who sits in the cube behind me, to peak over the wall.

"Congratulations, Jason!" Diya says triumphantly. All four of them appear giddy with this potential occupation that I can't ever imagine actually doing.

"Yeah, it's just that I don't think I'm interested," I say. "It's something I doubt I'll enjoy doing, so ... "

"But you can stay in Louisville, which is what you want, right?" Diya says.

"I think we all want to stay in Louisville," Barry says.

"If it were that simple, then I would be a lot happier about the situation," I say.

"Hey, there's no reason to be negative," Nelson says. "You have a job ... you can shop around for another without worrying you'll be fired. All in all, it's not a bad predicament to be in."

"Speaking of which, I have some opportunities to apply for," says Ken as he sprints back toward his desk. Barry and Diya follow, while Nelson returns to his regularly scheduled custom programming script.

I continue my trip to the break room. It feels odd to be the center of attention over something so basic as being called by a job recruiter. I suppose they realize that whether or not people are going to Cincinnati, it's imperative that everyone has choices. The Java/Unix job isn't a great option for me, but it is an option.

Everyone I work with is trying to find how he or she fits best. Sometimes it's easier not to have to make a decision, and not to have options. But rarely will someone voice an opinion as such. By having choices, people feel as if they are needed, which in turn gives them the confidence to choose appropriately what to do with their careers. It's like *Who Moved My Cheese?*, only the cheese has been taken out of the maze and shuffled across town to another pet shop. Hem and Haw would have no chance to find it then.

Spencer Johnson, the author of the book, wrote about the need to anticipate change.[15] How could I have known — and how could many of the people at Mettle have known — that we were being given a one-way ticket to a new pet store? *Credibility* authors James M. Kouzes and Barry Z. Posner write this: "People who do not exercise any choice can't feel responsible, nor can they make a difference within their organization."[16]

Another thing that I appreciate from the Mettle bunch is that the team wants everyone to succeed. No one displayed emotion other than joy when they discovered a recruiter had called me. It would have been easy for someone to show displeasure because I was the one phoned. It seemed like such a minor occurrence at the time, yet as I stroll back to my desk with my water glass, I again realize how lucky I am to work with such gracious individuals. Even though our side is losing the war, and our particular regiment is in dire need of supplies, the soldiers are keeping their spirits to a maximum.

Then again, we could be only days away from being taken as hostages to the North.

Wednesday, July 13

I've dug myself a small trench. The rain is pelting down hard so hard that I can't see above me, even though the dark sky is lit with bright lights. The wind complicates the matter as I see blurry white objects appearing from a short distance. It appears that there is one heading right for me, but with the rain beating harshly into my face, it's difficult to be totally certain what is about to strike me.

Bump! Thankfully, at the last instant, the volleyball comes into full view, and I make a decent pass to a teammate at the net, who sets to another teammate, who pounds the ball onto the other side. That's a point, which evens tonight's match at 1-1. It's time to switch sides.

At least for me, volleyball is a decent way to forget the current state of affairs. Not that things are really that bad; for starters, the job with Mettle enables me to pay my house mortgage. And because I just bought the house three months ago, that's pretty important.

Secondly, being in Louisville gives me the opportunity to see many friends and family. Even though I previously lived just two hours west of here, it wasn't always accommodating to visit. Another benefit to living in a larger city: It's exponentially easier to find dates with similar interests and tastes.

And now, back to the bad: As soon as I reach the pinnacle of new living, I may have to throw it all away. OK, maybe not the dating part, as Cincinnati is a bigger city than the 'Ville.

Besides, who can avoid a dating scene that involves a small town known for its prostitution heydays of the early 1900s (Newport, Kentucky) right across the river, and the fact that one of the many nicknames for the metropolis is "CinciNasty"?

However, now is not time to think about these things. Volleyball is my out, and it allows me to concentrate on practicing my spinning overhand serve, diving after balls that are at least three feet out of my reach, and yelling at Barry. OK, maybe "speaking loudly" is a better term to use for my diatribes with our team captain. He gets a little out of control sometimes, as I've seen so far in the handful of times I've subbed with his team. Today is the tournament, which means we could be here until past midnight, if we keep winning.

Then again, I probably don't have to worry about staying up past my bedtime with this team, which finished near the bottom of the standings. Next season starts in two weeks, and my sister is joining the team with me. That is, assuming I can make it through tonight without getting too pissed at Barry.

Barry is hardly volleyball great Sinjin Smith, but neither is anyone else in the tournament. Furthermore, he can be an above-average player, for this particular league's standards, when he concentrates. Tonight has been one of his best matches so far, and I have to believe it's partially because he's had a couple of beers to calm him down.

There are a billion ways to describe Barry. On one hand, he is the type of person who will manage to blurt out something catastrophic, even after he has said everything right for quite some time. It's sort of like building a gigantic house of cards, but when you're finished, running and jumping through it like a pile of leaves. While Barry has his moments sweet-talking the ladies (something he seems to indulge in more times than not), many of those moments end with an off-color comment or joke. I haven't deciphered yet whether Barry just tires of these conversations, or whether there's an avalanche switch that is activated within a particular time limit.

But on the other hand, Barry is also the type of guy who will put in the extra effort to help people at work, his family, and his friends. He's an honest, caring individual who is usually intent on finding a solution. Sometimes he can be a bit overbearing to others and even himself — for instance, he's still giving himself a pep talk after that last serve almost went backward — but as long as you understand that it's Barry's personality, it's not so terrible.

Speaking of terrible, we've finally ended the first match, and as expected, we are on the losing side. Barry's a little disgusted with his play during the game, but I quickly calm him down and change the subject.

"So how were the meetings today?" I say, trying to rub the sand off my legs.

"They weren't as fun as last week," Barry says. "But I can't complain too much. Monday, Tuesday, and today were all days to go over the general ideas behind fund transfers. And since I'm pretty much the only one here who knows all about it, I'm finally happy to see others take an interest in it."

"Well, I'm interested," I say. "Then again, I don't know how long that interest will last."

"The functionality is pretty nifty, I have to admit," Barry says. "We're moving millions of dollars around in different funds, depending on the day, the investor, the advisor, and so forth. There are a lot of duplicate processes that could probably be streamlined a bit, but it's also nice to have some of it as a backup."

"Are you in meetings pretty much all day? I haven't really seen you much at work lately."

"If I'm not in an official meeting, I'm discussing items with Chris, Mindy, Marty, and whoever else wants to listen. I've spoken to a few other big wigs at Northern Lineage, but I can't remember their names or what they look like. Meetings suck, but I don't have that much else going on right now, so it's OK. There was even a meeting about changing the Northern

Lineage logo. For whatever reason, they want to incorporate a moose in it!"

"Huh? Well, if you think of work I can do, I'll take a look. Jeff is keeping me busy with Annuity Profit Plus, but sometimes I have to wait for him to come back and tell me what's next."

"Yeah, sometimes he gets stuck in the bathroom ... it seems like he's in there for hours. So how did the interview with the recruiter go today?"

I tell Barry about my lackluster meeting earlier Wednesday with Katrina, the job recruiter. I suppose it could have gone worse; for instance, a meteor could have struck me as I walked to the restaurant where we had lunch.

As we sat down, Katrina handed me a folder labeled "IT JobSource," the name of the recruiting company. Inside, I found glossy color brochures about IT JobSource, Katrina's card, and my résumé. I wondered why I should be concerned with brochures because I already know what the company does (find people jobs, right?), but before closing the folder, I glanced at my résumé. I noticed that it wasn't the one I sent her two weeks ago, but instead, it was the one I sent her almost a year ago.

The waitress took our orders, and Katrina pulled out a notepad and pen.

"So Jason, it's really good that we are meeting today," she said. "Just this week I've heard about a few jobs that I think you are qualified for. One of the jobs involves Java. It is a change management position. The other is more for a IT expert that calls for 10 years experience."

Katrina handed me short excerpts on both jobs to review. I was not at all qualified for the IT position. The change management job called for five years' worth of application development, which I think I would be empowered to handle. However, it also called for one year Java of experience, so I'm not sure 21 days of Java would suffice.

While the Java job could be something interesting and challenging, it was not something that I would seek out. In the past, I haven't worked through recruiters much, so it's tough to know what they expect. I'm starting to realize that the only way a recruiter can help find a job is if you're specific about what you want. If not, someone like Katrina might as well throw darts at a job board. The dartboard approach can work if you're desperate for a job ... assuming you won't be disappointed fixing fax machines rather than doing actual computer programming.

"I appreciate your help with the job search," I said. "But I think that I may be wasting your time a bit. These jobs are vaguely similar to what I want to do, but in reality, they really aren't right for me."

"That's understandable," Katrina said. "I'm here to help you figure out what the right job is for you. I'm not the most technically savvy person in the world, but if you send me a list of programming languages, I can keep an eye out for you."

As I finish the story, I wonder if Barry is still listening.

"The meeting doesn't sound all that bad," says Barry, watching the end of a match between two teams in our league. "It sounds like she got it at the end."

"I guess it's the whole job-hunting thing that bothers me," I say. "I don't like it."

"I'm not sure many people do, really."

Although finding jobs can become a chore, eliminating unfavorable options and working within the Hollywood model suits many of the working class today. *The Opt-Out Revolt* explains how individuals work on a project-by-project basis, jumping from one job to another if interest exists.[17] When there's a lot of work around, and there are a number of job recruiters looking to make a buck by finding the right person for each position, it's not too difficult to job-hop and be satisfied.

And it's not necessarily that people in general want to look for new jobs. But it's apparent that most people in the marketplace now are eager to reach out for a new opportunity, as opposed to the earlier generation that felt more of an obligation to stay with a particular company for millions of years.

Fortunately, the other volleyball match ends, which means it is time for our team to play again in this double-elimination tournament. While I do appreciate talking to Barry and contemplating the relocation situation a little more, it is unnerving enough to have to deal with during normal work hours. I can only hypothesize that just about everyone else feels the same way. Well, except Don, who is essentially already past the decision-making stage.

Even those people who definitely know whether they are staying or leaving are, to my best knowledge, not satisfied. And how can they be? They are working at a job that will not be the same a month from now. The uncertainty is enough to drive people to make rash and illogical decisions.

While some people do appear to be frantic at times, Northern Lineage has allocated a fair amount of time to decide. But is a longer period better or worse? When taking tests, the experts agree to always go with your gut instinct, your first choice. The difference here, though, is the question keeps being altered slightly. One day, the choice seems blatant, but the next day, new information makes the options a bit fuzzier.

I'm inclined just to sit back and watch everything play out. I feel as if I'm sitting back and watching a disaster here, however. Our team is already down by seven points, and in the losers' bracket, we play one game to 25 points. But I'll try to enjoy every minute of it, because playing in the sand always trumps planning a career.

12
Responsibility

Thursday, July 14

I'm sitting in Chris's office, this time without my peers.

"Time for midyear reviews," says Chris, pulling out my file. "Since you've been here only a few weeks, there's not much for me to say. You're supposed to write things you think you have improved and other things you need to work on."

Rating employee performance seems to be all the rage these days because having this sort of data could come in handy at a later time when considering raises and layoffs. I prefer the term "ranking and spanking" to the "hell curve"[18] because it at least insinuates that there could be a bit of raciness involved.

Chris hands me the papers as I try not to laugh. I consider creating a paper airplane.

"When do you want this back?" I say.

"I'm supposed to have them all back in two weeks, I think. But with the move, I doubt they'll even ask for us to turn them in."

I think the "review" is complete, but Chris continues.

"Are you going to go to Cincinnati?" Chris asks.

"Honestly, I don't know," I say. "I just moved back here and bought a house, so it would be tough to move again. Still, it seems like a great opportunity."

"It's good you have an open mind about it. I hope you go. I think you would benefit, and I think the company would benefit by having you."

"You're pretty much already committed, right?"

"I haven't turned in the papers, but yeah, I've talked to my wife about it, and she understands it's something we have to do. We've been moving all over the last few years, and we knew this was going to happen eventually. I just didn't think it would happen right now. But at least by being in Cincinnati with the parent company, they won't move me again."

I leave Chris's office feeling somewhat sympathetic toward him. Chris has two-and-eight-ninths kids (the third should pop out any day now). So let's see ... a new kid, with a quasi-new job at a new location ... pretty easy stuff. At this point, the only thing that can rescue Chris is a complete stoppage of time. I should probably check an atomic clock and see if my date validation code takes this under consideration.

On the way back to my cube, I notice a woman with a grocery bag full of something that didn't appear to be groceries standing next to my desk.

"I'm supposed to give this to you," she says.

"Um, OK," I say. "What is it?"

"It's the company IT on-call phone and computer room keys. You were next on the list to receive it. Don't worry; you shouldn't have to use it. I kept the bag in my car the entire week."

Interestingly, this is the second on-call phone I've received today. Barry handed me the team on-call phone earlier this morning. It, too, rarely rings. Barry proved the battery wasn't dead by increasing and decreasing the ringer volume.

I still have no idea what I'm supposed to do as the on-call person — well, other than lugging around extra phones that no one calls.

Apparently, the IT on-call stuff circulates amongst the 50-or-so employees within Mettle's computer-related positions. This includes everyone from software engineers, systems technical support individuals, business analysts, and middle managers. I learned this on the intranet sometime last week, during one of those days I couldn't find much to do except scour our files for incriminating photographs of managers.

As I comb through the bag's contents, Jeff appears outside my cube.

"What's up, buddy?" Jeff says. "What do you have there?"

"It's the *other* on-call stuff," I say. "Do you have any idea what these keys are for?"

"I think they are for the computer room near the break room. I've never been in there. Let's go check it out!"

Jeff and I walk down the hallway and take a left, and before we get to the break room, we notice a partially concealed door across from a meeting room. We try the keys and find a match on the third one. Inside, there are computers (some with additional locks), modems, and a phone system with plenty of blinking lights.

"The meeting room across the hall used to have all of our servers," Jeff says. "Then they moved them all up to Cincinnati, so there's not much left here."

I pretend to be interested, but at this point, I'd rather fall asleep on a bed of keyboards that don't appear to be plugged into any systems. What I thought could turn into an adventure through the caverns of Mettle — not to mention the secret location of the employee dungeon — has turned out to be nearly as exciting as my midyear review.

Back at our desks, it's time for an impromptu meeting concerning the Annuity Profit Plus project. Jeff clues me in on more information concerning the progress. While he is working on the complicated form that the user fills out, as well as the storage of the information in the database, he asks me to work on the calculations. Because I have the date validation somewhat under control, it's time to focus on something else: actuarial fun.

Maybe what I'm about to embark on isn't normally be within the realm of the programmer world. But let's not forget what we are here. We are a performance troupe, with just a few more shows until we make it to Broadway. *There's noooooo business like finance business!*

Jeff hands me a stack of papers that, in essence, form the APP actuarial calculations.

"What I need you to do is look through these items and see if you can come up with a way we can code these calculations," Jeff says. "I'll also send you the Excel spreadsheet that contains some of the tables referenced in the notes."

"How are the calculations computed now?" I say.

"The actuarials have a Visual Basic program that handles all of the functionality. We need to build all of that into APP. I'm pretty sure the code for the VB program is in the handouts. Do you know VB?"

"I'm familiar with it, but I've programmed very little in it."

"Well, lad, I guess today would be a great time to reacquaint yourself with it."

While translating actuarial data (which I know nothing about) from one mostly foreign programming language (Visual Basic) to another mostly foreign programming language (Java) may seem a bit daunting, it's made exponentially better when you're told about it with a Sean Connery accent.

"Yessshh, this is quite a messsshhhh on your hands, boy," I say as Jeff returns to his cube.

Jeff has seemed a bit down the past few days. I still sense a tinge of uncertainty — not about making the moving decision, but about whether it's the right thing to do. Jeff has never appeared to be the type of guy who wants to be in a rigid business world, yet he also isn't avoiding it at the present time. Mettle is a good fit for someone like Jeff, but Northern Lineage might not be.

Maybe Jeff wants to be captured in the Death Star tractor beam, because that would buy him more time to devise a way out. He's not prepared to plunge into the graphic design world, but he could be soon enough. It's obviously easier to stay with a comfortable job with a company not known for sifting all the cream off the barrel. Not that Jeff would have to worry about termination; the managers apparently see a bright future ahead for him, and he gets along with all of his coworkers. The only sliding that will happen with Jeff is when he pushes his two-week notice under the door of his boss.

It's just that the door will almost certainly be in the new building in Cincinnati, not here in Louisville.

Throughout the day, I figure out some things with the actuarial calculations. I'm starting to understand what APP is going to do for the users, and I'm also determining what the old program does. I'm so inundated with work that I don't even notice Diya sneaking into my cube. She blows into my left ear and almost makes me jump out of my chair.

"Geez, Jason, did you not see me?" says Diya, giggling rather loudly. "I've been standing here for a few seconds."

"Wow, I guess not," I say. "I'm really concentrating on this stuff for Annuity Profit Plus."

"Well, you haven't been by my cube all day, and I am getting ready to leave."

"Already?"

It's almost 5 o'clock. I'd been staring at the numbers for more than three hours.

"Have you decided if you are going to make the weekend trip?" Diya says.

"I want to, but I just don't know when," I say. "I have some family things going on for the next three weekends. Are you going?"

Her brightly lit smile turned dim.

"I'm planning on going next weekend," Diya says. "Can you go with me? Since you aren't really looking for houses, maybe you can help me."

"I would like to go with you," I say. "I'm not sure I can. Let me figure out what's going on. I really want to go with you."

"OK," Diya says. "I need to leave or I will be late for dance class. Call me later if you want to talk."

Diya's feelings for me appear to hinge primarily on my decision. At the same time, she's not even assured she will go; there's still a decent possibility that she will have no other option but to return to India. It's too early to figure one way or another, though. In an email she sent earlier, she mentioned a meeting with some people in Northern Lineage's HR department that will take place next week.

Is there even time to think about a relationship? She has little free time, with dance and MBA classes. I want to prove to her that things can work even if she goes to Cincinnati and I don't.

I'm still in the dark about where our relationship will lead, but at the very least, we enjoy each other's company, and that makes the fiasco at work considerably more bearable.

Friday, July 15

Work is rather empty. Barry has started his vacation, Diya is working from home, and the rest of our team apparently has checked out for the week.

Jeff and I spent the majority of the morning hammering out more Annuity Profit Plus work, but there's only so much time one can spend analyzing code. After our productivity led us to stare at the screen, hoping that a 3-D image of a marine creature would appear, we decided our work for the week was complete.

"Let's see where everybody stands on the move," Jeff says.

Don was the easiest because he had taken off the day to look for housing in Cincy. Some speculate that as fast as he wants to move, he could find a place today; fetch his wife, kids and stuff during the weekend; and start working at Northern Lineage next Monday. I find this difficult to believe; knowing Don, he'd at least take off Monday to unpack a box or two.

As we walk the floor, taking an unscientific poll of our co-workers, we try to gauge who is staying and who is going.

One of the ladies in a window cube says she's out ... her

husband has a position in town that he doesn't want to give up. Meanwhile, Nitya, the lead DBA, is still more up in the air than most. She is in her late 30s and has two children. Her husband, also in the computer field, does contract work and can theoretically live anywhere.

Debbie, a Java programmer who is 30, recently returned to work from maternity leave. We gather she is looking to move, but she has an enormous task of selling her house for a decent price.

"We're thinking of moving, definitely," Debbie says. "But I don't know if we can get what we want for our house. It's the biggest house and biggest lot in our subdivision, so I bet everyone will try to lowball us. And we have to find a house with a three-car garage, so that we have some place to store our boat."

Reshmi, another Java developer in her early 30s, joins the conversation in Debbie's cube. She is a mother of a 1-year-old and is definitely on the fence. We learn that she had lunch yesterday with her husband and Marshall MacDougal, the VP of technology and Northern Lineage's best motivational speaker.

"Lunch with Marshall was great," Reshmi says. "My husband likes his programming job here, but he has been patiently waiting for a raise for a long time. Marshall said he could probably find him a job since he has a lot of contacts in the tech world. We are going back to India for almost all of December, so that may affect our decision. Those plans can't be changed, and I don't know if we'll have time to get everything taken care of here."

Another new participant enters the crowded cube. Vance, 52, is the business analyst on the Annuity Profit Plus project. I've talked with him briefly about APP, but amazingly enough, we have never discussed relocation.

"Which way are you leaning?" Jeff says.

"I'm not much of a leaner," Vance says. "I've been through company changes like this three times already in my life. The funny thing is that they call it something different every time.

Once, it was 'downsizing.' Next, it was 'restructuring.' Now it's 'relocating.' It all means the same thing: The company has found a way to save a decent amount of money. If I find something better, I'll stay in town. If I don't, I'll go. I can always move back. My wife won't mind either way, and my kids are already out of the house. I'm not going to lose sleep over it."

Two of the tech support guys jump into the conversation. Skip is set on going. He is single, but he doesn't think he'll have a problem getting rid of his house here and possibly renting close to the home office. Sam is the opposite of Skip. He's single as well but wants to stay. It seems that one of his hang-ups is the price of land near Cincinnati.

All told, no one has the same outlook on the relocation process. Everyone is identifying different important factors in the move. It appears to be a good exercise for everyone to discuss their positives and negatives because new things arise from these informal meetings.

The item that doesn't get mentioned often is the actual work being done at Mettle. Most decisions hinge on external factors and the work environment changing, which of course do involve actual job duty. This leads me to believe that either people here are fairly satisfied with their daily activities, or they have decided in unison that no matter where they go, they will be doing the same mundane thing. Whether you are sitting in a cubicle in Louisville or Beijing, you'll still be dealing with insane coworkers, clueless upper management, and unmanageable deadlines. In this way, people do at least have a choice and aren't just kicked to the curb to await a taxicab ride to a new career. Nevertheless, it's personal, and while everyone has his or her own story to tell, no one can clearly help another make an individual decision.

Saturday, July 16

Even though it's 10 p.m., I'm pulling into Diya's apartment complex. I had hoped she would go with my family and me to dinner, but she was finishing her schoolwork.

The weekend has been hectic already. On Friday, my sister's boyfriend, on leave from Iraq, returned to Louisville. Saturday morning, my brother flew in from San Francisco, and his girlfriend flew in from Minneapolis. Per our normal ritual, when everyone makes it to town, we eat a huge meal. But I promised Diya earlier in the week that I would see her during the weekend, and I don't like breaking promises.

Even though I was just in her living room last week, I was so focused on Diya (and nervous, for that matter) that I didn't pay attention to the décor of the place. It's your typical single-level, two-bedroom unit with a sliding door to the patio. Upon second glance, though, the cultural statues and colors that adorn the apartment are enough to separate it from any former date's home.

"Did you rent any new Indian movies?" I say as we enter her living room. "I really liked that last one ... with everyone dancing, it just seemed like a big party."

"I do have a few new movies," Diya says. "But none of them are like *Main Hoon Na* with the dancing. There are a couple of musicals and a serious one. Do you want to watch some of this one? It's about a lady who finds out she has AIDS."

"Sure, it doesn't matter to me."

She is right. There are no vivid colors or dancing in this particular movie. The film looks more like a documentary, although that may just have to do with the camera equipment. Most shots are dark, and the subtitles are barely legible. What's worse is some of the subtitling makes almost no sense. Diya explains that apparently, some of the movie houses in Bollywood can afford better translators than others.

While I'm trying to place verbs in their correct positions in my head, Diya redirects my attention.

"Tell me, Jason, why are you not romantic?" she says.

The needle not only scratches the record, but gravity seems to pause as well.

"What did you ask?" I say, even though I heard exactly what she said. I'm trying to buy more time for an actual response.

"You heard me just fine. Why are you not romantic? I thought American guys were more, you know, into the girls they are dating."

The line of questioning makes perfect sense and is completely bizarre to me. There's no question that I'm into her, but my mind goes blank when I consider her previous relationship stories, our cultural backgrounds, the relocation, etc.

In the meantime, I have plenty of resources to use for stalling.

"I do have two reasons, and I've been meaning to talk to you about them," I say. "First, I'm really not sure how you perceive me, and I don't want to mess up anything."

"Well, you are the first American guy I have been on a date with," Diya says. "I don't really know what is supposed to happen."

"I mean, I know your past and your opinions of what you think most guys want. I'm trying to tiptoe around those facts."

"That's OK, Jason. I know you are different than what I have seen from others. I think of you as a really great friend, and I hope you will always be my friend."

"Also, with everything going on at work, I want to keep us and the relocation separate."

"That's very sweet of you because I would prefer if people at work didn't know about us. Some of the people on the floor have asked me if we are dating. I just say that we are really good friends. Does Jeff know we are meeting outside of work?"

"I've mentioned it, but I completely trust him. He's not a blabbermouth."

"OK, but I would rather you didn't talk to Jeff about me and things."

"All right ... I can't promise I won't say anything at all, but

I won't tell him anything juicy."

Diya laughs. I don't think she would be having this discussion if she didn't have any feelings about me.

"There is another big reason that I haven't tried to get much closer to you," I say. "I met a girl a few weeks before I met you. She graduated from college with my sister. I've talked to her a couple of times, and I like her. But she lives in New Jersey. I decided, though, that I would attempt to figure out as much as possible about her before making any decisions about seeing just one person. I hope you understand."

"Of course, Jason, I understand," Diya says. "We aren't in a relationship right now, and I'm glad you told me about this."

I expect her to say more, but she doesn't. Then again, I'm not sure what more she would say: Maybe that she's not interested, or that she wants to be with me, or that she wishes I had a parrot on my shoulder. In the past, I have dated or been friends with girls who have set the parameters. Diya seems rather open to trying to figure this out as we go. Yet, she acts hesitant to make any radical moves. I appreciate it, considering I'm not sure how I feel about her. I've been enticed previously by beauty, intelligence, wit, kindness, and compassion. This time, however, honesty and maturity appear to be winning me over much more dramatically.

The movie ends, and it's really late. Diya has a full day of schoolwork Sunday, and I have more family events planned. She walks me to the door, and I stop for a minute to look into her eyes for answers, which I do not find.

"If you need a break tomorrow, give me a call," I say, reaching out for a hug.

"Don't worry," Diya says. "I probably will."

We embrace for at least two minutes. It crosses my mind briefly to kiss her, but it doesn't seem quite right ... not yet.

13
Trip Planner

Monday, July 18

I'm going to Cincinnati.

At least, that's what I'm telling myself at the moment. There's no use in continuing this fence-sitting exercise. Everyone else has been pouring in extra time at work to make his or her decision. By now, I've earned a little time to devote to pondering the move myself.

Besides, maybe I can debunk some of the untruths circulating about Northern Lineage. While it has been compared to both a sweatshop with a cafeteria and heaven (with a *bigger* cafeteria, naturally), I'm sure it sits somewhere in the middle. Then again, I don't recall any of Michelangelo's works depicting archangels wearing ties.

I find a bunch of propaganda, er, information, for the move in the break room. There are yellow expandable file folders containing a litany of magazines, pamphlets, and apparently everything else ever printed about Cincinnati. Of course, each comes complete with a folder from our friends in the real estate business, Community Choice. Also littered on the table is a plethora of Realtor business cards, as local agents are trying to capitalize on a number of movers.

There's even a paper brochure discussing Project Giza. The front reads, "We have built a great company in Northern Lineage. We must do our part to preserve it!" There are pictures throughout the leaflet showing NL employees doing random things, but in each, they are dressed in Egyptian attire. I'd much prefer the cloth robes to their current dress code. On my way out, I borrow the lone apartment booklet.

It is quiet back at my desk. Barry is on vacation, and I suspect Jeff and the others either are in meetings or have contracted smallpox. I stay in my bunker of a cube, just to be on the safe side.

The apartment guide is a bit overwhelming. It's not quite as large as the Java book, but it contains more options than I need. I may just try to contact some of the complexes Grant mentioned. I need to find an alternative to selling my house, but unless I can split the cost with someone, it may not be feasible. Luckily, we have up to a year to take advantage of the Northern Lineage house moving deal, including being paid in full for closing costs. Ken is already up for sharing a place; maybe we can get Jeff, his wife, and Diya to all go in together.

The yellow folder of treasure is a bit disappointing, especially because it does not include a coupon for free living arrangements. I thumb through each piece, again wondering whether I actually want to move to Cincinnati.

Next door, Jeff is speaking to Raj, who runs one of Mettle's e-commerce divisions. From what I can tell, Raj hasn't officially received an offer. That shocks me, considering that we were told everyone in "good standing" would receive an offer. Did Raj do something wrong?

Jeff scurries over to my cube and informs me that Raj might stay in the Louisville office. Why can't everyone stay in the Louisville office?

In the afternoon, the seventh floor is so quiet that even the rolling tumbleweeds tiptoe between cubes. Hardly anyone is here, although I'm almost positive Diya is at her desk. She sent me an email an hour ago, again mentioning that she wants me to join her this coming weekend for the house hunt. I want to go, but chances are slim, considering my family obligations. With Diya, anything less than a 100 percent "yes" is automatically translated into "no." Yet I think she believes that I don't want to go with her because I'm not planning to move to Cincinnati.

In fact, I have made at least one decision today: I'm not selling my house in the immediate future. If I go, I'll get an apartment, live in my car, or pitch a tent in my cubicle. The cafeteria is just a few floors away, and I can shower in the gym. Right?

I walk over to Diya's cube. She has wallpapered her desk with printouts. Upon closer inspection, I realize she is printing out information for practically every condominium place in Cincinnati and northern Kentucky. She steps out and walks past me en route to the printer, only to return with a handful of papers a few seconds later. The footer of one page tacked to the wall reads "48 of 90." Maybe she's working on the entire eastern half of the United States.

"Hi," she says, as she brushes past me, returning to the printer for the second time in as many minutes.

"Wow, lots of research here," I say. "Are there any in particular that interest you?"

"Not yet," Diya says. "My Realtor mentioned a couple of these places, and I am going to come up with a list to look at Saturday. I take it you are not coming with me?"

"I want to ... but I'm afraid it won't work out with my schedule. It depends on what my family is doing Friday night ... I might be able to go."

"Jason, it's no worry. I would like you to help me pick out the right place, because I trust your opinion. But you're not going to Northern Lineage anyway, so ... "

"But I don't even know if I'm going!"

She stops for a moment, gives me a "come on" look, and dashes back to the printer. I decide to change the subject.

"I found your city's website!" I say.

She immediately returns with a perplexed look.

"My city?" she says.

"Yeah, Mangalore, that's where you said you're from, right? They have a website, and I'm trying to learn some of the words."

The last time we hung out, Diya tried to explain to me the different languages spoken in her hometown of Mangalore, India. Tulu and Kannada are the main dialects, but people also speak Konkani, Malayalam, Hindi, and English. Diya had said that the two primary languages are known pretty much just by people from Mangalore, which is why I want to attempt to learn a few words.

"OK, I'm going to try this," I say. "You are a *porlu ponnu*. Did that make sense?"

She laughs.

"Yes Jason, but you have a lot of work in saying the words right!"

"But that means 'beautiful girl,' right?"

"Yes, but say it like 'pour-lou.' "

"All right. What about '*yencha ullar*?' "

"That's pretty close."

"I figure it's good to know how to say 'How are you?' "

"Yes, you almost have it."

"*Thondare ijji* (don't mention it)."

"Don't pronounce the 'h,' and 'ijji' is almost like 'itchy.' "

She smiles, steps past me, and heads back to the printer for more condo info.

"How's the status of the green card?" I say when she returns. "Have they taken care of everything?"

"No, but Ann in HR said Northern Lineage's lawyers are looking into it," Diya says. "I'm supposed to conference-call with them and Marshall later in the week. But I have to find some place in Cincinnati to live if I move with the company. If not, I can go back home and live with my parents."

"You would think that if they value you enough, they would find a way to keep you here."

"It doesn't work like that with the immigration laws in the

U.S. You have to follow all of the procedures. They don't have to process anything quickly, but you have to go through all three stages. Since we are moving out of state, I would have to start back at Step 1, even though I just entered Step 3. Besides the time element, if I have to start over, I have to pay the fees of about $2,000 again."

"Then how will the lawyers help?"

"If they can get everything processed faster, then it won't matter. My work visa is close to running out, though, so ultimately, I'm not sure if they have enough time to get it taken care of."

I wish I had the answer for her, but even supporting her has become laborious. It's not because I don't want to, and it's not because she is being standoffish. It's because I'm uncertain what she wants. She says I'm not going, but I'm not completely certain of that. I think she's going to go, but I get the feeling that she doesn't quite know what she wants.

Tuesday, July 19

As I try to focus on the menial aspects of the Annuity Profit Plus project, little things keep getting in the way.

Don is in his cube, barking away at his phone. It's possible he's talking to himself, but he seems to be obnoxiously nice to his conversing partner. Don has a way of disguising his true intent during discussions, which I find intriguing and annoying at the same time. I wait until it's silent in his cube and barge in.

"Hey Don," I say. "You're working today, huh?"

"If you want to call it that," Don says. "Having to deal with all the Realtor stuff is more work than my regular job."

"What do you still need to do?"

"I'm leaving the majority of it in Northern Lineage's hands. It's pretty nice to have them picking up the tab. I don't have to worry about taking extra days off to move. And they especially like me because I'll be the first."

"You are in the minority. Some people are interested in

moving to Cincinnati, but I don't think anyone wants to move immediately."

"From the day I started, I knew we were moving soon. In fact, on the day I started, someone predicted it would be a year when Northern Lineage decides to move everyone up. I started June 20 of last year, so it was one year and one day later ... pretty close guess."

It seems like a risky move to take a job someplace with the assumption that the job would be relocated. But Don's insider information paid off; instead of having to find a new job before moving, he found a job that was moving. Actually, in hindsight, it's pretty ingenious, assuming that Northern Lineage is going to pay the moving expenses. From what I've seen of the company so far, paying fees is the least of its concerns.

Five o'clock comes, and I leave work thinking fairly positively about the move. But by the evening, when I discuss the venture with family members, my ideas quickly change. Maybe I am placing too much emphasis on this job being exceptional. Not that I had ever claimed it as a dream job, but it definitely has perks: I don't work long hours; I work with great people; and I get paid a decent salary. From a personal standpoint, things are better than average as well. The biggest question, then, is what can be obtained faster: a new job, similar in stature to this one, or an equally satisfying personal life?

I decide to start writing pros and cons about moving or staying. At least one thing I can do to validate my decision is to put it on paper. I'm the only one who can determine the best approach for myself.

Wednesday, July 20

Today, for lack of better terms, is a financial business day. At noon, one of Mettle's lawyers conducts a seminar titled "Culture of Compliance." She discusses a multitude of recent legislation that will have an effect on the financial industry. Not many people attend, despite the free pizza. The seminar is mildly thought-provoking. The pizza is delicious.

That afternoon, perusing the Northern Lineage intranet to kill some time, I stumble across a news story concerning the company's growth during the last six months:

Northern Lineage Financial
Hits Record-Breaking Pace in First Six Months
I am pleased to report that Northern Lineage Financial had an outstanding first six months of this year. In fact, we experienced our best start ever.

Our recent successes can be attributed to a focus on margins, growth through the Indiana Life merger, and unwavering empowerment of holistic channels. For that, I want to thank each of you.

Without question, NL's associates are critical in meeting the needs of our customers, productizing end-to-end functionalities, and creating synergies across our businesses. All of these activities significantly impact our financial strength and ability to aggregate granular architectures.

So, take a few minutes to celebrate our record results from the past six months. Look around you, congratulate your colleagues, and reflect upon your personal contributions to our overall achievements. If the midyear results are any indication, we are closer to our goal of evolving into a true personal financial services powerhouse. Congratulations!

Is this one of the reasons they decided to move us now, as opposed to waiting any longer? I suppose anytime you can throw a number between a dollar sign and the word "billion," relocating a couple hundred employees isn't a paramount ordeal.

Still, the idea of a "true personal financial services powerhouse" frightens me. It sounds like either a large investment company or a robot from the future that spits cash out of its mouth. At the very least, I'm able to check off a number of terms on my corporate B.S. bingo sheet.

Thursday, July 21

Boredom rules!

In between numerous tests on Annuity Profit Plus, I try to catch up on new information for the relocation website. Even though we still have nearly four weeks to make our decision, there are already some people listed as relocating. I count four so far, each with a quote saying why they are going. While the comments vary in length, the main premise is the same: staying with Northern Lineage will be an adventure and could very well turn out to be the opportunity of a lifetime.

I also notice a new post on the relocation intranet question-and-answer section:

Q: If I move into an apartment in Cincinnati and for some reason I leave the company before the two-year commitment is up, will I be responsible for paying the company back money?

A: If you decide to leave the organization within one year of your relocation, you will be expected to repay 100% of the relocation expenses and bonus. If you decide to leave the organization after one year but before your two-year anniversary in Cincinnati, you will be expected to repay 50% of the relocation expenses and bonus. If you remain employed with Northern Lineage Financial for at least two years beyond your official transfer date to Cincinnati and then leave the company, you will not have to repay any of the relocation expenses or relocation bonus. Regardless of what you decide, we hope you give 110% while you're with us ;)

What it really comes down to is this: If you're going to relocate, and you really hate it but want to keep all of the bonus money, you're going to have to stay for two years. Northern Lineage isn't just going to hand out cash like an oblivious parent to a preteen wannabe diva. The relocation agreement comes with responsibilities, which most of the employees are now realizing. Even though the parent company relocating Mettle can be considered a disservice, precautions will ensure that Northern Lineage won't get royally screwed.

But the same can't be said for all of the employees ... or soon-to-be former employees.

Friday, July 22

After an adequate morning of Annuity Profit Plus testing, I meet with Vance about specific computation questions. We toss around a few possibilities regarding what some of the more cryptic things mean, and he jots down additional questions to ask our actuarial contact. But we set current work aside as Vance reminiscences about his fair share of companywide shakeups.

"I should have warned everyone this would happen eventually," Vance says. "I can't remember the last time I worked for a company that didn't have restructuring issues while I was there."

"Did you have to relocate?" I say.

"No, but I did lose my job both times. At my last job, they didn't dismiss a large number of people at once. Instead, they did it in spurts, and by surprise. Employees would show up for work in the morning and find all of their stuff packed in boxes, which had their names on them. The funny thing was that they didn't always get rid of everyone with their stuff packed away ... sometimes, it was just to move people around. If you stayed, you took your box of belongings back upstairs. If you left, you went to talk to the guy down in human resources ... some sort of hippie counselor."

"That's ridiculous."

"Yeah ... I never understood the whole put-everything-in-a-box rationale. Maybe they wanted it to be like a game show or something."

"You can go upstairs and take your job ... or you can have *what's in the box*!" I joke, even though with the explosion of reality TV, I think people would trade their jobs for a game show appearance.

"The sad thing is that wasn't the worst experience," Vance continues. "At another company, I gave a suggestion about the business, which they later used, and I ended up losing my job over it!"

"That's pretty harsh."

"It was a bit more than harsh. About seven to eight months before, the folks in the data center talked about rewriting their job descriptions. I heard about it and recommended to my supervisor that we do the same, just to clarify what everyone was supposed to be doing. It turns out that when that occurred, they realized they needed fewer people to do all of the jobs. So they let me and a few others go."

People who have been through the revolving door of the computer technology industry time and time again probably have similar stories. Every story I hear about resizing, restructuring, relocating, etc., is unique, yet the result is nearly the same. However, one huge difference appears to be that in our case, Northern Lineage isn't necessarily doing bad. On the contrary, the company is breaking revenue records.

So why would the head honchos think that now is the time to throw the Louisville office into disarray?

There's nothing wrong with having a business in Louisville. Look at United Parcel Service, which has its main hub located here in the Derby City. And what about Stride Rite, a children's shoe company that relocated here from Roxbury, Massachusetts, in 1992? The reason for moving was straightforward enough: according to *Corporation Nation*, Kentucky was closer to its consumers, it could pay lower wages, and of course, there was a $24 million tax break from the city.[19] On the flip side, many intangibles outside the business sphere — the nation's first in-house daycare center for employees, paid tutoring of inner-city kids on company time, and many other charitable events — disappeared after the relocation. Stride Rite had established a working relationship with Roxbury, sure enough, but due to competition and the bottom line, things had changed.

Maybe this isn't such a positive example after all.

"We are a huge part in the overall Northern Lineage company, which I think is one of the reasons they want us up there," says Vance, echoing sentiments that Jeff had mentioned before. "They initially bought us because we were doing things they hadn't even dreamed of yet. They could somewhat learn from us remotely, but they know it's better to get us under their roof."

The meeting with Vance continues longer than both of us had planned, but it's not a big deal. Friday afternoons are almost always barren, and even more so today. Numerous people from the floor, including Diya, have already left for the weekend trip to Cincinnati.

Vance mentions something that I remember seeing on the relocation website, so I open a new browser window and jump to it. Before I can get there, though, we notice a new feature on the website's home page. There's a large illustration of a bus, with a drawing of some skyscrapers, presumably in Cincinnati, in the background on the right. On the left side, there's a list of 10 names. The graphic is titled "Guess Who's on the Bus!"

"Well, that's a nifty little graphic," I say. "Are you going to add your name next?"

"Ha, I doubt it," Vance says. "I might get on, but I'll ask for a transfer, just in case."

14
Connections

Tuesday, July 26

The attendees on hand practically resemble our weekly team meeting. The only difference is that instead of Chris's desk between us, there's a volleyball net in the middle of the group. And, of course, we aren't in our work clothes, but instead, gym clothes and sneakers.

Barry and I have been playing pickup volleyball on Tuesday nights during the last few weeks. Nelson, my sister Katie, and a few random people also play every so often. We tried convincing others from work to play, but they are most likely still searching for Cincinnati living arrangements. Tonight, however, there are two special guests participating: Jeff and Diya.

Jeff had planned to play once before, but he had forgotten to bring extra clothes. Diya, though, astonishes us all, primarily because I mentioned playing volleyball to her almost as a joke. Not only did she appear, but she was halfway decent. At work, there really isn't an easy way to distinguish the athletes from couch potatoes. However, a few weeks ago, I watched Diya play badminton ... and I'm not talking about the backyard variety. I found out after seeing her play that she once defeated the U.S. Olympic representative in a match!

Yep, Diya's a cute, funny, intelligent athlete. Maybe I should switch to the other team so I can gawk less obviously at her.

The teams are fairly even: myself, Barry, Katie, and a random pickup, facing Jeff, Diya, Tom Nelson, and one of his friends. We aren't really keeping score; in fact, the only things being tracked are the number of times Barry attempts to record kills on top of Jeff's head.

"Come on fatty, fat boy," says Barry just before he whiffs at another kill opportunity.

"Wow, you're a lunatic both at work and on the volleyball court!" Jeff says.

For one evening, volleyball distracts not just me, but nearly the entire team, from the longest-running freak show in Louisville. Yesterday, things were pretty much status quo. Diya and a few others discussed their weekend Cincinnati excursions, and Debbie complained that she hadn't found any decent housing. Chris, with his recent Realtor fiasco, recommended that Debbie drop the agent.

I walked away before they finished the discussion. There was only so much I could take regarding the ongoing relocation saga. As a rough estimate, I'd say two-thirds of the people I know are seriously considering moving. Almost all of these people are looking at purchasing houses as well as selling their houses here in town. The age distribution stretches from the mid-20s to somewhere in the 50s. I am somewhat surprised that more people aren't considering the temporary housing, but at the same time, the majority will be moving their families.

I had a few questions for Jeff regarding Annuity Profit Plus. Jeff was starting his vacation soon, so I needed the info ASAP. Meanwhile, Ken was in Jeff's cube as they discussed the move. They didn't talk long, however, because everyone had deadlines to make for the week. Ken had to prepare for a special trip to Northern Lineage on Friday, where he was scheduled to train Grant on some of his Mettle duties. Jeff and I prepared for our 10 a.m. intranet training with the Northern Lineage team that will take over the internal website after we move.

As expected, both trainees wore business attire. Jeff and I

didn't dress up for the event, but we were prepared. We examined nearly every aspect of the intranet site, and we could tell that the Northern Lineage representatives were not ready for the wealth of information. They took fastidious notes, compiling four to five pages apiece.

After the training, Barry convinced Jeff, Ken, and me to join him for Chinese food. As we made it to the elevator, we passed Marty Valentine, the Northern Lineage technology manager. He was preparing to have lunch and wanted to know if he could join us. Barry shouted "Sure!" and we waited for Marty to catch up.

"Nothing against you, my man, but I don't think you'll be seeing me at the main office," said Barry on the walk to lunch. "They'd have to give me your job for me to move!"

"Barry rarely speaks for the rest of us," Jeff said. "I'm pretty close to turning in the form."

"That's what I heard from Chris," Marty said. "I think you'll really like it up there."

"I sure hope so, considering I've been working on finishing my basement here, and I won't really get to use it," Jeff said.

"That just means we should trash it before you go!" Barry said.

I expected lunch to be rather uncomfortable. True, eating during Barry's outrageous comments would leave anyone queasy, but this time, a Northern Lineage big wig would be sitting in on the action. Refreshingly, though, Marty seemed like one of the guys to us. He participated in the conversations, whether they touched on work, food, girls, or Barry's supposed recent rendezvous with girls.

One thing that easily gets lost in large corporations is the relationship between superiors and employees. I don't expect to go on binge-drinking escapades with the Northern Lineage or Mettle presidents. However, it is critical for those in charge to recognize the importance of keeping a strong rapport with the ones doing the grunt work. As noted in *Credibility*, all people, especially leaders, seek trust in a plethora of ways. But to be trusted, individuals have to be willing to volunteer information, share experiences, and make connections with experiences and aspirations of constituents.[20]

This means that if you are a monk, a fearful individual with a penchant of paranoia, or some combination of the two, you may have a hard time acquiring trustworthiness in the business environment. That is, unless you have psychic abilities, which can be convincing and may even confuse your cohorts into believing they can confide in you or purchase you a new brown robe.

I don't know if this was Marty's intention in joining us for lunch, but in the afternoon, we all agreed that his presence with the group was a positive one. It's too bad that Marty couldn't stick around for tonight's volleyball action.

We play for a couple of hours, until Nelson moves to court one for his league game. Jeff and Barry leave together because Jeff left his car in the parking garage at work. Katie is the next to leave, which leaves just Diya and me.

"Do you want to come over before you go home?" I say. "I can show you where I live ... it's just right down the road."

"Well, I shouldn't because of my parents, but since it's close by, then OK," Diya says.

Diya had told me last week that her parents were coming to visit from India. They started in California, visiting her brother. They are in Louisville and will be here for what Diya expects to last a month. I assumed that with her parents in town, our time together outside work would be drastically reduced. But playing volleyball and accepting an invitation to my house were good signs.

At my place, I pour Diya a glass of water and take it to her in the living room. We sit on the couch and drink. I hesitate to make any moves, but with her parents on this side of the globe, this might be my only chance at it for a while.

"So what are your parents doing ... are they at your

apartment?" I say.

"They probably are, but maybe not," Diya says. "When they go to new places, they like to go around town and find interesting things and other Indian shops."

"Did they rent a car?"

"No ... they usually just take the bus. That sometimes leads to them getting lost, but they always figure it out. And if not, I guess they can always call me to pick them up."

Diya lies down on my couch. It appears that she might be falling asleep, which would not surprise me. As much as she has been doing over the past couple of weeks, with school-work, dance rehearsals, and her parents visiting, on top of her already busy workload ... I'm getting an ulcer just thinking about it. I want her to relax a minute and try to forget about everything.

Maybe it's a little selfish, but I want her to just think about me.

I maneuver beside Diya, my right arm embracing her and my left hand playing with her hair. She smiles and takes two noticeable deep breaths. I wonder if she will pull away, but instead she turns toward me.

My heart races so fast that I can no longer distinguish separate beats. I look at her forehead, then her cheeks, then her mouth, and then her eyes. I have wondered for a while if this time would arrive, but it still catches me by surprise.

I keep thinking she'll turn away, but she doesn't. I squeeze her just a little with my right arm and lean in to kiss her on the right cheek. She shyly smirks and looks directly into my eyes. We kiss on the lips. And we continue kissing for at least three segments of eternity.

I feel as if maybe I'm doing something wrong, or maybe she doesn't want this, or maybe she's wondering what I'm thinking. But she doesn't pull away, and instead, returns the affection without question. And it is too wonderful to stop.

Eventually, we do; I guess she needs to go home, though

I'd rather she stay the night.

"I'm guessing that your parents are expecting you to show up tonight, right?" I say.

"Yeah, they would have a ton of questions for me if I didn't come home," Diya says. "I'm not sure how they would respond to me ignoring them for an American boy."

Although she doesn't elaborate, I finally start to realize a list of questions I have never seriously considered. Can we realistically be together? Will her parents frown upon us seeing each other? And will that make a difference to Diya?

Tonight is not the time. I walk Diya to the door, and we kiss one last time before she leaves.

Wednesday, July 27

I bounce between Jeff's terminal and mine. Mindy needs to use my computer for a host of things, although I try not to pry. She is using a floppy disk to carry her files. Yes, a floppy disk! I didn't even realize my machine had a floppy drive, but it does.

Over in Jeff's cube, I notice that the printer, which sits just outside his south partition, is abuzz with activity. Occasionally people print documents, even Diya with the booklet of condos she made last week. Maybe it caught my attention because I also need to print out a few things for a meeting that after-noon with Vance. When I approach the printer, I notice partial spreadsheet documents spitting out of the machine. Mindy's name appears on the entire lot of papers, creating a waterfall as they slide closer and closer to the table's edge, where some have already fallen to the ground.

"Mindy, I noticed you were printing out these spreadsheets, but it doesn't look like they are fitting on individual pages," I say, returning to my cube. "Do you need some help with it?"

"Maybe I do," Mindy says. "It looks like they are on one page, but why isn't it allowing me to do this?"

"Yeah, Internet Explorer isn't always nice about formatting

the printing. You could try printing landscape."

I walk over to my machine and try in Firefox, which seems to do the trick. I hearken back to a quote surely said by a number of past Northern Lineage employees: "Duplicates, triplicates, quadruplicates! Print, print, print like there's no tomorrow!"

Mindy runs to a meeting, so I close her documents. It seems more and more that she is the overseer of work, and not really a typical web person/programmer/carrier pigeon per se. Besides, most of her IT background, as she explained before, occurred during the mainframe days, without much of an actual public Internet. She has been instrumental in setting up Northern Lineage processes for her team and the interactions with other teams. So how high up in the priority list would landscape printing be?

Mindy runs off to a meeting with Barry ... only Barry. I find out later that they discussed Barry's cash cow: fund transfers. Without Barry, a complete system blueprint could take months to determine. Even with Barry, it could take awhile, but he is by far the most familiar with the code, mainly because he wrote it. While he has documented a decent portion of his work, it's not enough. Obviously, the prospects are not good for Barry to move to Cincinnati. Furthermore, Northern Lineage is a document-happy bunch. In fact, it would behoove the company to start utilizing this motto:

"If it works on paper, it works!"

At this point, Barry just wants to give Mindy a little better view of the process than just a general overview. But due to the complexity, there is no need to dig into the detail. Mindy will be scheduling other times for that, because it isn't something that occurs in a simple meeting. In my opinion, Barry's worries about being let go have all but dissipated. He is the Tree of Knowledge, and the fruit is blossoming at just the right time.

With Mindy disposed of for a while, I can resume working on my machine. I promised Jeff I would make a checklist of things that are complete and things that still need to be worked on when he returns. The biggest thing solely in my possession is the actuarial calculation mumbo jumbo that needs to be translated into the system. I am getting closer, but I still need questions answered, which seems to be a recurring theme in my life right now.

Thursday, July 28

It has been a fairly focused work day — at least until now (3 p.m.). I keep overhearing Nelson on the phone, presumably talking to job recruiters. At one point, I think he even had a phone interview. Does Northern Lineage care if we conduct job interviews inside the offices? It seems that as long as we aren't harassing anyone else, we can pretty much do as we please.

"Where is the job?" I say to Nelson after he hangs up the phone.

"Somewhere in Washington State."

"Are you willing to move that far away?"

"I wouldn't mind ... I've been out to the West Coast a bunch of times, and I really like it out there. I don't have anything really keeping me here. By the way, do you know if Diya is dating anyone?"

I'm a little surprised by the subject change, but with Nelson, I shouldn't be that shocked.

"I'm not really sure, but I don't think so," I say, remembering that I told Diya I'd keep quiet about us. Actually, it's an honest answer; I'm still not certain what she thinks is dating and what isn't and what "us" really is.

"Oh, OK," Nelson says. "It seems like you talk to her a lot, so I thought you might know. I thought she was married or something."

"Why would you think that?"

"Nothing in particular. It just seemed like awhile back, I overheard some people talking about her getting married. But lately, I haven't heard anything. So I thought I might ask her out. Does she date Americans?"

"That's an interesting question. I sure wish I knew the answer."

This is a risky line of questioning; I decide to return to work chatter.

"So are you definitely not moving to Cincinnati now?" I say.

"I have no idea," Nelson says. "I really don't want to move back up there. It's not so much the position itself, but if I want to find something else, Cincinnati is not the place. The IT job market doesn't seem that great up there. More than likely, though, I'll probably end up there at least temporarily. The only way that wouldn't happen is if I find the perfect job here. There's a girl up there I was seeing off and on, and it might be a good opportunity to move and try to make things work."

"At least it's a job, and it's not like you'll be fired from it anytime soon."

"Yeah, they can't really fire the handful of people who are actually moving."

Friday, July 29

I assume I will see Mindy at some point, but she emailed the team early this morning and said she was staying in Cincy. Not that this particularly matters to the rest of us; we have work to do, and that beats interruptions for meetings, at least for Barry and Ken. I really haven't seen them much this week, until now.

At the moment, I'm eating lunch in Diya's cube. My cell-phone rings, and as soon as I mention that it's Jeff, both Ken and Barry appear.

"Do you miss me?" Jeff says.

"Apparently we do, considering that everyone is gathering around me," I say. "You would think that you had been gone for years. Why are you calling?"

"Uh ... no reason, just to see what you were doing."

"I'm working, dumbass ... what else would I be doing?"

"Ha, sure you are. It's Friday. No one even comes to work on Friday!"

"I can't say a lot is getting accomplished, but Mindy isn't here. Reshmi helped me get the Java compiler working."

"Sweet!"

"All right, you should go back to your vacation."

"Good idea! Laura is telling me that we need to leave anyway. Talk to you later!"

Barry and Ken eagerly wait for me to transcribe the conversation. Everyone really wants to know what everyone else is doing at all times. In certain circles, that probably seems a little overboard, but within our small family, it's completely normal.

Barry and Ken retreat back to their cubes, and after talking to Diya for a few minutes, I do the same.

As with most Fridays, the seventh floor is almost empty. Finally, I can get some work accomplished, even though everyone else is enjoying a random holiday.

Now that I'm more familiar with what Annuity Profit Plus is supposed to do, I can actually test my changes. But with Jeff on vacation since Wednesday, I needed access to the items he normally controlled. I enjoy the silence, which lasts a total of six minutes, until my cellphone rings again. It's a Cincinnati area code. I decide to answer it, just in case it's someone from headquarters, making sure that all of the staff hasn't gone home for the weekend already.

"Hello, Jason? My name is Roberta Ford. I'm with Career-Start in Cincinnati. I noticed your résumé on JobImp, and I think I have the perfect job for you."

"Hi Roberta," I start. "I'm not looking for a job in Cincinnati. In fact, I already have a job there waiting for me."

"Oh, this job is in Louisville. It's a programmer position at Market Street Systems. Are you interested in this? The requirements are proficiency in HTML, JavaScript, and CSS programming. Would you like me to set up an interview for it?"

"Sure, that sounds good. If you can send me a full job description, that would be excellent."

"Certainly. I'll get back with you next week and let you know of the interview date and time."

Not that I expect much about this opportunity; I was just at Market Street Systems a few months ago, interviewing for approximately 216 different openings. Seriously, I spoke with eight employees in three different departments to determine the best fit for my capabilities. And each time I walked out of someone's office, I thought for certain that I would end up there. But before I accepted the Mettle job, I found out that they had gone in "another direction" with the hires. Considering that last week I received another email informing me that I didn't get hired, I can only assume the direction was down.

At least I got a free lunch out of having to wear a tie that day.

As I read the email that Roberta has just sent, Diya, with her bags packed to leave, stops at my cube's entrance.

"Are you leaving soon?" Diya asks.

"Most likely," I say. "I'm looking at another job here in Louisville."

"Oh? Does it look promising?"

"It might be decent. It's with Market Street Systems, but they turned me down before. We'll see how the interview goes."

"Well, that is wonderful."

Usually when someone says the word "wonderful," they say it with energy and pizzazz, as if there is a real belief in some wonderment. Diya, however, says "wonderful" the same way a person might say it in response to a someone's elaborate theory of swine respiratory diseases.

"Seriously, I'm considering all of my options," I say. "If I don't find an amazing job, I'll be heading up to Northern Lineage with you and everyone else."

"No you won't," Diya says. "You aren't going. I can tell."

"So you can predict the future?"

"Yes. I know you won't go. I want you to go, though, but I know you won't."

As Diya leaves, I can't find the words to respond. I have no idea if I will go. I have no idea if wooing her will result in any relationship. Ultimately, although I'm making strides to make the right decision, I'm lagging behind in coming up with the answers.

Unfortunately, someone whom I care about has found my answers extremely unappealing.

15
Talk Can Be Expensive

Monday, August 1

If Mettle is a circus, then Marshall MacDougal is assuming ringmaster duties — at least, in our divison. Last week, he sent an email to everyone on the seventh floor, saying that if anyone wanted to discuss the move, he would be available.

I jumped at the chance because I hoped Marshall would tell it to me straight. Regardless of the size of your company, finding trustworthy corporate people isn't always an easy task. Few leaders understand that unless they communicate, most of their employees won't give a damn. Sharing information, as *Credibility* suggests, lets everyone know the reasons behind decisions, including the way they are connected to serve a common purpose.[21] I want Marshall to tell me what he thinks is best for me and what's best for the company ... without trying to sugarcoat it.

"Jason, I'm glad you are meeting with me," Marshall says. "After our last discussion, I'm excited you are still pursuing the right decision, because I think there is definitely a place for you at Northern Lineage. Actually, while I was on vacation last week, I thought it might help if I drew out our organizational structure for you."

You have to hand it to Marshall: He is being creative with his tactics now. Off the clock, Marshall has constructed a map of various technology teams that report to him. It's a maze of bubbles with lines connccting them, akin to something one may contrive from playing the old Adventure computer game.

But Marshall doesn't have to leave gold or an oil can behind to find his way back.

"Since it seems that you are interested in how everything works at Northern Lineage, this diagram may give you a better idea of who reports to whom," Marshall continues. "Your skills fit within a few of these teams, and as you can see, Mindy's team is in the middle of the action. But there are other ways you can help support our systems. With the number of people involved, there are always going to be more procedures. That's why we want to get the right people in the right places. If we can do that, we can avoid potential bottlenecks. Let's face it, we're not trying to boil the ocean here."

Marshall again makes it tempting to move. It's pretty cool that important people are taking the time to understand the employees — even someone like me, who has been with the company a mere seven weeks.

But this isn't the end of why I wanted to have this meeting today.

"I'll look at this blueprint a little bit later ... thanks for putting this together," I say. "I also wanted to ask you about Diya. Do you think she will be able to go to Northern Lineage?"

It's not any of my business, true, but if I'm talking to someone who will tell me the truth, I might as well ask.

"I know the lawyers are working on the green card issue," Marshall says. "I can't really say anything for certain, but we are trying to make it so she can continue working here in the States."

"She is a dedicated worker, and it would be bad to lose her," I say. "I can tell that much from the short period of time I've worked here."

"It's good to know she has other people in the company who can vouch for her."

My scheduled 20-minute meeting has already exceeded 40 minutes; I say goodbye and return to my cube. I plan to tell

Diya soon about my morning encounter.

During the weekend, I mentioned to her that I might say something to Marshall about her. She didn't seem reluctant, but she also didn't act as if it were a great idea. Because her parents are still in town, we spent a few hours together at my place rather than hers. I still haven't met her parents. I wonder if she has told them much about me, or even about me at all. I can't be certain they don't disapprove of us having a relationship ... if that's what it is. And I don't know how to ask her about any of it.

Diya couldn't stay out too late, so we just grabbed a Dairy Queen Blizzard and watched another Indian movie, titled *Aankhen*. The movie stars Amitabh Bachchan, one of the most well-known Bollywood actors, in an intriguing role. He plays a bank manager who is fired from his job for a trivial reason. To retaliate, he kidnaps a boy and blackmails the boy's older sister into training three blind men to rob the bank.

Stop for a minute to dissect the movie plot, if you will.

The movie is pretty decent; I like any movie where I can't guess the ending midway through the story. The movie does tend to drag at the end. But I didn't even really notice because Diya and I were kissing. We tried not to get too carried away, especially because she had to return home. Besides, with our decisions looming — only two weeks until we have to make a final decision — it wasn't too hard to contemplate just how close we should get at this time.

Then again, at that moment, we were pretty damn close.

Back at work, I defer to talk to Diya until after our weekly web meeting. As usual, the focus is not on current work but instead, the housing situation.

"We've finally decided on something," Chris says. "It's still about 30 to 40 minutes away from work, but at least we can afford it."

"I have a feeling we'll end up near you," Jeff says. "Ken, aren't you looking in northern Kentucky, too?"

"Yeah, but the situation here is still complex," Ken says. "I don't want to move the entire family right away."

"Take advantage of the temporary housing," Chris says.

"It's either that or rooming with Jeff for a while," Ken says.

"It looks like your bed is going to be full!" Barry says to Jeff.

"If we can work out a deal for the house we want, there will be room for you," says Jeff to Ken. "But I'm not making lunch for you every morning."

"That's no problem ... lunch is on the house at Northern Lineage!" Barry says.

There's a bit of apprehension in Ken's comments. He needs more time for the decision. I'm not sure, though, whether the problem is a matter of deciding to relocate or of finding something else here in town.

"How did the meeting with Marshall go?" Chris asks.

"It went well," I say. "He is very convincing. And he seems really genuine."

"I would agree," Chris says. "He has always done great things for the employees. Obviously, it's a pretty big thing, especially considering you are new to the company. But I know we can use you up there."

I thank Chris and leave his office. My resolve swings back in favor of relocating, but it doesn't last long. When I return to my desk, I notice an email from Roberta, the recruiter I spoke with last week. My interview at Market Street Systems is scheduled for 11 a.m. tomorrow. Immediately, I go back to Chris's office to tell him. While others in the office may have a reason to keep things secret, it's not going to do anything for me — at least not at this point. If Northern Lineage is going to be open with allowing us the opportunity to search for jobs while in the office, the least I can do is be honest.

Before I get back to the actuarial calculations for Annuity Profit Plus, I make a break for Diya's cube. I want to update her on the interview with Marshall, but she isn't there. I haven't actually heard from her this morning, so maybe she's running late ... extremely late because it's after 11.

For once, everyone at work seems to be busy with real work. I slip back to my cube and go unnoticed. Maybe my welcome has finally worn out, or maybe the tension has reached a new pinnacle. Regardless, there's plenty of work for me to do, and there will be time later in the week to contemplate my coworkers' dispositions.

Tuesday, August 2

"We need someone who can take Photoshop designs and code them in HTML and CSS. We have a fair amount of projects, but currently, this is a one-year contract position. It's definitely possible it could turn into a full-time position, but as of now, we are just working with contractors. Also, we are very particular about coding standards, and we make sure everyone adheres to those."

Bruce Stanley is the design team leader for contractors on the Market Street Systems Consumer & Industrial Marketing IT team. I listen closely about the job and give my normal spiel regarding my experience, minus my stint in the circus.

My best dress pants do not fit well anymore. Yeah, I should probably be wearing a suit to these things, but that hasn't been high on my list of priorities. I am wearing a gray oxford shirt and a patterned tie, which made me stand out this morning at Mettle. It was painfully obvious to everyone that I had an interview, and I didn't care. Besides, I wasn't planning on going back to work in dress attire. The noose can wait until I'm totally bound by Northern Lineage.

Bruce is a nice guy and thoroughly explains the details involved with the contract work. The job appears to be moderately appealing, but I'm not enamored. Bruce mentions that he'll send along a test Photoshop file, and after I complete the task, he'll make a decision.

Back at the office (minus the tie, of course), I talk to Mindy about the move.

"Are you any closer to making a decision?" Mindy says.

"Not really," I say. "But I am exploring it from every angle."

"I get the feeling that most people are still up in the air," Mindy says. "After this week, more of the forms will be turned in, but right now, most departments are still in the dark."

I wish I could tell Mindy one way or the other. I don't enjoy waffling on making decisions, but just like everyone else, no one wants to make the wrong one.

I could tell Mindy about the interview, but I don't. She might just assume that I'm definitely not moving, and that's clearly not my aim. I'll revisit the situation tonight and clear my head while learning Java. That can only benefit me at this point, whether I move or not.

In my email inbox, I notice I've received a message from JobImp. Of course, I've been receiving occasional job offers from the site, but this looks different. Maybe it's a job to work from home and make six figures!

Hello Jason,

My name is Reggie Macklin. I am an Operations Manager for JobImp. We are looking for web content professionals to help us at our prodction center in Jeffersonville, Indiana. Would you be interested in working in a GoLive/Dreamweaver, Photoshop, CSS, HTML, MAC/PC environment?

Please respond with your availability for an interview, samples of your work and an updated résumé.

~ Reggie

It's a good thing I posted my information on JobImp.com. I just never thought that the perfect position might be with the career website giant itself.

Wednesday, August 3

Barry is acting strange this morning. And when I say that Barry is acting strange, I mean he's acting subdued and extremely low key. Maybe he's sick.

"Hey man, what's going on?" I say, entering Barry's cube.

"Nothing much, newbie," Barry says. "I'm trying to get some of the documentation finished before my interview this afternoon."

"Interview?" I say. "Who is it with?"

"Key Printing," Barry says. "They need a systems analyst, and most of their stuff is in Java and Unix. On paper, it would be a great fit."

"Well, good luck with it," I say.

"I hope that if they offer me something, they'll be lenient on the start date. There is still plenty I need to do here, especially training. I suppose I shouldn't get too ahead of myself."

Barry is a rare commodity in today's workplace. While he's concerned about finding a new job and staying in town, Barry doesn't want the fruit of his previous work to be all for naught. Barry is pretty damn good at what he does; it's a bonus that he wants to transfer that knowledge, with or without the help of a mad scientist.

Because Barry is so upbeat about the interview, he wants Ken, Jeff, and myself to go to lunch. We stroll down to Fourth Street Live and find a booth in T.G.I. Friday's for an early Wednesday meal.

"I'm going for the barbecue ribs today," says Barry to the waitress. "Today is a big day."

"Is it your birthday?" the waitress asks.

"No. He's creating his first stuffed animal at Build-A-Bear this afternoon," Ken says. "So Barry, are you going to stick with the bear, or pick a different animal?"

The conversation derails even further as Barry discusses his "special" methods of barbecuing various animal parts. Jeff and Ken look as if they've heard the tales before, and I'm too famished to pay much attention. I perk up when Barry mentions the idea of changing his last name to "Quixote," and his middle name to "Bartholomew," just so he can initial any used cookout napkins with "BBQ."

As they prattle on, I start thinking about the effects of relocation and all of the talk about it. Barry's demeanor hasn't changed a bit; if anything, he is more comfortable at Mettle now than he was when I started. He has an inordinate amount of job security, considering he's the only one at this stage who knows the processes inside and out. Then again, that was the case seven weeks ago as well. So why is there a lack of tension now?

It's simple: Northern Lineage is giving Barry the attention he craves, which in turn has created a much more relaxing environment for him. He's still the same determined worker ... but he's a bit more carefree with his emotions about many company dilemmas. It must be a weird feeling, knowing that you essentially have control over your lifespan at a business, pretty much regardless of what happens.

Ken is in a similar scenario, yet it scares the shit out of him. Unlike Barry, he has notions of moving, and from my standpoint, it looks as if he will go. But lurking in the back of his mind are different thoughts. He's feeling that while this could be an amazing opportunity bestowed on him, it will come with risks, and those could lead to hardships. Being a fence-sitter isn't necessarily a bad thing, but it can be if there isn't a discernible difference between the sides.

At the same time, Ken is taking precautions in case something doesn't work out as planned. He is searching heavily for local jobs, and he has made it a point not to move his family immediately. He still can back out during the next few days. I'd be mildly surprised, but I wouldn't call it totally unexpected.

Jeff, I assume, will submit his form today and sign up for the Northern Lineage dungeon. The strange thing about Jeff's choice is that he acts confident about relocating, but in reality, he doesn't want to be there. He wants to be in California, working in the graphic design industry. He thinks that hiding in Cincinnati will give him time and allow him to save money to work toward his aspirations. Why, then, wouldn't he consider just finding something else in Louisville? Why is he dead set on purchasing a house in Cincy when he may live there only a couple of years?

The answer lies in a couple of areas, one being Laura, his wife. She's ready for a change, and she's willing to move, even though her family is in Louisville. I wonder if Laura could theoretically find a job here in town, but I suppose that when couples make a decision, it's increasingly tough to turn back. Considering that Jeff doesn't have a definitive reason not to move, he'll go anyway.

As for me, I just want to make the right decision. I have very few dependencies, so I know I'll be all right. In a weird way, having more responsibilities seems to make large decisions easier.

***

Late in the afternoon, I notice that just about everyone has gone home except Jeff, Barry, and myself. While Barry is busy with his phone interview, Jeff and I tend to the Annuity Profit Plus project.

"I've finished a good amount of work on the date validation stuff, and I think I have these actuarial calculations figured out," I say. "So that's pretty much all that's left to do, right?"

Jeff gives a hearty laugh.

"Oh, I wish," Jeff says. "I'm sure things will change again ... and again ... and again."

"What do you mean 'change'?"

"At first, this system was supposed to be just for new money being invested, then they modified it to allow current contracts. So I had to add another page in the step-by-step process through the form. That was a real pain in the ass. I'm sure they'll find something else to throw in there before we're finished."

Website modifications can be anything from simple text changes to overhauling a project. More often than not, the people requesting the transformations are so detached from the work that they have no idea into which category the edits fall. Imagine constructing a two-story house, and as you are adding the last shingle on the roof, you are told that the house should have a third story. That might be what's happening with APP, but we won't know until I see the other changes.

Fortunately, Jeff has made the fixes already, and now he's determined to finalize the validation and start plugging in numbers. Because my computer doesn't have a license to run Visual Basic, we decide to trade cubicles for some of the work tomorrow.

Barry, apparently finished with his phone interview, enters Jeff's cube but doesn't say anything. For once, he waits for someone else to start the conversation.

"So ... how did it go?" Jeff says.

"You know, I'm not really sure," Barry says. "They seemed nice enough, but they asked pretty specific questions about Java. I think I answered them correctly, but they didn't act like I was either right or wrong."

"Do you remember the questions?" I say.

"Yeah, the first one they asked was something like 'What is an abstract class?' " Barry says. "It seems simple enough, but I don't really know exact definitions."

Upon hearing this, Jeff almost falls out of his chair.

"Wait a minute!" says Jeff, spinning his chair to face his bookshelf. "I've read that question before somewhere."

He grabs for a book and pulls down *Conducting the Java Job Interview*. Turning to the first chapter, we find, word-for-word, the exact same question.

"Holy shit!" Barry says. "That was the question. Let me see

that book!"

Jeff gives the book to Barry.

"They asked me the second question, the fourth question ... almost all of these questions!" Barry says. "No wonder they didn't know if my answers were right. They were just reading straight out of a book!"

"Wow, I never realized companies just took those questions verbatim," I say.

"Yeah, really," Jeff says. "Did they just start using Java?"

"Hell, I don't know," Barry says. "This is really fishy, though. Next, I'm supposed to go there and take a personality test. The guy said it's like 1,000 questions. After this debacle, I'm not sure I'm even interested."

"Hey man, it is a job programming in Java close to home," Jeff says. "It's not like you have a better alternative at the present time. Well, unless you plan to go to Cincy."

"That's a good point," says Barry, handing the book back to Jeff. "I guess this job is better than no job. But I'd rather not be managed out of a book."

"But what if it were a cookbook?" Jeff says.

Thursday, August 4

I'm finally running Visual Basic on Jeff's computer this morning. The process isn't that exhilarating, but it's worth mentioning. The basic function I'm in charge of is determining how this VB script is coming up with its results. By dissecting the actual tabulation, I should be able to mimic that in the Java environment. I've completed some of the syntax conversion, but the numbers are nowhere near right, which is probably just because I don't know what I'm doing.

During the monotonous testing, I finally communicate with Reggie Macklin at JobImp. We had been playing phone tag since I received his first email. I schedule my interview for tomorrow afternoon.

More testing ensues for the remainder of the day. My only

solace is that finally, Jeff returns from his nearly endless meet-ings.

"Did you figure it out yet?" Jeff says.

"Oh, of courshhh," I say. "I'm making millions of dollars as we speak, and I plan on sh-pending it on lots of hot bodies."

"You'd better alert Moneypenny, or else your super spy agent duties might be suspended."

As we're talking James Bond again, Jeff rolls over the chair from my cube and appears to prepare for a serious chat. Because Jeff is never too serious, I'm curious to hear what's new.

"I was just in a meeting with an interesting combination of people, mostly managers and me," Jeff says.

"Why were you in the meeting?"

"Beats me ... Chris wanted me to go."

"He's grooming you to be the next great superior! You'll have your face carved on the Northern Lineage version of Mount Rushmore."

"The meeting was about how all of the different depart-ments connected, but nothing really got accomplished."

"You should have taken the picture that Marshall drew for me."

"Oh, he was in there, too. Anyway, I talked to Mindy about our team. She said she is filling four positions when we move."

"What if everyone decides to go?"

"That's what I asked her. She said she would take everyone if that happened, but she doesn't think it will."

"But if everyone goes, maybe they'd eventually get rid of one of us. Seems like I would be the first to go."

"I don't think they would get rid of you."

"I also wouldn't think a company would hire me and then, on my eighth day, say they were relocating."

"But look on the bright side ... if they fire you, you'll still get to keep the bonus!"

16
Potential Lurks

Friday, August 5

Another day, another interview, another opportunity to wear a tie.

This, of course, is an obvious indication that I'm serious about wanting this job at JobImp. I will readily admit that I've been to interviews for jobs I had no intention of taking, and I still succumbed to the powers of the necktie. I have always been told that even if you're not interested in a job, you should go for the interview to practice. I don't disagree with the adage that practice makes perfect, but unless you have problems with job interviewing, you'll probably need just one or two before you're ready.

Hell, in this state of the universe, if you are reasonably intelligent, you'll probably be turning down those jobs you consider practice interviews. You might even be able to get away with being a slob, but I'd at least wait until the second interview.

I know little about the interview with JobImp. The company has an office in Jeffersonville, Indiana, which is just a short drive over the bridge from Louisville. It's unbearably hot today, which just makes dressing up that much worse. My fear is that inside, there won't be any air conditioning, and I'll end up dying tragically because I couldn't remove that top collar button.

Thankfully, it's much cooler in the building. I take the elevator to the sixth floor and attempt to find a receptionist.

Instead, I see scavenger hunt-like signs, directing patrons to an office a few doors down. I tell the people inside that I'm here to talk to Reggie Macklin, and they flag him down after a myriad of phone calls. After a short time, Reggie enters and leads me to his office, which is roughly the size of an average walk-in closet.

"What type of job are you looking for?" Reggie says.

Carnival positions notwithstanding, I try to explain a combination of what I've done previously, what I'm doing now, and what I hope to do in the future.

"I don't think there's one thing in particular that I'm looking for necessarily," I say. "The job description you sent me sounds interesting. In the past, I've worked directly with clients and I've managed website builds and ... "

Reggie hesitates and looks at my résumé.

"You know ... I just had a great idea," Reggie says. "We've discussed hiring a full-time person to do some management of the contractors here. Judging by your résumé, you might be an ideal candidate for that. Here, why don't I get you to fill out all of the paperwork, and we can always come back to it. I need your driver's license to make a copy for our files."

I hand Reggie my driver's license, and he hands me a stack of papers. I rifle through them and wonder why I should fill out tax information during an interview. It doesn't sound as if Reggie even knows what I'll be doing.

Reggie reenters the room and hands back my driver's license.

"Did you fill out the paperwork?" Reggie says. "I'll go ahead and put you into the system."

"Honestly, I'd rather fill it out later," I say. "I really don't want to be bound to anything just yet. Did you find out about the full-time job?"

"I want you to talk to Lloyd Backman. He's the general manager, and he'll give you a better understanding of what we can offer you."

Reggie leads me to the open foyer, and I sit on a couch. A few minutes later, Lloyd introduces himself and sits down beside me while glancing at my résumé.

"Thanks for coming over, Jason," Lloyd says. "So why are you looking for a job?"

"My current job is moving to Cincinnati, so I'm looking at my options right now," I say. "But if I find something more enticing here, I'll stay, considering I just moved back to Louisville not too long ago."

"I see. There's definitely work for you here. Looking at your résumé, I know we could use someone like you."

"Reggie mentioned something about a full-time position. Is that available?"

"We hope to fill it in the near future. Let's get you in here started at our normal contract rate, and take it from there."

Lloyd goes on a bit about the history of JobImp and how the global company selected Jeffersonville, for web development because office space is cheap here. He also tells me that Reggie will follow up with me regarding a simple web job as well as the full-time position. I consider the interview a success, and I'm grateful to unlock my oven of a car and remove my tie.

Back at the Mettle office, there are a handful of faces standing outside Jeff's cube. This isn't unordinary, but it is 4:30, and most of them seem to be awaiting my return.

"So how did it go?" Barry says.

"Pretty well," I say. "They are going to send some additional information, and I'm going to go over one day next week after I'm done here."

"You have a job!" Ken says.

"Well, it's still contract work," I say. "They did mention a full-time position."

"Oh, you have it made now," Barry says. "Say goodbye to Northern Lineage!"

"No final decisions yet," I say. "I really don't want to give up a full-time position for a part-time one ... unless it's really lucrative. This one pays enough to start with, assuming I have 40 hours a week. And that's a fairly large assumption."

Jeff, Barry, Ken, and a few others continue talking, but I notice my cellphone lighting up. I usually keep my phone on silent, but the green pulsating light shows that Diya is calling me from her desk. I give my phone a look of surprise, as if it is the device's fault for leaving me bewildered.

"Who is calling you?" Jeff says.

"Diya ... for some reason," I say.

Jeff and Ken both look toward her cube, as if she's standing on her chair and peering over the top of the cubicle castle.

"I know she's back there; I just came from there," Ken says.

"Yeah, she's calling from the office phone," I say.

Jeff and Ken look puzzled, so I walk over to see Diya. She is working on schoolwork when I arrive.

"Hey, I was over at Jeff's cube," I say. "What's going on?"

"I heard you come back, but I didn't want to come over there," Diya says. "So everything went well? I am happy for you."

"Yeah, I'm going to try it out and see if it's something I want to do. The people there seem nice enough, and it looks like there might be an opportunity for me there."

Diya continues working, but I know she isn't ignoring my words. I feel as if she thinks I'm giving her the inevitable resolution that I'm not moving to Cincinnati. It's a precarious position because I want to stay optimistic about moving with her, but I can't blatantly lie about this new possibility.

"I haven't decided anything," I say. "There are still numerous things I need to weigh before the deadline. That's why I want to get over there next week and check out the work. Maybe I won't like it at all, and it will make the decision that much easier."

She doesn't budge. It's useless to continue talking about the situation. I return to my cube with the hope that I'll be able to discuss everything in greater detail with Diya during the weekend.

At my desk, I catch up on email. I actually have messages. I open one email that pertains to the "Indecision Party," which will be a glorified happy hour for all of Mettle. Even though the party is scheduled to take place the Friday after the forms have to be turned in, I bet that most of Mettle's partygoers will be in attendance.

It's already 5 now, and everyone on the team has left for the evening. But I notice Mindy working on something in the office across the hallway. She has been using this office the last day or two, but mostly as a pit stop area between meetings. Now, however, it appears she has made it her own place of business.

"How were the meetings today?" I say, strolling into the office.

"Thrilling as always," Mindy says. "I'll be happy when we are finally finished with all of the synergy meetings. It's tough to get anything accomplished when all you are doing is learning about other teams' processes."

"I can believe that. So how much longer will you be coming down on a daily basis?"

"Depends on the number of items going on each day. After the decision forms are turned in, we will start working on knowledge transfer stuff from the people who are not going. So hopefully everything will be documented before those people leave us."

As Mindy talks, I notice a decent number of notes on yellow legal pads scattered on her desk. From what I can tell, she has been taking notes and then, at the end of each day, typing the notes on her computer. Looking at the volume of notes and pieces of paper, it seems as if it would take an eternity to compile the information.

"So when do you usually get out of here at night?" I say.

"I don't stay too long ... maybe 6 o'clock," Mindy says. "Then I grab something to eat and finish at the hotel. I have to put all of the notes into a format for our training and documentation sheets. If I get behind, I'll never catch up."

"With the number of notes on your desk, I can believe it!"

"Are you closer to making a decision?"

"Not really. I actually had an interview today for a possible position. It sounds as if it will just be contract work, and I really don't want to give up a full-time position."

"Is it with a local company?"

"Sort of ... it's with JobImp. They have a web integration office just over the river in Indiana. I'm supposed to go back next week after work, so maybe I'll know more then. I just wish this could be an easy decision."

"I've seen a lot of people struggle with decisions like this. We hope you come along for the ride to Cincinnati, but I'm sure a lot of people won't be going. I get the impression that Barry won't be making the trek, but I'm not that positive about everyone else."

"What will happen on decision day? Are you coming down? Will there be a lot of people from Northern Lineage in Louisville?"

"We haven't really discussed it. I'll probably stay up in Cincy, considering I'll be down here most of next week. There are more meetings there that I'm missing because I'm here."

The way Mindy makes it sound, August 15 — just 10 days away — will be a mostly anti-climatic event. Not that I expected confetti, beautiful models, and a bottle of milk to drink at the finish line, but I thought there would be a little more than just signing on the dotted line.

Then again, the more I think about it, anything outside the decision itself will just be fluff. And like holiday sales at any department store, time is running out to take advantage of the outstanding deal.

Sunday, August 7

It's time to start the list.

With barely more than a week remaining, I have to compile tangible evidence for my decision. And the easiest way to do that is to come up with a list of pros and cons. First, I have decided to focus on the positives and negatives of relocation.

PROS:

• **Leave open the possibility of going**: Whether or not I'm actually going doesn't have to be decided next week. But if there's any inclination that I will move, I need to check "Yes" on the ballot.

• **Full-time position**: I have a full-time position waiting for me.

• **Cafeteria**: It's free food. How can this not be a major positive?

• **Gym**: While I'm still fuzzy on the hours the gym is actually open, it's still a gym.

• **Money for moving**: Northern Lineage will pay closing costs on my house, and there are other benefits within the relocation package.

• **Bonus money**: They're giving me $8,000 to move. That's tough to pass up.

• **Live close to work**: Maybe I could live within walking distance and not even have to worry about traffic.

All of the preceding items are great, but they are ancillary in comparison to the three main reasons I have for moving:

• **Opportunity**: I have the chance to learn an exponential amount of programming and business knowledge by staying with Northern Lineage. From Marshall's perspective, the company plans to stay on the cutting edge of technology, and I would be able to research and analyze new options as they come along.

• **Working with Jeff**: I have worked within a team atmosphere many times before, but rarely have I worked with a team that can focus on just the tasks needed to complete the process. Sure, we have other minor items of business coming to our desk, but with Annuity Profit Plus, we are shielded from taking on additional large projects. My talents mesh well with Jeff's, and I think we could handle anything thrown at us. We would, however, prefer to avoid the messshhhhes as much as possible.

• **Diya**: Despite all that we converse, I still have no certainty in her feelings toward me. Is this a legitimate cause for moving?

Case in point: Friday night, we went to the movie theater. I thought the flick was pretty funny, although Diya seemed to miss a lot of the pop culture references. Afterward, she said she liked it OK. I thought maybe I should have picked a different movie.

We walked back to Diya's car. Diya got into the driver's seat, turned on the radio, and then jumped into the backseat. Taking this as an invitation, I got into the backseat next to her; just like in high school, we started kissing and trying not to squish each other into the floorboard.

Yes, I realize that two fully clothed 20-somethings making out in the backseat is a bit of an anomaly. Or even an anachronism. And as much as I wanted to be nowhere else but in the back of Diya's SUV, there was something awkward about it. We were at most 10 minutes from her apartment, but she didn't take me there. I assumed it was because her parents were there. Shouldn't I meet them?

I moved past the paranoia stage regarding her not introducing me to her parents because they would not approve. It's true that she hadn't met my parents, either, but they are not living at my house.

Maybe Diya shouldn't be solely in the "pros" list. If we

don't end up together, even after I move, would that be considered a negative? Or what would happen in the remote chance that I move and she moves back to India?

I can't answer these questions, but I can at least list items that will definitely have a negative impact if I embark on the Cincinnati journey.

CONS:

• **Dress up**: "I'll gladly pay you Tuesday for a necktie today!"

• **Buy new clothes**: It's not that spending a few dollars for a few shirts is a big deal. The problem, as I've mentioned before, is I just bought new clothes for this job. At this rate, after I move to Cincinnati, they'll change to all-spandex attire at the end of the year, followed by a choice of overalls or wet suits next summer.

• **Housing fun**: I just bought my house, and because I won't be living in Louisville, I'll have to do something with it. The real estate wing of Northern Lineage might help, but at the same time, I'll probably have to give up a healthy commission check.

• **Don't go, don't get the bonus**: If I say "Yes" but find something better here in town, I lose the 8K. Not a huge deal, but something to consider.

• **Volleyball**: During the last few months, I've found plenty of teams to play on and sub for. I have no clue if I'll find the same fervor in Cincinnati, and even if I do, it won't happen overnight.

• **Moving away from friends and family**: Cincy wouldn't be that much farther away, but I would miss many of the items I'm actively involved in now.

• **Commute**: If I don't live close enough to walk to work, things could get ugly. I have a 12-minute commute now, and that's plenty far enough. Jeff, Ken, and Chris plan to live in a subdivision that is nearly 45 minutes away during rush hour from headquarters. With no traffic and going 100 miles an hour, I might be able to get to Cincinnati from Louisville in that amount of time.

• **Misleading if I don't go**: Even if I say I'll go, I don't have to. But I have to consider what Ken said previously: By saying you're going to go, you leave the door open, regardless of the final decision.

• **Diya, again**: While it may not be probable, what happens if I move and Diya's green card expires?

All things considered, the list looks nearly even to me. I put together a shorter list for the pros and cons of saying "No" on my decision form:

PROS:
• **Bonus money**: I'm pretty much guaranteed the severance pay, assuming that I stay until the end of my term.
• **Already have contract work at JobImp**: It's not as if I would be turning down the job for nothing, although I don't know how much of a job the thing with JobImp is.

CONS:
• **Can't go**: I would effectively resign the option of staying with the company.
• **No full-time position**: See above.

Even though many of the items within the "Yes" pros and cons still exist on the "No" side, I definitely limit my options by turning down the job outright. At this stage, I conclude that I almost have to say I'll go.

On Saturday, Jeff invited me out to check out his basement. I could see that he had invested a lot of time in it, but I could also tell that he was not finished. Before I could mention his spectacular handiwork, he wondered aloud about D-Day.

"There's no way Barry is going," Jeff said.

"Yeah, even Mindy knows that," I said.

"I'm pretty sure Ken will at least say he's going, but he's pretty shifty. Of course Don is already in, and Diya pretty much is as well. I hope some of the other people on the floor go. The more people who sign on, the fewer people they will have to replace immediately. What are you going to do?"

"I'm pretty sure I'll be saying 'Yes,' but I still have a few possibilities in town for jobs. Are you definitely going?"

"Yep, Laura and I have already made the commitment. I'll put in my two years, though, and then I'll be gone."

"Then why bother?"

"It's too stable to pass up. I haven't even worked on my portfolio lately because I've been working on the basement. I can't get into the graphic design industry without a portfolio."

"You still have a few weeks at work when no one is going to be working ... just do it then!"

"Yeah, and avoid the only project going on at Mettle. It would be nice to get Annuity Profit Plus in working order before we leave."

"Do you think that will happen?"

"Hell no. I'm sure it will be changed another thousand times. But at least we aren't sitting around doing nothing. Then again, if I had nothing to do at work, maybe I could get the portfolio finished."

"Well, at least you have a goal, other than just to move and become another Northern Lineage drone."

"I can tell you for certain ... that's one thing that won't happen."

17
The Final Countdown

Monday, August 8

Subject: Integration Update

Synergy teams entered the "Planning Stage" of the assessment portion of the project. This stage will begin developing the deliverables, start and stop dates, and resource requirements of all activities for transitioning Louisville-based operations to Cincinnati. This planning process should conclude at the end of August when all teams will submit their respective plans to the Integration Office for consolidation into a single project timetable. We anticipate that Executive Management will review and approve by the third week of September.

We do not anticipate associate separations earlier than the fourth quarter, with some separations not occurring until year-end processing work is completed at the end of the first quarter of next year.

Updates will continue to be posted to the website on a weekly basis regarding the integration effort.

Ann Singleton
Human Resources Manager

NL FUN FACT: When Thomas Edison traveled through downtown Cincinnati, he remarked on multiple occasions that he noticed "Synergic Occurrences" coming from the Northern Lineage office.

Decision Day is a week away, and this email tells me ... basically nothing. There are a few guesses about time frames, a lot of company-speak and a general feeling that the big wigs just used the B.S. Generator to come up with the message. It's possible that Northern Lineage is in the process of creating a Mad Libs-type of email creator so that employees and customers alike can keep abreast with all of the latest made-up terminology. We're not just talking about Web 2.0 ... we're all the way on Web 4.6 here.

Now there are 20 names in the "Guess Who's on the Bus!" graphic on the intranet, including Jeff's, and a few new question-and-answer comments. If 20 people are on, that leaves more than 200 who haven't made a decision. I predict that 30 to 40 percent will say they'll go, but in the end, only about 25 percent will realistically make the journey. I think Northern Lineage will be happy with anything over 20 percent. If head honcho Claude Simpson can get everything out of the people already here, he can find plenty of work for them. And I can say for sure that unless people were exponentially more productive before I got here, there's definitely a lot of wasted time.

While trimming the fat helps economically, the same can't be said for the people being left behind. In *The Opt-Out Revolt*, workplace consultant Bruce Tulgan estimates that from 2001 to 2004, 3.5 million people between the ages of 40 and 58 not only lost their jobs but also completely disappeared from the American workplace.[22] Some of this, though, could amount to early retirement, but that's a big chunk of missing people I haven't yet seen on the side of milk cartons.

To make matters worse, it's evident that as individuals race toward retirement age, it becomes more difficult to find a new job. Many of the people at Mettle must consider this while making their decisions, while younger people like myself don't necessarily need to worry about it.

Checking my personal email, I notice two new Java jobs from recruiters. I forward them to Barry and others in the office who might be qualified. I've decided that if I'm going to stay with Java, I might as well stay with Northern Lineage. As Jeff said Saturday night, it's at least stable, and it's an environment where one can learn, even if that means moving.

I overhear Chris in Jeff's cube, so I slide over.

"We went in with a higher offer than I wanted," Chris says. "My new Realtor thought I should do that to ensure we have a shot at the house. Is your house up for sale?"

"No, not yet ... still working on the basement," says Jeff while smiling in my direction.

"It's pretty nice," I say.

"You mean it's *going* to be nice," says Jeff.

"It can't hurt to go ahead and put it on the market," Chris says.

"Possibly, but I'm not convinced I'll get lowballed since the basement isn't finished," Jeff says. "It seems like that's such a big deal and can really raise the value of a house."

"It's the truth!" says Barry, barging into the party in Jeff's cube. "If you get your basement looking good, you're probably looking at another 15 to 20 grand."

"I'd be happy to at least get back what I spent on the materials," Jeff said.

"Let me know when you want me to come back over to help with the drywall," Barry says. "I'm a master at that."

"A master of doing the work or telling others how to do it?" Jeff jokes.

"I've built houses before, Jeff," Barry says. "I'm no novice. But I would say that what you've done so far is pretty good."

"Thanks Barry; that means a lot coming from you," Jeff says.

"Pretty good for a wannabe graphic designer," says Barry, leaving the area.

Chris returns to his office. I head back to my cube, but then I notice Barry ushering Ken back to Jeff's cube. Barry motions for me to join them.

"I had a great idea over the weekend," Barry says. "I decided to start building a cornhole set. Remember how they were talking about how everyone in Cincy is playing cornhole now? I think I might be able to make a business out of it. I can purchase the plywood and do the finishing. But I'll need help making a website for it."

"You do realize that there are already companies that make these sets, right?" I say.

"Yeah, but they charge absurd prices," Barry says. "I can make them far cheaper than that by buying the materials."

"How much time did it take you to make the board?" I say.

"I don't know, three to four hours," Barry says. "But it was the first one I made. I'm sure I can make them faster, once I get it down."

"Are you making the beanbags, too?" Jeff says.

"Yep," Barry says. "They are filled with dried corn, so I would just need to sew the bags together."

"That's more time, though," I say. "You need a factory to produce them as fast as the manufacturers."

"I bet I can make two to three a day," Barry says. "And another idea I had is putting logos for teams. I can make them pretty cheap. So who wants to help me with the website?"

"I think you should finish the first one before you build a factory," I say.

Barry walks back to his cube. Ken, Jeff, and I just look at each other.

"Was he serious?" I say.

"Sort of," Ken says. "He's always coming up with these get-rich-quick schemes."

"He's never short of ideas," Jeff says.

I return to my cube, still a bit mesmerized by Barry's ideas. I envision Barry turning his backyard into a cornhole factory, with gnomes moving plywood in assembly-line fashion just in time for the college football season. Gnorm, the head gnome, would inspect each board personally, while his two supervisors,

Gned and Gnigel, would review the bag weight and packaging. All gnomes would be required to wear ties. Bow ties would be acceptable, assuming they were clipped directly onto beards.

My daydream soon turns to hunger. I notice that the others have already gone somewhere for lunch. Even Diya isn't at her cube, although I haven't seen her all day. I decide to take my peanut butter sandwich and Chex Mix to the waterfront.

Mettle's office is a few blocks away from the Belvedere, which is a great place to relax while overlooking the Ohio River. As I walk up the brick-laden pathway, I remember a few of the statues decorating the route, including Daniel Boone, a Kentucky trailblazer, and York, a slave and tour guide for Lewis and Clark. I can follow in these brave men's footsteps by journeying to Cincinnati in a few months. But I don't own a coonskin hat, nor do I have paddles to maneuver a boat up the river. And I use the term "brave" loosely here.

As I scarf down my food, I enjoy the view and reflect on what I should be doing. I have to make a decision by next Monday. I don't see myself moving, but every time I consider staying, I can't stop thinking about Diya. Obviously, there still is no answer.

On my way back to the office, I see Vance enjoying the weather as well. He appears to be playing a banjo as I walk closer.

"Hey man," I say. "Where's your cup? Here's a quarter."

"I'll need a lot more than that," Vance says, "if I don't get on the bus."

"I think I might have a dime too."

"Actually, I'm working on a little ditty about the move. It's called 'The Northern Lineage Blues.' I'm almost finished with it."

"Cool! Are you going to play it at the Indecision Party?"

"Yeah, probably ... unless they confiscate my banjo and make me wear a tie."

As I walk away from Vance, I'm not quite sure why I think

I'm late. I have suddenly become the White Rabbit, eagerly waiting for what's next, but having absolutely no idea what that is. If Alice is following me through Wonderland, she will be sorely disappointed when she finds out her blue-and-white outfit won't pass as business attire.

Tuesday, August 9

Originally, I was supposed to go to JobImp tonight after work. But Reggie Macklin never phoned or emailed me to say when I should arrive. Instead, I will be doing something much more worthwhile: entertaining Diya.

Even though we talk almost every night, and even though it seems that she has feelings for me, I am reluctant to call our friendship anything more than that. At work, Diya continues to be inundated with request after request, and by the end of the day, she's spending more time determining why she's even considering the move in the first place.

We leave the work realm for only a brief period at my place. We kiss for a few minutes, and I urge her to stay. But she claims that she has to be at work early in the morning to finish all the work that has been piled on her desk.

"Do you think this will change after the move?" I say. "Personally, I like Chris as a boss because he knows we are working on the stuff we need to be doing. He'll still be your boss, unlike our side of the team. Who knows how Mindy will be."

"I'd rather work for Mindy," Diya says. "She seems to know more about Northern Lineage and its procedures."

"That might be true, but that's not my litmus test of a good manager. I will say, though, that I do like Marshall ... he is straightforward enough."

"Oh, I talked to Marshall today. He told me that I should try to convince you to move."

"I'm not really worth that much to the company, especially compared to someone like Barry."

"You do have something in common with Barry, since

you're both not moving."

I initiate another long kiss with Diya, but I can tell a slight difference in intensity with her this time. Whenever she brings up the fact that I'm not going, she instantly isolates herself. It's as if there is suddenly an infinite amount of cubicles between us, even if we are connected mouth-to-mouth.

I've already forgotten that Diya needs to leave soon, or that I still haven't met her parents. I constantly come back to the notion that the only way Diya will be happy with me is if I accompany her to Cincinnati. But will the joy exist outside company walls and into a longer relationship?

Wednesday, August 10

The days are passing swiftly now. Just about everyone in the office is feverishly rummaging through as much relocation information as they can, whether it be on the relocation website, during Realtor phone calls, or via email from coworkers.

Meanwhile, I'm at my desk learning Java and actuarial calculations. It's a great way to take my mind off the inevitable.

More importantly, we have made, as Sean Connery would say, eckshellent progresshhh during this week. Considering that Jeff has already made his decision, and I'm still playing with my fate, we've been able to focus on Annuity Profit Plus.

I hope that Jeff has thought this all of the way through. He appears confident that relocating is the answer, but at the same time, it's not in line with his career goals even a small amount. What's worse is that he assumes this is his best alternative, even though there are plenty of options available. I want to discuss this in more detail with him, but I don't want to constantly harp about the possibilities. He's a big boy, and he should be able to decide on his own.

I finally snap out of my reverie when I realize it's time to leave. Unfortunately, I'm not finished with work just yet. I drive down the parking garage ramps and make a right, toward the Ohio River. Because I couldn't go to JobImp last night, I'm headed to the Jeffersonville office now. But I don't make it too far, because I'm stuck in traffic on the interstate.

I check my car clock more times than I lift my foot off the gas pedal. It's already past 6, which is when I was supposed to be there. I have been stationary on the interstate for at least 10 minutes. I start to call JobImp, wondering if a devilish monster with four eyes will answer. I found out earlier in the day that Reggie won't be there, and instead, I'll be working with someone named Benoit. My only hope is that Benoit will be easy to find, and that I'll be able to avoid the office-seeking carousel that I rode last time.

I exit the elevator and head straight for the previously cloaked receptionist/programmer office. There, I'm told to make a left out the door and walk all the way to the end of the floor, where I should find Benoit. Most of the offices I pass along the way are closed or empty, with the exception of one room that houses three individuals. Maybe I'll be working with them by the end of the night, but until that time, I need Benoit to tell me what I should be doing.

"Are you Benoit?" I say to a man walking out of the corner office.

"Yes I am ... why?"

"I'm Jason ... Reggie told me that I was supposed to meet you and determine what I should be working on tonight."

Benoit sighs and turns to look back toward the office he just left. I realize that he had just packed his briefcase to leave for the night.

"OK ... come back in here," says Benoit, flipping the lights back on. "No one told me about this, but that's not unusual ... I'm usually the last to know."

"If it's a problem, I could come back some other time," I say. "Or you could send me the work and I'll do it from home."

"But if you're already here, I do have something for you do. You can use that computer over there. Hold on and I'll send you the files. You can go ahead and login to our file server."

"How do I do that?"

"Just use the login credentials you used last time you were here."

"This is the first time I've been over here to work."

"Oh, I see. I guess you can just use mine. So what do you know about the systems here?"

"I guess nothing really."

"OK. Not that that matters anyway. I just need you to do some coding on one site. There's a problem that another designer was having with getting something to work. Do you want to take a look at it?"

"Sure. At least that's a start."

"That's great. I'll send you the email when I get home because I really have to go. Until then, go ahead and get set up on that machine. Do you have an IM screen name?"

"Yes."

"OK, I'll send you mine in an email and we can chat. I'll be back on in about 45 minutes. Talk to you then."

Benoit leaves, so I try to deduce what I am supposed to do. He left me a couple of printouts, one of which contains information that shows where the files are located on JobImp's file server. An email somewhat spells out the problem Benoit had mentioned, although there's little information about whether it's a web browser issue or something else. After quickly reviewing the documents, I notice that there is no information regarding where the live files are located or how to test them.

I make duplicates of all of the files and review my edits. While doing this, I hear people, presumably the individuals I noticed in one of the offices, in the hallway. Their voices trail off in the distance, which is followed by an elevator noise. Silence ensues, so I walk out of the office I'm sitting in and peer down both hallways. I see and hear nothing.

Have I been left here alone? Barring any catastrophes, I suppose I'll be OK, so I walk back to the computer I'm using. Benoit has signed on to instant messenger, and he has also sent me a job to do.

Benoit: I just sent you an email with work stuff.
How are you doing?
Jason: OK ... I think I'm the only one left here.
Benoit: Ha, yeah, it's usually pretty empty this
time in the evening. But others show up later.
Jason: Oh. Well, I was planning on leaving at 9, so
whatever I don't finish here, I can do from home.
Benoit: Sure. Did you look at that problem?
Jason: Yeah, I figured it out. I'll send the files.
Benoit: Cool. I'll be online, so let me know if you
have any problems.
Jason: OK, cool. Talk to you later.

For the next two hours, I code a JobImp advertising client website. It isn't a glamorous task, but it isn't devastating, either. Looking ahead, I don't think this type of work can keep my interest for a long time. However, just the novelty of having an entire six-story building to myself at night might be worth it.

Thursday, August 11

Barry is entirely too giddy for this early in the morning. He races over to Jeff's desk, then back to his, clicks a few buttons, and then races to the printer. I think he's jumping up and down as well. Did he just win the lottery?

Barry, document in hand, joins Jeff, Ken, and me in Jeff's cube.

"I was contacted about this great job offer yesterday," Barry says. "I just had to share it with you guys. It's a job with Northern Lineage selling annuities!"

Sure enough, the email mentions a sales office in Louisville, where the company is looking for additional staff. We do not bother to ask what job site produced this match for Barry. While he obviously has experience in the annuity and life insurance business — on the programming side — you would think that the algorithm used to produce matches would possibly eliminate current employers.

In this case, Barry could remain with the company, stay in Louisville, and become the greatest salesman in the history of the financial industry. Instead, Barry has other plans.

"So I've been thinking more about building those cornhole boards," Barry says.

The rest of us try to look disinterested, but it doesn't matter.

"I have started researching what it would take to open the business and also incorporate the logos on the boards," Barry continues. "Would someone like to help me build a website for it? I would like to have something up for football season this year, but it might be too late."

"Yeah, considering that football season is starting in the next few weeks, I think you're a little late," Jeff says.

"Wow, really, it starts that early?" Barry says. "Oh well, I guess we can shoot for next year. At the very least, I'll have the first boards ready for my party next month!"

Barry walks away, leaving us to contemplate the length of time it will take Barry to realize that this might not be the best endeavor.

"At least he has drive," Jeff says. "He's one of the few people who's motivated to do anything here. Speaking of work, D-Day is Monday! You guys are coming with me, right?"

"I guess," Ken says. "I'm taking off tomorrow to work on my house porch. We have a prospective buyer coming on Sunday."

"Sweet!" Jeff says. "So you won't have to live with me after all!"

"I'm still looking for jobs here because I don't want to move the family," Ken says. "But it would be easier to go up there and look. I will at least say I'm going, regardless."

"What about you?" Jeff says to me.

"The JobImp thing isn't bad, but there's so much confusion over there," I say. "It wouldn't surprise me if a full-time position never appears. If I don't go, it would suck to give up the bonus money."

"I think you guys should both come," Jeff says. "If we keep everyone together, we'll probably get to stay on task with our projects. I think there's even opportunity to get the other group up to speed with some of the new functionality we are building. I think we are ahead of them, so they may even let us lead."

"Maybe, but aren't you the same person who was trying to get off the web team?" Ken says.

"Yeah, but I changed my mind," Jeff says. "At least, for today."

Leave it to Jeff to try to convince the rest of us that moving is the right thing to do. He somewhat cornered himself into going, in the same fashion that a mass murderer can convince himself that he did nothing wrong.

I'm all for "sticking together," but everyone here has vastly different goals toward where they want to be 10 years from now. Jeff wants to be a 3-D graphic designer; Ken wants to learn new database technologies; I want to be anywhere except the corporate world; and Barry, I guess, wants to be in his cornhole factory.

And these are just the people I've spoken with in the last five minutes. Who knows where Diya, Don, and the others on the floor are situated. It's sad because I never sensed any dissatisfaction at Mettle before the relocation announcement. Then again, I was here for only eight days, so maybe people were unhappy with some aspects of the working conditions.

Right now, I have a feeling that nearly all 250 people would love to step into a time machine and return to June 22, before the announcement was first made public. Most people would be content with making this portion of Northern Lineage into a sentient being, rather than just another subsidiary that gets handed procedures from corporate headquarters.

Unfortunately, H.G. Wells and Doc Brown aren't here, and unless they visit us shortly through a space wormhole, the relocation march will be coming to a theater near few.

18
Decisions, Decisions

Friday, August 12

I'm sitting in Jeff's cube when I hear a phone ringing. I assume it's Tom Nelson's phone, but then I realize it's mine. I've received a total of four calls since I've been here. Three were wrong numbers.

"Hello Jason! This is John Sanderson from Northern Lineage. Marshall MacDougal passed along your contact info. How are you today?"

I don't know a John Sanderson from Northern Lineage. Maybe I stole his pineapple cake on our visit, and he's finally caught me.

This John character proceeds to ask me if I have any questions about the move, because he's in IT and a Notre Dame graduate like me. I can't think of anything to ask except what he's having for lunch today, but I decide against it. It's cool and bizarre that Marshall would have this guy call me because he's a Notre Dame grad. I still find it difficult to believe that Northern Lineage wants me to come to Cincinnati, but it's impossible to overlook items like this.

I check my email while I'm in my cube, and I notice an email from Lloyd Backman at JobImp. Reggie informed him of my superior work on my first project, so he is raising my pay rate. Furthermore, Lloyd wants to schedule a meeting with me next week to discuss a full-time position in greater detail. I'm up for a discussion, but it would be nice to have some inkling of what regular employment with JobImp would entail. At this stage, I still don't know if it would be designing and coding, programming, management, or riding a unicycle and pretending to be a circus bear. I could definitely go for the latter, provided that JobImp supplies me with a decent hat.

I return to Jeff's cube and continue working in Visual Basic. Jeff is out today; Don has been on vacation this entire week, I think; Ken is here but leaving early; and Diya is MIA for the time being. That leaves Barry, who at the present time is pacing in the hallway.

"Hey newbie, why are you in Jeff's cube?" Barry says.

"Haven't I been here long enough to not be called 'newbie?' " I say. "For crying out loud, it has been more than a month!"

"You're still much newer than everyone else. I just wanted to make sure you knew that I am leaving early today."

"Oh, that's cool ... I have plenty of things to do. Why are you leaving?"

"I have a job interview today, and I'm pretty excited about this one. It's with a company called Excelsior Computing. The job requires a Unix sys admin and some other IT support. It won't be as good as the job here, but it's pretty decent, considering the circumstances."

"Is today your first interview with them?"

"In person. I had a phone interview with them last week. But I feel good about the people there. If I bomb at this interview, then I'm moving!"

"That would surprise me ... and Mindy ... hell, it would surprise everyone. Is that what you are wearing to the interview?"

Barry is wearing a polo shirt that has been in his wardrobe for at least 15 years.

"No, newbie, I'm going home first to change," Barry says. "The interview is at 3 and it's 12 now ... well, I might as well leave. See ya!"

And with that, Barry exits. I didn't realize that "leaving

early" meant leaving immediately.

I hate to be the one to bring up interview attire to Barry. But lately, it's difficult to go through the day without some reminder about having to dress for the corporate world. Why must I sit in front of a computer all day and have no visible contact with anyone outside our building, and still have to dress like a game show host? I overheard other people on the floor talking about not even being able to wear white socks to work. Who cares if I wear white socks, gray socks, no socks, or Christmas socks with kittens on them?

I always thought that work dress was just something to show off your stature among peers. It seems that Northern Lineage is trying to keep this intact by establishing the dress code in which managers have to wear a jacket, while regular employees do not. But the clothes that make a man run deeper than just pecking order, according to the 1899 satiric novel *The Theory of the Leisure Class* by Thorstein Veblen:

> *"It goes without saying that no apparel can be considered elegant, or even decent, if it shows the effect of manual labor on the part of the wearer, in the way of soil or wear ... Much of the charm that invests the patent-leather shoe, the stainless linen, the lustrous cylindrical hat, and the walking-stick, which so greatly enhance the native dignity of a gentleman, comes of their pointedly suggesting that the wearer can't when so attired bear a hand in any employment that is directly and immediately of any human use. Elegant dress ... not only shows that the wearer is able to consume a relatively large value, but it argues at the same time that he consumes without producing."[23]*

Maybe the folks at Northern Lineage took this book a bit too seriously. Veblen never saw a computer during his lifetime, but he most certainly saw the anguish of harnessing a tie around a neck for trivial purposes.

And now, time winds down on the last workday before Decision Monday. Barry runs past Jeff's cube as I'm trying to finish one last calculation.

"What are you doing here?" I say.

"I left a few papers here that I need for the weekend," Barry says.

"How did it go?"

"It went really well. They seem to be willing to work with me with regard to the separation date. That is, assuming they hire me ... but prospects look good."

"Congratulations!"

"They're supposed to let me know something in a week or so. This would be a big relief. Things might work out for me after all."

Barry doesn't stay long, and I'm ready to go, too. I don't have anything in particular that I need to take home, with the exception of the agreement paper. I need to read over it one last time before signing. I'm still looking for the loophole that will allow us to work through this for an indefinite time period.

Sunday, August 14

It probably seems as if I've been ignoring Diya, but that couldn't be any further from the truth. Diya has been so busy all weekend, and even though I've been contemplating every five minutes what I need to say to her, I haven't had the chance. That is, until now; I'm on my way to meet her for dinner and a final discussion about the relocation. Best-case scenario, I convince Diya that regardless of me moving, we can still be together, potentially, over time. Worst-case scenario, she serves an ultimatum: We get married tomorrow or she takes the first plane back to India with her parents.

I pull into the parking lot, but she's not there yet. I've never been here before, but as I walk up to the restaurant, it appears closed. I return to my car when Diya pulls up next to me.

"It's closed," I shrug.

"What else could go wrong?" Diya says in a joking but practical manner.

I'm thinking the same thing. She then suggests a Chinese place down the road. I wonder if Bob has added this particular location on his magic Chinese eating map?

"Did you finish your work?" I say after we order.

"Most of it is done for this week," Diya says. "But I'm trying to get ahead because my dance recital is next month, and I will have to practice for that."

"How do you have time for everything? And more importantly, what are your parents doing while you are working all of the time?"

"My parents don't mind. At least my mom and dad have been making good dinners, so I don't have to make something to eat when I get home. So you talked to my mom today?"

I had almost forgotten about the call. I tried calling Diya's cellphone and the DBA on-call phone, but there was no answer. Instead, I tried calling her home phone and spoke to her mom.

"Yep, we talked," I say. "I thought it was you at first ... I didn't know what to say."

"You should have talked to her," Diya says. "She was interested in talking to you."

"How do you know that?"

"Because I talked to her about you. I showed her your website so she could see what you look like."

"Oh ... what did you say about me?"

"I'm not going to tell you that!"

"So when do I get to meet your parents?"

"Maybe at the dance recital, or maybe sooner, I'm not sure."

Maybe the whole meeting-the-parents thing was never a big deal to her after all. Nevertheless, I keep thinking about this throughout dinner. Afterward, Diya jumps into her vehicle, and I climb into the passenger seat, even though we both drove to the restaurant.

"This is long overdue," I say. "But since tomorrow is the big day, I need to at least tell you where I stand. As of now, I think I will say that I'm going, but it's looking more and more like I will stay in Louisville. Even if I do stay, I don't want you to think that I don't care about you or want to continue what we are doing."

"That's nice of you, Jason, but I still don't know what will happen to me," Diya says. "As of now, I will be trying to go to Cincinnati, but I may not have a choice. If the green card isn't taken care of, I will have to go back to India."

"Do you know if they have made progress?"

"Honestly, I do not. Marshall and Anita have been working with the lawyers to see if I can stay on. They are doing as much as they can, but that might not be enough."

"When will you find out? I mean, it just seems as if this is something you need to know immediately. Your life is sort of hanging in the wind."

"It is very frustrating to me, knowing that I don't have control over what will happen next. This is one big reason that at times lately I have been distant to you and others. I like working at Mettle and in Louisville. I have made so many good friends here, and I don't want to leave. But it looks like I'll have to leave regardless ... either to Cincy or to India. I don't like either of these ideas."

I lean over to hug Diya and give her a small peck on her forehead.

"I totally understand, Diya. But assuming that you are able to stay in the United States, it's not like moving to Cincy is a permanent thing. You could eventually move back, move elsewhere, or do anything. You are very intelligent and can find a job at a bunch of different companies."

"Thank you, Jason, for the compliment. You are a really good friend, and I am glad you are helping me deal with this. But at the same time, you need to make your decision based on what you want to do, not me."

"But why is that? If I want to have a relationship with you, then I have to consider where you are going to be."

"What if I am in India?"

"Well ... I'm going to hold off on thinking about that until that really happens. So hopefully it won't happen tomorrow."

I don't know Diya's expectations during the next few days, much less the next few months.

"So what do you want to happen?" I say.

"What do you mean?" Diya says.

"Well, you have your options, and you don't like them, yet at least for the immediate future, one will happen ... right?"

"Yeah, I guess so. But I do not want either of them."

"OK. And that means ... you'll move to Cincinnati?"

"Probably."

"And if I go to Cincinnati as well ... "

"But you are not going."

"How do you know?"

"Your friends and family are here. You want to stay. My friends are here, but I can't stay right now."

"Cincy is not even that far away. Why is it such a big deal?"

"But it is. I could come down only on the weekends. I like to see my friends during the week."

"You can adjust to that, right?"

"Jason, it is different with me. I have close friendships with Reshmi and Nitya here. I don't think any of them are going now, and I won't find that up there."

"You won't find it if you don't try!"

"It's not about trying. It's a different atmosphere. I won't have the same relationships as I do with the people at work now. All of the people on our team get along so well together. I have made other good friendships at work with people on our floor. We have spent so much time together ... the people up there are not the same."

"There are other people in Cincinnati than just those at Northern Lineage, you know."

"But I won't have time to seek out these people. I've been

burned enough by people in my lifetime. I know that there are
people here I can trust. I can talk to Ken like a brother. I have
known you only a short time, yet I trust you fully. Even Barry,
as silly as he is, I know that he would help me out."

"Although if you need help from Barry, you must be in a
sorry state!"

We laugh, even though we both continue to be absurdly
frustrated. Diya really doesn't have a short-term solution, and
in the long term, things appear to potentially be much worse.
I've struggled from the beginning to understand just what I
can do to help her. I want to be with her ... I think. But I can't
pick up and move based only on that. I need to be certain of my
feelings for her.

But how can I be, when I'm so uncertain of how she sees
me in the future? She could be pushing me away because her
nomadic journey could be starting. Or maybe she doesn't want
either of us to get hurt, and she knows that I have a place here.

I could ask her the reason, but I won't get an answer, at
least tonight. She's focusing on her own dilemma, separate
from me. I respect that, to a certain extent. The only negative is
that ultimately, I am doing something she requested that I don't
do: consider her in the equation as I make up my mind.

We kiss for a little longer. It's suddenly 11:30, and we both
have to work tomorrow.

"It is really late," I say. "I don't want to leave you, though."

"I don't want to leave, either," Diya says. "I bet my parents
probably think I got lost."

"Let's talk more tomorrow. Just remember that you can talk
to me about anything, all right?"

"Yes, Jason, I know. I really appreciate everything you have
done for me. I hope that I don't ever lose your friendship."

"Hey, I'm not going anywhere."

I kiss Diya and return to my car, too late to realize that I
just told her the exact thing that she didn't want to hear.

19
D-Day

Monday, August 15

With all of the momentum building for today, Decision Day, I was expecting something noteworthy when I made it to work. I wasn't positive what it would be but assumed it would include flying paperwork, monogrammed ties, or frozen yogurt machines.

Instead, few people are in the office, and even fewer people are discussing the relocation factor at all. I count three empty workspaces: Ken, Reshmi, and Nitya. Barry and Debbie are at their desks fixing a bug in the annuity system. Diya is retrieving a backup of the weekend's data to do a comparative analysis. Jeff is cleaning up his email and trying to take care of a maintenance request. Don is in his cube, but I don't dare determine what he's doing; he's probably singing the University of Cincinnati fight song.

Everyone has essentially made his or her decision already, so today is a letdown. Maybe I expected more drama to unfold, or penalties for people who made the wrong decision. Sort of like they signed the wrong line and a pneumatic tube would suck them to Cincinnati. Or Hades.

Although I've pretty much made up my mind to say "Yes," it can't hurt to check the relocation site one last time. Maybe I'll be the one millionth site visitor and win an iPod nano.

Of course that doesn't happen, but there's a new post on the Q&A portion of the website:

Q: What happens if an employee changes his or her decision after 8/15? If I submit a form indicating I'm going but then decide not to go, will I still get a severance package? If I submit a form indicating I'm staying in Louisville but decide later that I would like to go to Cincinnati, will I still get a relocation package?

A: If you make a commitment to relocate to Cincinnati and then decide later not to come, that would be considered to be a voluntary resignation. You would not be eligible for severance or any Mettle performance bonus this year that is paid. If you indicate that you are not relocating to Cincinnati but then later decide that you do want to relocate, you would be considered under the following conditions:

    * The position offered is still open

    * Management approves placement of you in the position.

Should you be accepted into the position, the relocation bonus would be honored.

This certainly changes things. According to this, I can say "No," but with manager approval, I can go and still receive the bonus. How is that even possible?

"Hey Jeff," I shout over the cubicle. "It looks like we might be able to say we're not going and still go."

"What do you mean?" Jeff says.

Jeff jumps from his chair and walks over to read my monitor. He laughs and shakes his head.

"That could be a bit risky," Jeff says. "Mindy said they already determined the number of spaces on our team."

"I remember ... you said there are four," I say. "So you and Debbie are definitely in. Barry is out. Reshmi is out, right?"

"I think so, but I'm not sure."

"If she's out, that means only two of the four spots are taken, unless Ken is being counted."

"I don't know, man. It still seems crazy to try it."

Though I agree with Jeff, why would Northern Lineage post something so open-ended on the website? Isn't the point of today that you *have* to decide, one way or another, so that management can proceed with calculating how many bodies are still needed?

I email Mindy to ask her what this new information means. My decision will hang for a bit longer.

I alert the others to the new information on the site; some of us huddle between Barry's and Debbie's cubes to have a final discussion about the decisions.

"I turned mine in this morning," Barry says. "I'm not going. Let's just hope I get that job!"

"I'm assuming Ken already turned in his form?" I say.

"I don't know if he officially turned it in yet, but he emailed me this morning and said he was saying 'Yes,'" Jeff says. "I gave mine to HR a while ago."

"I handed mine in last week," Debbie says. "My husband will be able to transfer with his company."

"What about Reshmi?" I say.

"I think she was going to say 'No,' but I'm not positive she had made up her mind," Debbie says.

Surely Diya knows what Reshmi will decide. I walk just a few steps to Diya's workspace, where she appears to be having fun looking at a black screen full of data.

"Hey," I say.

"Hey," says Diya, although it takes longer than usual for her to respond.

"Is Reshmi moving to Cincinnati?"

"Hold on, I need to finish this and send an email. Why do you need to know whether Reshmi is moving?"

"I guess I don't have to know it. But there was a new posting on the moving website about saying 'No' and still going."

"That is ... interesting."

"Since Barry definitely isn't going, that leaves four spots. I assume they don't mind hiring one person pretty quickly, but if only two people say they are going, they might give me a little more leeway with my decision."

"But you are not going anyway."

"Then why did I decide I would say 'Yes'?"

"I don't know, but you aren't going, Jason. I already know this about you."

"Well, regardless of me, do you know if Reshmi is going?"

"Actually, I do not. I know that it depends whether or not her husband gets a raise and also whether or not she gets a job she interviewed for last week."

"So you're saying she hasn't turned in her decision slip? How will she do that if she isn't here?"

"I'm not sure. Maybe I will talk to her later today."

"If you do, let me know what happens because my decision may hinge a bit on hers."

I leave Diya's cube, more frustrated than before. It bothers me somewhat that she is partially right. No, I'm not uprooting my life immediately to go to Cincinnati. But that doesn't mean that I won't possibly go for a bit.

You know, just to spite her, I should put "Yes" on my form and move up ASAP. That way, every day we see each other in the cafeteria, I can gloat that I was right and she was wrong. Then again, that may interfere with our ability to have a long-lasting relationship.

But why worry about that when there's a frozen yogurt machine at your disposal?

Barry is sitting on the corner of Jeff's desk, so I join them.

"What's the word on Reshmi?" Barry says.

"No one seems to know ... not even Diya," I say.

"Wow, that's surprising," Barry says. "I thought those two talk about everything."

"I guess I'll wait and see what she is doing," I say.

"You aren't going to turn your paper in now?" Barry says.

"Why bother?" I say. "Something new may pop up. The deal may change."

"The deal can't really change," Jeff says.

"It can change any time," Barry says. "I remember a couple of years ago, when Northern Lineage first bought us, there were three or four network engineers who were promised four weeks' severance when they left. I heard they ended up with only two weeks' worth."

"What?" Jeff says. "You can't be serious."

"Hey, I'm just telling you what I heard," Barry says. "I just hope I get my bonus."

Jeff and Barry both have good points. The document can be construed as a legally binding agreement, but there is enough vagueness with which Northern Lineage could have the propensity to slightly alter the bargain. Then again, considering how many people would be affected by a clarification at this stage of the transfer, it seems that the parent company would be best served to stick to its commitment.

As I return to my desk in an attempt to do a little work, I again contemplate the reasons that they feel it's a good idea to move everyone from Mettle. According to the website, there are 37 people on the bus, less than 15 percent of Mettle's entire workforce. There's little doubt this is a cost-cutting measure, but the philosophy doesn't always work, even when there's a slim offering of choice.

In *Corporation Nation*, author Charles Derber reviews a multitude of ways that companies attempt to cut corners to make more money. Derber acknowledges that downsizing and even outsourcing, to a certain extent, are sometimes used as a last resort by businesses that have been managed so inefficiently that they may have to shut down without an emergency escape plan.[24]

"But there is another side to the story," Derber writes. "Annual American Management Association surveys show that downsizing and outsourcing do not tend to increase profitability. The AMA surveys show that only one-third of companies who downsized between 1990 and 1995 reported increased operating profits after the first year of layoffs or outsourcings, and even fewer firms report such gains in the following years.

"By hacking permanent jobs off the organization chart and replacing them with virtual ones, companies frequently undermine rather than improve their long-term competitiveness. One analyst dubs it 'dumbsizing,' pointing out that hundreds of companies are living to regret downsizing and outsourcing decisions."[25]

Of course, firing people at random does tend to draw the ire of employees, so that won't solve any problems. It's hard to fault Northern Lineage for not trying to save money. After all, how much did the company make last year? The total revenue just reached something like $30 billion.

I return to the Java code in front of me. For the sake of my sanity, it would be best to work on things I can control, like Annuity Profit Plus. I'm in the process of compiling another list of questions that either Jeff, Vance, or the last King of France, if available via satellite feed from the late 1800s, will have to answer.

The hours pass, and I still haven't heard from Mindy. I eat lunch at my desk a little later than usual, as everyone else seems to be on a different schedule today. It's back to being obnoxiously quiet in the office. I stroll to Diya's cube.

"Guess what?" I say. "I still haven't turned in the form."

"It's almost 3," Diya says. "What are you waiting for?"

"I sent Mindy an email, but I still haven't heard from her."

"She's not going to tell you anything new."

"I don't know about Ken, so she can at least tell me that. Have you heard from Reshmi?"

"I just talked to her. She's pretty sure she's not going."

"But she might change her mind? Should talk to her?"

"I told her about your discovery on the website and that you were still up in the air. But something monumental would have to occur for Reshmi to go."

"Oh, OK. Well, if I don't hear from Mindy by 4, I'm going

to call her again."

"All right, let me know what you are doing, even though I already know."

Diya looks up from her screen and winks at me. I shrug my shoulders and start to walk away.

"Hey Jason, how is your friend in New Jersey?"

"My friend?"

"Your new girlfriend, Jason, how is she doing?"

"She's not my girlfriend ... I've seen her only once! She's doing fine. We talk a couple of times a week right now, but she is really busy too."

"Yes, everyone's life is busy these days ... too busy to live."

Diya has a knack of changing focus from work or herself to something completely different. I guess she has the right to know if I'm in another relationship, considering that I explicitly stated that this girl exists. It's just strange timing, based on what has happened during the last few weeks, and what is going on in the office.

At first, I thought that Diya and I had become closer recently, but that's up for debate. We have spent more time together, we have talked more often, and we have been in more affectionate situations. Even still, the chasm exists between a friendship and a platonic relationship. Strange questioning like this doesn't quite make things any better, either.

Back in my cube, I check my email, but my cellphone rings. It's Mindy.

"Hi Jason, how are you doing?"

"Hello, Mindy. I'm guessing you got my email."

"Yes, I did. Now what are you asking about again?"

"On the relocation website, it states that we can say 'No' and then potentially change our decision, depending on the number of people going, with the manager's approval."

"What does that mean?"

"I don't know ... that's why I was calling you."

"I'm not aware of what it means. I've been told that we

have four spots on our team, and that includes Ken."

Now my work phone is ringing. Unless it's a bomb threat, I don't see how that could be important. I stand and move to Jeff's cube, because I'm sure he'll be interested to hear the news about Ken.

"Sorry, Mindy, I just wanted to make sure I understood you right. Since Ken counts on our team, you are saying that there are only three additional spots?"

"From Mettle, yes. We may eventually hire someone else to add to the team, but we're not going to do that until we assess a little longer."

"OK. That's good to know."

"I have a feeling that some of the current team tasks will get moved elsewhere. For instance, I know there has been some talk that our team won't be doing the weekly website builds. But we'll figure all of that out after you guys get up here. You are coming, right?"

"I guess I'm saying 'Yes.' As you know, I've been looking here in town. But I don't want to pass up this opportunity."

"If you come, you'll be working with the best. You'll be exposed to a lot of different things, a lot of different technologies. It's definitely a great career move, but I'm a little biased."

"Thanks, Mindy. I appreciate you keeping me updated."

"No problem. Just let me know if you need anything else."

I hang up. Barry notices that I'm off the phone and joins us in Jeff's cube.

"So what's the verdict?" Barry says. "Have you made up your mind?"

"Why does it matter to you?" Jeff says. "You aren't going anyway."

"I'm just curious as to what the newbie is going to do," Barry says.

"Dude, he has been here almost two months!" Jeff says.

"Mindy said that Ken counts as a spot, and that we might not be doing the weekly website builds," I say.

Barry laughs.

"Who will be doing them, a different team?" Barry says.

"I suppose," I say. "I didn't get any details."

"Ha, I'm sure that will work just great," Barry says. "They won't know anything about the code or how to fix it. I can already tell you guys are going to have so much fun up there!"

Barry bounces away. I check my voice mail to find out who called while I was conversing with Mindy.

"Hi Jason, it's Marshall MacDougal. I just wanted to call and see if you have any additional questions on Decision Day. Just give me a call ... I'll be around the rest of the afternoon. I know you'll make the right decision. Talk to you later."

As I place the phone back on the receiver, I laugh. Here's the vice president of technology calling me at 4 p.m., an hour before I have to make the choice, to see if I need any more info. Am I the only one within his jurisdiction that is still on the fence? Doesn't he have something more important to do at work besides checking on my status? The man is really on top of things.

Regardless of what happens, if I don't end up in Cincinnati, it won't be Marshall's fault. He has shown me that even inside a decent-sized corporation, there can be individuals who show empathy to their subordinates.

I see no reason to wait any longer. I check "Yes," grab Jeff, and head up a flight of stairs to human resources on the eighth floor. I walk directly to the HR manager's office, but it is locked. Jeff and I shrug at each other. Should I knock? Should I slide the paper under the door? Should I nail it to the door and attach my own version of Martin Luther's "95 Theses?"

While debating this, I notice Nicole, who is also in HR.

"Do you want my decision paper?" I say.

"Sure," Nicole says.

"Has everyone turned it in?"

"I hope so! But I really don't know."

"Are many people going?"

"There are a few ... but I've seen a lot more with 'No' checked."

I doubt that Nicole wants to know the play-by-play of what transpired today, so I thank her. Jeff and I check out the eighth-floor break room, but much to our chagrin, we don't find any free snacks. So we return to our cubes.

"That was fun," Jeff says. "Now it's time to go home!"

"Already?" I say. "It's only 4:30!"

"Look around ... no one else is here. We can start hammering away on APP again tomorrow."

"I guess so. Do you think things will change tomorrow?"

"No way. It will be the same as it has been the last few days. When they start actually moving people, though ... things will probably start to change."

***

On the evening of signing over my life, I realize I have work to do for JobImp. It's nothing too difficult; I just have to spend a few hours coding a website. I don't consider it challenging, mainly because it's not worth it. There are numerous ways to code a site, including those that are more standards compliant. However, the pages I build for JobImp, at least to this point, are far from achieving compliance. They still work just fine, though, and that's all the client really wants.

This gives me enough time to consider moving in the near future and, of course, Diya. I never even had the opportunity to say goodbye to her this afternoon; she must have left while I turned in my paper. I've tried calling her tonight, but she's not answering. Maybe she has dance class, and that's why she isn't answering. Or maybe she thinks this is a good time to make a break for it. After all, she knows I'm not uprooting myself to move north, right?

So why did I check "Yes"?

20
Uncertainty and a Party

Tropical cyclones have specific names, depending on their location and strength. A tropical depression doesn't have a storm eye and has maximum sustained winds of 38 mph. The next strongest, the tropical storm, has higher sustained winds (39 to 73 mph), and while it doesn't quite have an eye, a cyclonic shape starts to take form. Finally, a hurricane, or typhoon, has winds of 74 mph or more and a defined storm eye.

Hurricanes don't hit Louisville, so I'm not really sure how to characterize the storm I'm walking through this morning. The rain hits me horizontally, rendering my undersized umbrella useless.

Next time, I should probably go for a golf umbrella, rather than the ones used for a Long Island Iced Tea.

It seems fitting that this torrential downpour occurs the morning after Decision Day. I arrive close to my normal time, but the place seems mostly vacant. Before I can unlock my computer, I notice Debbie walking to the break room. It makes sense that I see her already because she usually comes in around 7 and leaves at 3.

"So, you said you're moving, right?" says Debbie with a filled water cup in hand.

"Yep, it went down to the wire," I say. "But I might as well say I'm going, even if I don't."

"If you said you're going, why would you not go?"

"I'm still looking for jobs here, so if something better comes up, then I won't go."

"Well, then you shouldn't say you are going, if you aren't going."

"Why is that?"

"There's no reason to train you on anything if you aren't going."

"But I don't know if I'll go, and I don't have another job lined up ... so that's where I stand right now."

Debbie hurriedly leaves my cube. She's pissed, understandably, but I really don't know if I'm going or not. I would hate to lose my job if I can't find a better one. Do I owe my coworkers anything? I want to be upfront with them, but I also don't want to speculate. There's no easy way out of this one.

I finally get to my email. I initially notice an email from Mindy.

Subject: Welcome to the Team!!!

Mindy Green
Northern Lineage Financial

NL FUN FACT: Northern Lineage has a time machine.
Really, we do!

A three-exclamation-mark subject is a great sign! I wonder how many Jeff got, assuming he received a similar message after he signed on. Because I didn't call Marshall back yesterday, I decide to write him a short email to proclaim my honor, loyalty, and dignity to Northern Lineage (at least this week).

The rest of the team starts to trickle in, but everyone looks glum. I'm not quite sure if the depression stems from the final countdown ending yesterday, or the fact that there's actual work to be done today, or possibly the sheets of precipitation cascading down outside.

I enter Jeff's cube to find him back at work on Annuity Profit Plus. A glance across the way at Barry's cube shows that he is most likely compiling documentation.

"So guys, you're actually doing work today?" I say.

It takes a minute for either to respond, but eventually, Barry joins us in Jeff's cube.

"Well, newbie, I got an email from Mindy about training," Barry says. "She's going to be here tomorrow, so she wants everything that I have."

"Is that exactly what she said?" Jeff says. "Because I'm pretty sure you said your last three dates said the same thing."

"Very funny," Barry says. "Let's put it this way. If I don't train you guys on all of the fund transfer stuff, you'll have a terribly difficult time maintaining it."

"I can believe that," Jeff says. "But I really don't want to maintain it either. Ha!"

"Who's going to be involved in the training?" I say.

"I would assume everyone," Barry says. "Well, at least, everyone who is going."

"Come on, Barry, you can still change your mind," Jeff says. "Cincinnati will be fun! And there are lots of hot chicks there as well."

"Really?" Barry says.

"Um ... sure!" Jeff says. "OK, I have no idea. But they have to be somewhere, right?"

"I wonder if they play volleyball," Barry says. "Speaking of volleyball, Jeff, I'd like to spike on your head a few more times. You should come out to open gym tonight."

"I think I'll pass, man," Jeff says. "I need to work on my portfolio, and the basement, and ... "

"You're just scared, I know!" Barry says. "You don't want to get hurt, right big boy?"

"Ah, here we go again," Jeff says.

While Barry and Jeff continue to trade volleyball banter, I escape to Ken's and Diya's cubes. Because Ken isn't there, I sit in the extra chair inside Diya's cube.

"I tried to call you last night," I say. "Is everything OK?"

"Yeah, I was just taking care of some stuff for work," Diya says. "What did you need?"

"Oh ... I just wanted to say 'Hi' because we didn't talk much yesterday."

"It's OK, Jason. Yesterday was a crazy day."

"So how are you feeling about all of this?"

"Honestly, not very good. All of the people who are not going are telling me horror stories about Northern Lineage. Why would they do that? I thought they were my friends."

"What are they saying?"

"Just that I won't like it and I shouldn't move and this and that. It just doesn't seem right."

"That is strange ... but they aren't going. So I wouldn't rely on them to tell you how it's going to be."

And I thought the people walking past my cube looked sad: Diya seems mired in depression over the relocation ordeal. Then again, she is hypersensitive to anything that would take her out of her comfort zone, so it's not that surprising. I'm not positive who is telling her what, but why they would want to make her feel more miserable is beyond me.

As the day progresses, the mood fluctuates between minor turmoil (the goings versus not-goings), malaise, and sheer nothingness. Most of it seems to happen within the confines of Diya's workspace, although Ken isn't a willing participant. He continues to mind his own business and not speak too much to the rest of us.

"Have you talked to Ken today?" I say to Jeff, who just returned from an Annuity Profit Plus meeting.

"Not that much," Jeff says. "He's really out of it. The house thing is getting to him. He can't afford his house, so he doesn't know what to do."

"I guess buying a house wouldn't be the best thing to do."

I decide that talking to Ken will be on tomorrow's agenda, assuming that we will have a minute or two in between training sessions to focus briefly on our real lives.

Wednesday, August 17

I'm a little tired today from staying up late to work on another project from JobImp. The good news, however, is that I talked to JobImp Reggie, and we are finally going to discuss a full-time position. I'd like to stay with Mettle a little longer, but if the JobImp position is available immediately, I would be a fool not to accept it. That is, assuming that I finally decide I don't want to move.

Apparently, we aren't starting training today. Mindy is here, but she's meeting with other people. We won't discuss training stuff until tomorrow, and then maybe it will start next week. It doesn't matter to me. I have work to do with APP, and I'd rather do that anyway.

Jeff isn't here, which gives me the freedom to toggle between his computer and mine. I'm still attempting to run the Visual Basic calculations and regenerate them within Java. I think I'm making headway, but it's somewhat tough to tell, considering I'm not really sure I know what I'm doing.

It's sometime after lunch. Yes, my computer has a clock, but between looking at actuarial calculations and numbers zipping across my screen, I've forgotten how to read a digital clock. Mindy stops by our workspace to provide pertinent information for the weeks ahead. She stops in Jeff's cube, where I'm sitting, and nearly everyone else gathers around.

"I wanted to fill you in about what's going on," Mindy says. "I've been in meetings all morning, and I have more this afternoon. We'll start the training tomorrow. At first, I think we just need to make a list of things that we need to train on. Then we'll make a timeline to get everything done."

"Do you know yet when everyone is moving?" Barry says.

"That's a really good question," Mindy says. "But unfortunately, I don't know. They've told me that they'll give at least a 60-day notice. The biggest thing we're trying to do right now is take WebSphere out of your department. We already have a team familiar with WebSphere, so they'll probably handle anything that needs to be done."

While Debbie, Barry, and Reshmi stare blankly at Mindy, let me explain. WebSphere is a piece of software that allows websites to be published in their entirety and in an efficient manner. In our department, we create the website builds and use WebSphere to "turn off" the old site and "turn on" the new one.

The good thing is that assuming all of the code works, upgrading is pretty fast. The bad thing is that if you have just a minor change, or if you realize a problem with the new website build, you often have to start over.

"How can a different team be in charge of our code without knowing anything about it?" Debbie says.

"Yeah, what happens if there is an issue?" Barry says. "It doesn't seem like you guys could get another team to do this."

"It might be a challenge, but we think it can happen," Mindy says. "I mean, we already do this now. The development team hands off to the WebSphere team, and then they deploy the new code. That way, there are fewer people with access to the live server."

"Are you saying that we won't have access to the production server?" Debbie says.

"I don't know yet," Mindy says.

"What if you need to make a small change," Reshmi says, "and you don't need to do a whole new build? Who would take care of that?"

"We haven't gotten into the details yet," Mindy says. "It would be nice, though, to use the WebSphere team for both Northern Lineage and Mettle items. That way, we can cut down on costs by utilizing both technologies together."

This is worrisome on a few levels. First, as I've mentioned before, Northern Lineage codes mostly in .NET, whereas we use Java. Meshing these two together in a haphazard format would be the equivalent of building a bridge with steel and then deciding to finish it with a few planks of wood.

What's even more difficult to grasp, though, is how portions of the corporate world are built on mistrust. If we don't have access to the live server, then anytime there's a problem with the Mettle websites, the following has to happen:

1. We test in the development area.
2. We make a build of the entire website.
3. We send the build to the WebSphere team.
4. That team deploys the site.
5. That team alerts us.
6. We test in production (the live site).
7. If there's a problem, we start all over.

Steps 3 to 5 are being added to our already busy schedule. If that's not bad enough, we'll have no idea whether the WebSphere team actually knows what it's doing. Maybe something is wrong, but it's not our fault. Adding layers onto what we're doing complicates things and, even worse, shows that the parent company doesn't believe we can do what we are already doing.

Does anyone trust corporations? *Corporation Nation* mentions a 1996 national poll commissioned by the Preamble Center for Public Policy in New York that showed nearly half of the participants claim corporate greed is the main factor behind economic difficulties.[26]

Then, when you factor in companies not even trusting their own employees, the issue quickly deteriorates even further. It's a shame that admirable checks and balances within workflow become, for the most part, just checks and more checks. In this case, Northern Lineage will be swallowing a mouthful of procedures just for the satisfaction of knowing Mettle programmers can't touch the code on the live website.

Mindy returns to her meetings. We return to our work. I finish with Jeff's machine and go back to mine. I see that Marshall has returned my email.

Subject: Re: Decision

I'm very excited that you are coming to Cincinnati.
I'm looking forward to working with you!

Best regards,
Marshall

NL FUN FACT: Our life insurance sales staff is the
best in the business. Once, a sales rep sold a policy to a polar bear.

While I'm at it, I check my personal email. Lloyd from
JobImp wrote back as well.

Subject: RE: JobImp opportunities

Jason,
Keep me posted on your situation. I did receive an
approval from my boss last night to add a full-time
person to payroll. If you are interested and would
like to discuss, you can arrange to visit with me
on your next trip, or we can talk over the phone.

I feel as if both Northern Lineage and JobImp are just
dangling carrots in front of me. What really annoys me is that I
don't like carrots.

Thursday, August 18

"We're going to start from the top and just go over everything. We need to gather all the information Barry and Reshmi
have and make sure that Jeff and Jason have it before the move.
And since Jason is the newest, he should probably sit in on all
of the trainings, even those that Debbie and Jeff own."

Mindy, our fearless leader, has just scheduled the rest of
my time at the Louisville edition of Mettle. I don't think she
quite understands my involvement with Annuity Profit Plus,
because that is one project (or possibly the only project) that is
being worked on in the entire place. Unless that cloning project

works, I don't see myself finishing that plus sleeping, er, sitting through hours and hours of training.

"Since the announcement," Mindy continues, "I have been putting together an integration roadmap, so that we make sure all of our bases are covered with respect to the projects and systems. Grant has helped with a lot of the details, but what we need to figure out now is in what order we should knock off these tasks. I'll just go down the list and we can add or move around the items I have."

There's no doubt we have a lot to do. Even though our team has a fair amount of documentation, it's not enough, and it's not in the nice, Northern Lineage format. The philosophy here is that as long as it's on paper, someone can read the paper and figure it out. But because technical documents like these have to be constantly updated when new items are added, it appears that the originals will collect more dust than use.

I hear my name called out frequently because I'm considered a trainee on nearly every item. Barry will be the primary trainer on most of these items, and Debbie has already volunteered to take notes. Mindy, as usual, will also be taking notes.

Even though Jeff has been here five years, he doesn't know about all Mettle website processes. Every person on the team can't be the expert for every piece of code. But that will change, to a certain extent, because the Owner of the Lonely Code, Barry, will be staying put as we sail up the Ohio River.

We return to our desks. I was really trying to keep track of how many training sessions I have to attend, but I lost count at 34,105,124. I know that Mindy will fill in her spreadsheet and send it out, so I'll just look for my name on every line there. The Northern Lineage way is revolutionary, in that the managers make lists to make documents, which leads to transcribing more documents that will be listed in a spreadsheet. Revolutionary in an 1100s, monk/scribe-type way.

I hear Ken talking in Jeff's cube, so I torpedo over there. The everyday Ken has been replaced with a suave-and-slick

Ken, who appears in a more sporadic fashion. Ken is wearing a new dress shirt and tie. The shirt is sea green, with maybe a hint of turquoise. The tie is a darker design and complements the shirt perfectly. Ken's hair even seems styled, which leaves me pondering why he would be dressed like this.

"Hey Ken, where's your interview?" Barry yells from his cube.

Ken starts to tell Barry to keep quiet, but it's obviously too late now.

"Five years with the guy, and he still can't keep a secret," Ken says.

"Well, where is your interview?" I say.

"Oh, there's no interview," Ken says.

Jeff and I laugh.

"No, honestly, there's no interview," Ken says. "The only place I'm going today is to get my hair cut. I dressed like this to get a response from everyone else."

"What type of response are you looking for?" I say.

"I don't know," Ken says. "Just any response. People on our floor are giving me a second look."

"But Ken, that's because you're hot!" says Jeff, almost falling out of his chair.

Ken retreats to his desk. I talk to Jeff about Annuity Profit Plus, and then I stop by Ken's cube for a bit.

"So are you getting out of here, or are you still moving?" I say.

"I don't know anything anymore," Ken says. "I thought I had a sure thing a couple of weeks ago. If anything, I was over-qualified. But I still haven't heard back from them."

"Maybe they are just slow to get back to you?"

"Possibly ... but it has been two weeks, and from what I understood, they were making a decision this week."

"Are you saying you don't want to move now?"

"I don't want to move my family, at least not initially. We are trying to sell our house, but there's some work that still needs to be done. I've been trying to finish up the porch, but people are coming to look at it this weekend. If I sell it right away, then everyone has to move. But if I don't attempt to sell it now, then I can't buy a house in Cincinnati."

"Man, that's a nightmare."

"No joke. I just hope Jeff will be OK with me living with him for a little while. That way, I can at least start to make arrangements on the other place, assuming I find something up there. It just seems like no matter what decision I make, I'm going to question it."

A forced decision is no decision at all. I have it easy, considering I have just myself to worry about. Ken, on the other hand, has a wife and kids and a career to consider. It's not like he can change his mind overnight and find a solution. I can't say I envy his dilemma at all. Ken's hell isn't just the relocation; it's his state of mind and the fear of the apparent future.

Friday, August 19

Work was worthless today. The only thing remotely interesting was Marshall bought five-dozen doughnuts for the seventh floor. That's a lot of doughnuts!

After work, I drive to the bar. I walk in, but I have no clue where I'm supposed to go. After a minute or so, I notice a Mettle employee leaving the restroom and walking out the back door, so I follow.

It's excruciatingly bright outside, so much so that I have already lost the person I was following. However, the party room is pretty evident, to the right. I open the door and hear, "JASON HARRIS IS HERE!"

My eyes adjust rapidly, and who else but Barry would be standing right in front of me. Most of the other 30 or so people in the room glance at me momentarily and then continue what they are doing. Jeff and Ken, who are sitting next to Barry, giggle and shake their heads.

"Hey buddy, here's a seat!" Barry yells while patting the

chair next to him.

I didn't eat much lunch, so I'm looking for food, which seems to be the case for everyone. As we chat, I notice pizza being placed in the far right corner of the dimly lit party room.

"Can someone tell me who these people are?" I say. "I recognize maybe three of them."

"Most of these people you don't need to know," Barry says. "There are only a few who are going to Cincinnati."

I learn the names and ranks of some Mettle partygoers. Because Barry is the self-anointed party greeter (he should have worn a blue Wal-Mart vest), we keep our heads down and gossip about all the people we do not know.

I didn't plan on staying too late, but between eating, drinking, and people watching, the time goes by fast. While the other guys are talking, I step outside to call Diya.

"Hey ... everyone's asking where you are," I say.

"Jason, I won't be able to make it," Diya says. "I have a lot to do since I'm leaving tomorrow to visit my friend in Florida. Plus, I'm feeling tired after this week."

"But it's the Indecision Party! Everyone is here."

"Maybe next time. I'll talk to you later."

Next time? There is no "next time" for something like this. I'm sad I won't be able to see Diya tonight, but hey, I'm not going to let that spoil my fun.

I walk back into the party room, and I see Tom Nelson on the dance floor with his posse. They have started the Indecision Party's dance revolution. We join in, albeit gingerly. Even though there are plenty of people on the dance floor, Jeff and I seem to gravitate toward each other. After dancing in close proximity four or five times, we decide it's best to take a seat.

Jeff, Ken, and I continue to watch Barry, Nelson, and his friends on the dance floor. While tonight's party has been an opportune time to relax, especially after the furious last few weeks of contemplating life-changing decisions, the end results for most of us are far from being determined.

21

Preparations

Tuesday, August 23

Well, this is different.

The first person I see this morning is Don. On top of that, he's at his desk. Presumably working.

During the past few weeks, I can count the number of times on one hand that I have seen Don at work. Some of us assumed he had already moved to Cincinnati, though his computer was still in his cube. Barry thought maybe Northern Lineage gave him a new machine up there, and eventually, a man in cufflinks would be sent down to retrieve the old one.

"Hey man, where have you been?" I say.

"Mostly at home, packing," Don says. "I went to Cincinnati for a few days. We visited people around town. Nothing too unusual."

"We thought maybe you already moved."

"Ha, I wish!"

It's still rather strange to discuss the relocation with Don, considering that he's taking it as if it's a vacation. If Claude Simpson were to appear at Mettle right now and proclaim he was changing his mind about this, the pandemonium would cease, the office would surely become bright, and a Broadway musical might even break out.

Instead, we are left with Don's glee and the possibility of someone tossing him a cane, top hat, and a tie; being surrounded by a gaggle of dancing girls; and singing a chorus that would go something like, "I'm mooooooving! I'm mooooooving. The sound of relocation is so soooooothing. So soooooothing!"

"So, when are you mooooooving?" I sing, er, say.

"I thought it was going to be this week," Don says. "Now, I guess it will be next week. Either way, I don't care. I'm ready to go when they have a spot for me in the office."

"You'll have to let us know how things are up there."

"I'll just do what I did here and try to avoid everyone. But I'll definitely be visiting the cafeteria on a regular basis."

With training looming later in the week, and with the dust mostly settling for relocation items, I expect to have ample opportunity to work on Annuity Profit Plus. Monday was a pretty productive day, with a small timeout for Chris's baby shower. His wife is due next month, so we pitched in for presents, pizza, cake, and ice cream.

Also on Monday, a new employee began working in the cube on the other side of Jeff's. I saw one of the IT guys set up a computer in the previously vacant area, and I saw an unknown man, probably in his 50s, walking over there periodically. Maybe he's on the web team, maybe he's on the DBA team, or maybe he's on the janitorial team. Today I walk over to Diya's cube to ask, but I remember she is still in Florida.

Instead, I step sideways into Ken's cube.

"Looking for jobs today?" I say.

"Actually, no," Ken says. "I'm working on training docs for the CRM. Grant is coming down later this week, and we are going to discuss what I know. I'll be glad when I'm not the only one who knows how to use it."

"I still don't understand how you are going to be on our team. Will you be doing web development?"

"I don't think so, but if someone else is taking over my CRM duties, it's possible. They haven't told me what I will be doing. Have you seen Mindy?"

Now that Ken mentions it, I can't remember the last time

Mindy was in Louisville. Or is she here today, in meetings? Ever since we scheduled training, she has been missing.

"I haven't seen her," I say. "Doesn't training start tomorrow?"

"I don't know," Ken says. "I don't think I'm involved in most of the training that you guys are doing. It's a good thing, because it will take me awhile to finish these training docs."

Jeff and I have something to do today, too: Annuity Profit Plus. Earlier, Vance delivered another round of modifications. Besides that, we are still ironing out the current calculations. I would say that we are definitely getting closer to completion, but the more I learn about it, the more I realize it isn't finished. We may engage in the proverbial pyramid-on-top-of-the-completed-pyramid scheme. This occurs when a single project turns into something that no longer makes sense, given the initial specifications. Assuming we can get the cornerstone in place, via a complex system of pulleys and a rickshaw, we may survive.

Surely we'll get it to work right, so we can make more money for all of the rich people.

In the afternoon, Jeff and I take a break with Nitya and walk to a local coffee shop. I figure it will be nice to get some fresh air, even though it's approximately 451 degrees out there. I heard some employees started a bonfire with file folders, but that's purely speculation.

"Have you given your notice yet?" Jeff says to Nitya as we cross the street. "I overheard you saying you might have a job."

"I do have a job, with Waveland Healthcare," Nitya says. "I was planning to give notice, but today, I received a call from a job recruiter for something different. The hours are a little more flexible and the pay is better."

"But you already accepted a job with Waveland?" Jeff says.

"Yes, but I could turn it down," Nitya says.

"You could have the shortest term ever at Waveland!" I say.

Nitya picks up her coffee, and Jeff orders some sort of

iced cappuccino beverage. I consider a drink or a cookie, but I change my mind. A treat won't complete my extra pyramid any sooner.

Wednesday, August 24

Diya is back!

She still looks tired, but at the same time, refreshed. In a non-zombie way.

"Florida was a lot of fun," Diya says. "My friend and I went to Disney World, SeaWorld, and some other places. I have a few pictures that I'll show you."

Diya was pictured next to a man. Did the friend take pictures of Diya and a stranger? Oh, I see … her friend was this guy. I'm not sure why, but I assumed the friend was an Indian girl she had known for a long time. Right ethnicity, wrong gender, I think, while trying to hold back a pang of jealousy I never knew existed.

"I'm glad you had fun," I say. "So how long have you known this guy?"

"We met when I first moved to the States," Diya says. He's a really good friend who would do practically anything for me. But we would never be more than just friends."

"Why not?"

"That's just not how our relationship is. Besides, he was dating a girl for a long time, and they just broke up. He calls me to talk about her, and I tell him to find another girlfriend!"

"Sounds like you're supposed to fill that void."

"I don't think so. Anyway, I have something for you."

Diya reaches into her purse and pulls out an object wrapped in white tissue paper. She hands it to me, and I unwrap the paper. I find inside a key chain: a gold-colored round piece, vaguely similar to a pocket watch. It's thicker, though, and hollow in the middle, except for a "J" that's attached at the top and bottom by small springs. I flick the "J" to spin the letter.

"I was thinking about you, so I wanted to bring you

something back," Diya says.

"Thanks," I say. "You didn't have to get me anything."

I immediately attach it to my current set of keys.

"So what did I miss?"

"Not much. A new guy started. He's sitting next to Jeff's cube."

"Oh, I know who you are talking about. His name is Brandon Mallard. He is also a DBA, from Northern Lineage, but he will be working down here for a couple of weeks."

"Let me get this straight. Don is moving to Cincinnati any day now. But another guy is coming down to Louisville on a daily basis to do the same job?"

"Brandon will be doing knowledge transfer with Nitya."

"So Don already knows everything?"

"No, but he wanted to move already ... so they're letting him go."

Don and Brandon Mallard, the new guy, have to be the same person. I have yet to see them both at the same time, and it makes no sense that we're sending someone to Northern Lineage while they send someone down here. Is this like having high school exchange students at the workplace? Maybe they don't want to send all the new people up at once, for fear that they may tip the scale too fast, and a single fleeing employee could evolve into a lemur-esque escape.

I leave Diya's cube, satisfied that at least she didn't forget about me while she was gone. Back on my side of the floor, I look up as Jeff suddenly slams his phone.

"Shit!" he says. "We've been downgraded!"

I have no idea what that means.

I still don't understand financial ratings. We were rated AAA, which could mean the exclusive auto members club or minor league baseball. Maybe we've been moved to AA?

"Why did our rating go down?" I say.

"No idea, and I really don't care," Jeff says. "More importantly, we have to immediately change all of our marketing information. We have our rating scattered all over the websites. It could take days to make all of the changes. I just talked to Raj downstairs. They are already making the changes on the printed literature."

I decide to do a little research on the Internet. I find three major rankings systems: Standard & Poor's, Fitch Ratings, and A.M. Best. The highest ranking of the first two systems is AAA, while the best of A.M. Best is A++. Northern Lineage holds all three of these distinctions, as did Mettle when I showed up for work this morning.

The ratings depend on certain aspects of the overall financial institutions. Standard & Poor's focuses on financial strength; Fitch Ratings are based on insurer financial strength; and A.M. Best looks at financial strength, operating performance, and market profile. It works sort of like the college football BCS standings, only no former Heisman winners get to vote.

I'm not certain that all of the rankings changed. But my job isn't to keep the rankings elevated. Instead, I'm helping Jeff identify all of the changes necessary on the public website. When I say "help," I mean clicking on random links on the corporate website, with the hope of finding those rankings. I find three altogether. Jeff groans.

Before I resume APP work, I check my personal email. Katrina Henderson, the recruiter with whom I met previously, sent me a job for a PHP developer position in Santa Ana, Calif.

"Hey Jeff, come over here for a second," I say.

In mere seconds, Jeff is reading the email.

"Whoa, that's really close to where we went for vacation," Jeff says. "I'd love to move out there."

"Are you interested in this job?"

"I wish."

"What's stopping you?"

"The Cincy trip is a done deal. Laura's already looking for jobs and stuff. I don't think she's ready to move all the way to the West Coast now."

"But why not now? With the way this is worded, there might be multiple positions. Maybe I could go, too!"

"Awesome! Well, you can find out the info about it. But I can tell you that the likelihood of Laura going for it is pretty low."

Jeff exits. He told me that his dream is to move to California, so I don't know why this wouldn't work. Then again, there is a catch: It's just a contract position.

If Jeff does relocate with the company, I think he's making the wrong decision. Not a bad decision, per se, but the wrong decision. Then again, maybe I'm the one who's confused about the move, and I'm just projecting the craziness onto others.

Thursday, August 25

The good news is that we know when the training will begin: next Monday. The bad news is that I'm scheduled for pretty much the entire week to just sit through training. Barry is already here, so I attempt to ascertain from him the importance of being involved in everything.

"That's not my call," says Barry. He's busy installing a new program on his machine.

"Understandable, but what is going on during these training sessions anyway?" I say.

"I'm supposed to go over everything I know, which is a lot!"

"Can't I just read the manuals and stuff that you are compiling? Jeff and I have to work on Annuity Profit Plus. It's the only project going!"

"Yeah, I guess you can talk to Mindy about it. I'm just the trainer. Say, have you used Google Earth before? I'm installing it. At least that will give me something to do between writing all of this documentation."

"If you need me to, I'd be happy to look over it and help with edits."

"That's great! I'll send over what I have. It's like 70 pages now."

Whoops. Maybe I shouldn't have volunteered to review Barry's handiwork. Even though Barry acts as if what he's doing is a lot of work, I can tell that he's happy to leave a legacy behind. I heard from Jeff that Barry received an offer from Excelsior Computing, the place that interviewed him recently. But he probably doesn't want to leave immediately, or he'll have to forfeit the separation bonus.

Other tidbits permeate the floor throughout the day. Chris received an offer on his house in town yesterday. If things go well, he'll probably be casting off for Cincinnati in the next few weeks.

I see less and less of Chris every day. Everything we do now pretty much goes straight to Northern Lineage via Mindy. Management probably had to beef up security at the money vault due to a presumed excess of tie wearers in the immediate vicinity.

Tom Nelson found out that his team will be moving in December. We are scheduled to move before then, but at last check, it depended on the completion of the new building. Nelson is still on the bus, but he is also furiously looking for a legitimate alternative, like a solar-powered rickshaw.

After lunch, we return to workstations to find black travel totes in our seats. I find out from an email that a business that did recent system upgrades left behind the bags. Why the company gave out travel totes, I have no clue. Maybe to help us pack.

I try to make headway with APP, but I become stumped with a single figure that my calculation is giving me. On that note, I decide to leave work early. I'm normally one of the last people to leave our floor, primarily so I can avoid fighting traffic. As I grab my tote, I notice Diya walking out, too. I'm surprised to see her still around.

"I thought you had class tonight?" I say as we head toward

the elevator.

"No, the class is over," Diya says. "But a new one starts next week."

"Then you must have all sorts of free time."

"I've had so much work dumped on me that I don't think I'll ever have free time."

"Extra work?"

"Since Don is gone, I have to do his stuff. And Nitya is training Brandon Mallard, so I have to do her work. Chris must think that I'm not doing anything."

"Why do you say that?"

"He keeps telling me I need to get it all finished. And he said I won't be moving until February! Just about everyone else will be moving before next year, but not me."

"Have you talked to Chris about the workload?"

"I haven't because I haven't had time!"

I originally wanted to talk to Diya about her weekend plans, to see whether they included me. But as she fires off her complaints, I have a problem getting in a word edgewise.

"The move is really putting a burden on me, since I also have to find a place to live up there and do all of this work," says Diya. We step into an empty parking garage elevator.

"But everyone has to do it," I say. "I mean, Chris has a wife, two kids, and another on the way! It's not really easy for anyone."

"You are right, Jason, but don't forget that I'm still fighting the green card issue. From what I can tell, I'll be able to go to Cincinnati without starting over the process. I'm not even sure I want to move, though. Everyone still keeps telling me all sorts of bad stories."

"But the people telling stories aren't even moving! You have to make the decision for yourself, not everyone else. They made their own decisions."

"I guess so, but it seems so awful."

Northern Lineage could be great, it could be terrible, or it could be the same as now. I'm not going to sugarcoat the place. I begin to mention that as of now, I'm still going to Cincy. Before I say anything, Diya spins toward me, tiptoes, and kisses me on the cheek. The elevator opens to the floor where Diya's TrailBlazer is parked.

"I really did miss you when I was in Florida, Jason. I missed talking to you a lot."

"I missed you, too! Do you think you'll have time to talk or do something over the weekend?"

"I'm not sure. Maybe we can go to a movie or something tomorrow night? I have a wedding to attend Saturday with my parents. And I have schoolwork to do the rest of the time."

"OK ... we can talk about it tomorrow. I need to go home and cut my grass."

Diya nods and locates her car.

"Goodbye, Jason. Think of me tonight, OK?"

I stand there for a minute before turning and continuing down another level to my own car. Either she undoubtedly does want more than a simple friendship, or the stress has made her delirious.

Regardless, how can I not think about her tonight?

22
Alternatives

Monday, August 29

I have another interview Friday. This time, it's for a full-time position at TurtleWeb. The name sounds almost like a company that makes kids' toys. For the right price, I can be a good elf.

Today, there's no time to revel in a potential new future. My outlook consists of learning the Mettle systems in their entirety. Personally, I'm not so excited that I just can't hide it.

The training table in the conference room is fairly full: It's me, Jeff, Barry, Debbie, and Mindy. I have no idea what we'll be doing.

"We should begin with a general overview of just how fund transfers work," Mindy says.

"I can do that," Barry says. "I think we should go over the fundamentals of why the fund transfers are set up the way they are. Then, later in training, I can go more in-depth about each segment of the process."

"Just tell us everything you know," Jeff says. "We don't know anything!"

Barry describes the fund transfer procedures and why the complexity exists for certain days of the week, holidays, etc. With the stock market, especially the New York Stock Exchange, being a primary dependency of the funds, Barry had to sync the open and close times for the Mettle systems.

The actual training disintegrates after about 20 minutes,

as Jeff and Debbie seize the opportunity to interrogate Mindy about various relocation items.

"Do you know yet when we're going to be moving?" Debbie says.

"I heard they changed their minds, and instead, they are moving everyone from Cincinnati to Louisville!" Barry says.

"Is he serious?" Mindy says.

"No," Jeff says. "He is never serious."

"Well, you can move up any time you'd like," Mindy says. "We can make space for you."

"I think what she wants to know," Jeff says, "is when we have to move up there."

"The new building is supposed to be ready November 14," Mindy says. "Any time after would be OK. But even before then, we can set up a makeshift workspace for you."

"Hell no," Debbie says. "I don't want to move up there, then move again. It's hectic enough already!"

"So everything will be ready to go by that date?" I say.

"I would hope so," Mindy says. "But there are no guarantees. It was supposed to be ready a month before. And if they don't get it finished by then, it probably won't be functioning until March."

"March?" Debbie's voice elevates. "We won't move until March? How are we supposed to plan for this?"

"If it's really that late, we'll have to find space in one of the other buildings," Mindy says. "Let's just hope it doesn't come to that."

"The new building will have parking in it, right?" Jeff asks.

"Yes, the first few floors are for parking," Mindy says. "And they should be ready before the office floors."

"At least we'll have that set up for us!" Jeff says.

"Not necessarily," Mindy says. "You guys might be parking across the street, where we park now. Most of the spots are tandem parking."

"What's tandem parking?" I say.

"There are spots that people share," Mindy says. "So if you get to the spot first on a particular day, the other person parks behind you. You can exchange keys with them, so whoever leaves first can move the other car, if necessary."

"Seriously?" Debbie says. "You have to move people's cars just to get home?"

"Most people seem to work it out fairly well," Mindy says. "And only a few spots are like that."

Of course, those few spots will be the ones dedicated to the Mettle team. How convenient.

"I'm not sure I'd be too hip on the tandem parking thing," Barry says. "I'd find some other place to park."

"Yeah, that will get old fast," Debbie says.

"It's definitely not the optimal solution," Mindy says. "I'd like to think they'll do away with the tandem parking, especially with the new building."

We get back to training, although it's a pretty ominous way to start. First, we still have no clue when our team is moving. It looks as if the choices are November or March. So if we sell our houses now, what will we do? Furthermore, the parking situation sounds outrageous. When I want to leave for the evening, I really don't want to spend time moving other cars around. Mettle is paying me to code, not to be a valet.

Besides, those guys are always dressed in tuxedos, so that's definitely not my calling.

Tuesday, August 30

The number of suit-and-tie people walking around the seventh floor grows day by day. This morning, I rode the elevator with a few Northern Lineage posers. Now, I walk past the break room and conference room and notice a repp, two foulards, and two club ties. There's a paisley and two dots hiding in the back. I would call this nothing short of an invasion.

But wait! During an invasion, people usually don't switch sides in the middle of combat, unless they are taken as prisoners of war. We're being treated far superior to that, minus the stuffy clothing.

Jeff and I are skipping the WebSphere training. First, Mindy already told us that this was being moved to a different department. Second, this is one thing that Jeff knows pretty well. Third, and most importantly, we have the APP project to build. Sometimes, it's nice to have real work to do.

I read an email from Don, whom I asked earlier to chronicle his first day at headquarters.

I just got back from lunch. It was much better today. I had spicy fried fish, mashed potatoes (no gravy — some Yankee must make the menu), salad, Greek salad, mixed fruit, two good-sized slices of watermelon, and steamed vegetables. I also had breakfast in the cafeteria. They didn't offer too much, but I was able to get a doughnut, a muffin, some cream of wheat, juice, and milk. On the down side, no break room. No coffee provided in the work-space. No access to a microwave oven and only two urinals on the whole floor.

So far I have continued to do my job as before. I suppose it would be more correct to say I have started doing my job again, because the scale of my effort suffered after "The Announcement." As yet there has been no integration. It seems like these guys would like to farm out the development/data part of the job to the development/report writing staff here. That would just leave pure DBA stuff for us, which means we could quickly integrate into the Oracle staff here.

Everyone here seems interested to know when the next Mettle person is going to arrive. Heard anything? Has anyone gotten a final date yet? Anyone get hired away yet?

The tie still sucks.

NL FUN FACT: We have a new flavor of frozen yogurt in our cafeteria this week: Cincinnati Chili!

I wish I had answers for him, but no one here knows what will happen next. Meanwhile, it seems as if Don can somehow predict the future, given that he anticipated when the relocation would happen. Even the employees who have been at the Louisville office for a few years were left in shock. I suppose they expected something to happen eventually, or maybe they conveniently decided to ignore the possibility.

Don, on the other hand, had already sold his house! Even though he has a wife and kids, he has been a step ahead of Northern Lineage with his relocation plans. Is it feasible that he had insider information about the integration, and that he knows the plans of the parent company so far in advance that he is pulling some strings of authority? I'm guessing no ... that he just got lucky. But it wouldn't surprise me to see a large picture of Don and Northern Lineage president Claude Simpson, both giving the thumbs-up sign, unveiled at the next companywide dinner. You can purchase autographed prints after the entertainment.

I shoot Don a quick reply and then stroll over to Jeff's cube.

"I just found out that they use Java at Indiana Life," Jeff says. "Just about all of the programming at Northern Lineage headquarters is .NET. It'll be good to have other systems on Java, too."

"Do you think they'll move?" I say.

"They probably have a similar deal as what Mettle had: five years and then move. It's funny that they realized they needed to buy life insurance companies."

"What do you mean?"

"I think one of the reasons our rating went down is that our offerings aren't as diversified as they used to be. It seems that Northern Lineage isn't making as much from life insurance as they were before."

"We're Mettle Life Insurance, yet that's not our major offering ... maybe this company is the same way."

"I looked at their website, and that's their main gig. But who really knows. Maybe they sell pizza and ice cream."

I don't completely understand Northern Lineage's overall plan of financial domination. I think the steps, in chronological order, are as follows:

1. Purchase a company.
2. Let the people at the newly acquired company think they can run things the way they want.
3. Slowly filter in how they should be running the company.
4. Announce they are moving to the home office.
5. Make sure to enunciate the great benefits of moving.
6. Let them try out the gym and the salad bar.
7. Send the imperial troops to the company to conduct transfer of knowledge seminars/experiments.
8. Lop off the fat, i.e., the people who don't want to move.
9. Reserve a few tandem parking spots for the brave individuals leaving their lives behind.
10. Profit über alles!

And who controls the profit? Is most of the balance just being thrown into the heap for a handful of individuals to become filthy rich, while the rest of us toil away? It's not completely fair to compare Northern Lineage to the stockyard companies in Packingtown depicted in *The Jungle*. And it's not as if our friends in Cincinnati are trying to squeeze employees entirely out of record-breaking profits. However, someone seems intent on shaking up the Risk board and not completely taking into consideration the point of view of every employee.

But then again, if Northern Lineage tried to do that, I suspect that no work would ever get done.

Mindy and Grant appear in my cube and startle me.

"So the training is over?" I say.

"At least for today," Mindy says. "I thought you were coming to it?"

"Jeff and I decided it would be best to work on Annuity Profit Plus," I say. "We have to make sure we hit the deadlines."

"Oh, that's really great," Mindy says. "I haven't been totally involved with that, but I'll try to catch up eventually. In the future, just let me know what training you won't be able to attend."

I want to say "all of it." I decide to hold back for now.

"When will you be moving?" Grant says.

"I honestly have no idea," I say. "There's a lot to think about."

"If I were you, I'd take advantage of everything they are offering, especially the temporary housing," Mindy says. "It's pretty close to work."

"The thing is, I really don't want to sell my house immediately," I say. "I just bought it three months ago!"

"Wow, that's crazy," Grant says. "Let me know if you need any other help with apartments or anything."

"We are going to type up the notes from the WebSphere meeting," Mindy says. "But keep me posted regarding when you want to move because we want to get you guys up there ASAP."

Mindy and Grant exit. It's funny that they're so insistent on knowing when I'm going to move. Can I tell them "Never"?

Thursday, September 1

Once again, we're herded into the basement. As much as I wish this were only a tornado drill, it is an integration meeting. Maybe we will find out when, exactly, we will be moving. Or how many people are going? I have a few key pieces of information I'd like to know as well — for instance, is it OK to wear clip-on bow ties at the home office?

"We have completed the master prospect schedule," says host-for-all-seasons Ann Singleton as she moves to the second slide of the PowerPoint presentation. "As of yesterday, 54 people have accepted a position with Northern Lineage, which is a pleasing result.

"Each department is still gathering information for accurate move dates. We should have those sometime in the middle of September. At this juncture, if you are moving, and you plan to sell your house, it would be best to obtain a house appraisal through Cardinal Realty. If you are not relocating, we are in the process of setting up a job fair with local employers.

"However, it's imperative to remember that there is still a great deal of work to be accomplished. There's a certain sense of satisfaction of seeing a project to the end. Everyone has an important role to play. It can be stressful, both personally and professionally, during a time like this. There is support available for those who need it. Most importantly, there will be rewards for all at the conclusion of the transition."

After that first piece of information — the final tally of employees relocating — the meeting has quickly disintegrated into a pep rally. The issue, of course, is making sure those people who aren't moving — especially those who actually know something about the company — stay long enough to transfer their information to Northern Lineage colleagues. As the separation bonus dangles in front of people's faces, people could definitely forego the money if the price is right someplace else.

Most people I have talked to are shooting for the bonus. A problem at this stage is that we still don't know when the separation date for our team will be. Initially, it was an October time frame. More recently, Mindy said November or March. Does that mean Barry and Reshmi would have to stay until then to be eligible for the bonus? These unstructured target times would work for bears, because they could hibernate in Louisville or Cincinnati and be all right. Other than Barry mysteriously getting his head caught in a jar of honey once as a youngster, I don't see how there could be a mixup.

Even though we made our "decisions" August 15, it's rather

apparent that Northern Lineage still has a stranglehold on the actual choice, at least if you take into consideration the bonus. That's acceptable, although I'm not interested in being subjected to vague stipulations. I'll pass up the bonus for something better in Louisville and get out in a heartbeat. But Northern Lineage doesn't have to worry much about me. I'm not hoarding any business knowledge.

We think the meeting is finished, but Ann stops us from exiting.

"We would also like to unveil our new Northern Lineage logo today," Singleton says. "We worked with a leading New York design firm to enhance our logo and bring it up to date."

Ann clicks the mouse to show the final PowerPoint slide. It displays a scripted "NL" that appears to be wearing a pink party hat, with confetti surrounding it.

"This marketing endeavor cost the company $500,000," Ann says.

I scan the room, and there are a lot of stunned looks and open mouths. After a particularly long uncomfortable silence, people start exiting the room.

"Fun meeting, huh?" I say as I catch up to Barry and Ken at the elevator.

"Don't they realize it's sort of tough to figure out what to do when we don't know how long they are going to keep us?" Barry says.

"But that's the trick," Ken says. "They want to keep you on a short leash."

"Well, if they want help from me, they should give us at least an idea of when we'll be leaving," Barry says. "Or I'll just take all of the information with me."

Back on the seventh floor, I skip my desk for Jeff's to see why he didn't come to the meeting. He is examining two somewhat equal stacks of paper. Both are approximately 8 to 10 sheets.

"Great news!" chuckles Jeff. "Annuity Profit Plus is

changing again!"

"What's changing?" I say.

"Who the hell knows? I'm trying to figure that out by comparing the new specs with the old ones. The biggest thing is that they want to be able to create quotes based on existing contracts."

"Will that be difficult?"

"No idea. I'm trying to get a data sample from Vance to see what it entails."

"Dear boy, you are in quite a messshhhh."

Jeff is silent. I return to my cube, thinking about tomorrow's interview with TurtleWeb and hoping there are no more surprises today. Before I can check my email, Barry pops into my cube.

"Hey Jeff, come over here," yells Barry over the partition wall.

Jeff appears.

"I've pretty much finished my first cornhole set," Barry says.

"Congratulations!" Jeff says. "Let me go get your diploma. You did it!"

"Ha ha, very funny," Barry says. "Anyway, I'm going to unveil it at my party. You guys are coming, right?"

"When is it?" I say.

"In three weeks, on Sept. 25," Barry says.

"Sure, why not?" Jeff says.

"We'll have barbecue and cornhole ... what could be better than that?" Barry says.

Jeff and I try not to laugh, although I'm uncertain why. It's truly debatable right now as to what is the most hilarious: Barry making cornhole boards, Annuity Profit Plus changing on a whim, Mettle relocating, or some twisted combination of the three. How can a job be so much fun and so stressful at the same time?

Friday, September 2

My interview is at 10 a.m., so I head to Mettle, check email, say hi to everyone, then drive out to Louisville's east end.

I check the lobby's business directory and walk up a center flight of stairs to TurtleWeb. I see a collage of the company's recent design work before opening another door to the office. There were actually two doors to choose — one on the left and one on the right. I choose the right, primarily because there's a sign in front of it that says, "Welcome, Jason Harris."

To my right, through the entrance, is a pool table. Straight ahead is what could be a receptionist's desk, although there is no one there. I walk toward the desk and then look to my left, which is an open work area. Finally, a guy approximately my age appears outside the office next to the front desk. I ask for Vic Carmen, and the man goes back into his office.

At this moment, I have a strange revelation. I am wearing business attire, with a tie, for the interview, yet it doesn't bother me. Perhaps all of the interviewing I've done lately has made me accustomed to the formal coverings. But as I notice my neck slightly strained from the tightness encircling it, I also see that the man with whom I've just conversed is *wearing shorts*.

I wonder if this is a dream. A man wearing jeans and a flannel shirt approaches me.

"Hi, I'm Vic. Follow me to my office."

It's insanely dim in his office. The walls are green, and I can tell it's partly cloudy out his window. But the overhead lighting is nonexistent. He has just a small light perched above his Mac.

"I just started here a few weeks ago," Vic says. "If you want to know things about the company, you should ask Alex or Denny ... they are the guys in charge. We have about 400 to 500 websites that we host and work on. Most of the sites are in PHP, but we do support some ASP sites."

"What's a typical day like?" I say.

"I'm not sure there's a typical day. We have two other programmers, two designers, and a design intern, and everyone works on different aspects of each project, depending on what's needed. You would probably be the main PHP programmer because that's what the guy before you did. One of the guys does website maintenance, but he also does some project management. Everyone just fills different roles when people are busy."

"How many people work here?"

"I think it's 25 or 30, but we've hired a few new ones. The environment is pretty causal here ... you can pretty much wear whatever you want, we have informal get-togethers and parties and that sort of thing. It's a lot different from when I worked at one of the big hospitals in town. I was working 60 hours a week with people who acted like robots."

"Do you work a lot of overtime here?"

"Not a whole lot, but we just finished up a project this week, and I was here until 1 on Thursday morning. But I just took off part of Thursday to make up for it."

I tell Vic a bit about my background and what I have been doing at Mettle. Of course, I also mention the relocation saga. So far, TurtleWeb is definitely more my taste than Northern Lineage. The work here would be similar to the programming I did before I came to Mettle, which is enticing.

Vic hands me a coding test to complete in the next few days. He says he might have me in for another interview, depending on his schedule and the other potential applicants.

"I'm trying to hire two people in my department right now," Vic says. "One will be developing client sites and the other will be on the R&D side of things."

"I know a guy who might be interested," I say. "I work with him now. He seems to be set on moving, but I really don't think he wants to move."

"Tell him to send in his résumé. I'm not supposed to start looking for the R&D position until I have another programmer in here, but it can't hurt."

Will Jeff go for something like this? At least it's an alternative to moving. I leave TurtleWeb, wishing I didn't have to take the coding test. But it's a reasonable request, assuming that anyone, from a 10-year-old kid to a three-legged dog, could walk in off the street and claim to build a websites. There are a lot of pet websites out there, you know.

Back at Mettle, the normally loquacious bunch is rather quiet. As we work on the newest changes to Annuity Profit Plus, Jeff tells me that Ken left early to look at houses in Cincinnati, and Barry is at a job interview but should return soon. However, Nitya informs us of today's real story: Chris's wife had the baby!

"This calls for a celebration!" Jeff says.

"There is ice cream from the baby shower in the break room freezer!" I say.

"Eckshellent work, young lad. Prepare the ice cream!"

"I'll see if anyone wants to join us."

Because no one else seems to be available, it doesn't take me long to notice the paltry ice cream social attendance. As I stroll toward the break room, I notice Diya returning to her desk.

"Chris's wife had her baby," I say to Diya, following along to her area.

"Yeah, I heard," Diya says. "That's great."

"Jeff and I are having ice cream to celebrate. Would you like some?"

"No, I don't think so. I have a headache and haven't been feeling well. I think I'm going to leave early."

"Is there anything I can do for you?"

"No, I'll be OK."

I notice that Diya's water cup is empty. I grab it, walk briskly to the break room, fill it with water and ice, and hurry back to her cube.

"Here, you should drink some water," I say. "Maybe that will help your headache."

"You didn't have to do that," Diya says. "Thank you, Jason. That was very thoughtful."

Diya and I really haven't talked much at work this week, and hardly at all outside work. She is busy preparing for her dance recital and finishing her classes. I decided awhile ago to just give her space. After all, last week she said she missed me. Maybe she's still deciding what she wants in her life right now.

Jeff has already scooped two bowls of ice cream for us. There's still at least half of a container full, so I don't feel guilty that I have four scoops in my bowl.

"I like ice cream!" Jeff says.

"Who doesn't?" I say. "Oh, get this: TurtleWeb is hiring two people, one programmer and one for R&D. I mentioned you could send over your résumé."

Jeff laughs.

"I don't even have an updated résumé!" Jeff says.

"Hurry up and update it then," I say. "It shouldn't take you too long. Just write, 'Mettle: Dealt with projects and some B.S. for five years.' Then you're done!"

"What would I be doing there?"

"I guess research and development."

"As much as I want to ... I think I'm already committed to moving. Laura is ready to go."

"Come on, man, you don't have to give up yet. Just send your résumé. You know you aren't a Northern Lineage type of person."

"That is true. But I can do my time and get out."

"Why not just get out now?"

I would like to convince Jeff not to move, but I can't make the decision for him. Maybe he'd fall for a cleverly disguised spam email about a design job in Louisville. Or maybe I should just tackle him and tie him to a chair with neckties. There must be a way to do it.

Jeff and I silently finish our colossal bowls of ice cream.

23
Join Me

Tuesday, September 6

I stare at my computer screen, contemplating more Annuity Profit Plus work. I have a list of changes, but I still have questions before I can begin. I could guess at the calculations and let the numbers scroll across my screen for the rest of the afternoon, hoping that at some point, my figures will deposit millions into my bank account. It should be a rather simple formula. They do it in the movies all the time.

Instead, though, I'm focused on Diya. I haven't spoken to her since Saturday night ... or was it afternoon ... or wait, was it Friday? It has been so long that I can't even be sure. The only thing I remember is that she attended a wedding the Saturday before last and has buried with homework and dance practice since that time.

Lately, I've been thinking about her more than usual. During the weekend, I watched two movies I borrowed from her. The first, *Mr. and Mrs. Iyer*, involves a Hindu woman who, with her newborn, travels across India by bus. However, the bus is hijacked by Hindu rebel forces who are attempting to eliminate as many Muslim citizens as they can. The woman befriends a photographer, whom she does not trust at first because he is Muslim. The man manages to conceal his religion long enough to organize an escape. At the same time, the woman clearly becomes attached to the man and continually wrestles with their differing faiths. Although religious hatred exists in the U.S., it seems mild compared to that in some developing nations, especially when there are large numbers of people on both sides constantly at odds. This movie aims at decreasing the tension between Islam and Hinduism in the most basic way: Love is not based solely on people's religious values but, instead, involves how individuals treat one another.

The other movie also focused on aspects of love. In the musical *Dil Chahta Hai*, an innocent friendship between a man and a woman turns out to be rather serious, even after the man finds out the woman is engaged. The woman acts unhappy with her fiancé but has no alternative due to his societal status. As expected, the other man has very little clout but spares no cost to be with the woman whom he deems his soul mate. He waffles throughout the movie until finally, on the eve of the wedding, he finds the courage to make his move.

The themes of these movies seem too coincidental. In both flicks, a man and a woman fight the fact that they are from opposite backgrounds, and they both find ways to be together. Is she expecting the same outcome for us? Furthermore, how can a word like "waffle" mean both flip-flopping and a delicious breakfast choice? Just like the characters in the movies, though, I can't give up, especially before running out of syrup.

Speaking of food, I recall that Reshmi and Diya were recently discussing the Ganesha Festival, which is a 10-day Hindi celebration that involves large feasts nearly every day. Ganesha is the elephant-headed son of Shiva and Parvati, and he is said to be the supreme god of wisdom, prosperity, and good fortune. I suppose this means my time with Diya outside of work will be severely limited, especially considering that celebrating good fortunes within the confines of this building hasn't happened in quite some time.

After tweaking my APP calculations for a brief period, I go to Jeff's cube to see if he has any answers for the project.

"I haven't heard from Vance about my questions," I say.

"Me neither," Jeff says. "But I closed my mail so I could

focus on getting the contracts working. I've actually made pretty good headway, if I may say so myself."

"You may."

Jeff opens his mail and quickly reviews.

"The only new email I have is about our mandatory meeting and training with Mindy tomorrow."

"Great, another break!"

"I don't think she cares much about our project. I think she just cares about finding out our current business logic."

"How important is APP anyway?"

"Considering it's Bender's baby, and it's the only project I know of that's being worked on during the integration, I'd say it's pretty important. So when is your next interview? Didn't you say the place you interviewed at wants you to come back?"

"I go back Friday. I still have to take a coding test for the job. Did you send your résumé yet?"

"Not yet. But I think you are right. It can't hurt to get my résumé together. Actually, I told Chris I was going to take off on Friday. I'm going to work on my portfolio a little, as well as the basement."

"Awesome!"

"I don't think I can get out of moving, though. But hey, I need a portfolio eventually, so I might as well start working on it."

Jeff is at least entertaining the notion of not moving now. Now, if I can just convince everyone else, maybe we can start a revolution.

Wednesday, September 7

During the past three to four weeks, I could guarantee seeing, at some point during the day, a group of Northern Lineage employees. They are generally easy to spot: a combination of oxford, chambray, gingham, and tweed fabrics. However, I see the same people today, and they are not wearing their normal garb. Instead, they're wearing polos and khakis, a corporate-issued camouflage. Who ordered the dress code change?

"I have no idea, but that's pretty funny," Jeff says.

"So if they are wearing that stuff down here, why can't they wear it up there?" Ken says. "And why can't we wear it up there, too?"

"They're probably just trying to blend in," Barry says.

"Maybe, but why now?" Ken says. "It seems a little late to start blending in."

Our Wednesday late-afternoon discussion came about for no particular reason. Jeff, Barry, and I are supposed to be meeting with Mindy in the afternoon, while Ken is waiting for Grant to start another session of knowledge transfer. The transfer must be going well, as the needle on Ken's knowledge gauge appears a little low. Or maybe that's just his I-couldn't-give-a-shit meter that's nearly empty because he looks peeved about something.

Ken seems to be taking the relocation the hardest. It's completely understandable: He's concerned about moving his family; he's concerned about selling his house and buying another; he's concerned about what his job will entail; and he's concerned about what he really wants to do with his career. Ken's uncertainty about everything can't help him even begin to make level-headed decisions, because ultimately, each item on his list affects the other. Unless he strikes it rich at the lottery, or a meteor strikes Cincinnati, I'm not sure how Ken can find happiness, given the current situation.

Grant appears, wearing a blue polo shirt and khaki pants. I have to take another glance to make sure it's Grant, considering that I've seen the man wearing only a white dress shirt and dark ties. A casually dressed Mindy is not far behind.

"Hi guys," Mindy says. "Are we still on for the meeting this afternoon? I have a few other meetings before then, but I should be ready by 3 p.m."

"Sounds good to me!" Barry says. "What are we going to

discuss, anyway?"

"I would like to start with the fund transfer process," Mindy says. "Since we had a bit of an overview the other day, I would like to delve more into where on the servers the scripts are, in case we need to make modifications."

"Sure thing," Barry says. "We just need to meet somewhere so I can map it out on a whiteboard."

"OK Barry, but no more drawing dirty pictures up there," Jeff says.

Grant follows Ken to his cube, and Barry and Jeff head to lunch. I eat at my desk and then review some of the newer APP project changes. There seems to be enough information in a recent email from the actuarial to move forward. I immerse myself in the code, so much so that I don't realize the other guys returning from lunch, or that it's now already 2:55 p.m.

"Time for the meeting!" says Barry as he skips past Jeff's cube.

We walk up to the eighth floor and wait for Mindy in one of the corner conference rooms. Barry immediately begins drawing on the board.

"What are you doing?" I say.

"We might as well get started," Barry says. "I have to show you newbies where everything is."

"I've been here five years, and I'm a newbie?" Jeff says.

"It's new to you!" Barry says.

As Barry writes, Jeff and I ask relevant questions as to what we need to know so first, we can fix stuff if it breaks and second, we don't accidentally break it. The training is moving nicely when Mindy shows. It's almost 3:30 now.

"Sorry I'm late, guys," Mindy says. "The last meeting ran long, and I couldn't get out of there."

"No problem," Barry says. "We started without you."

"Oh?" Mindy says.

"Yeah, and unless Barry is totally making up stuff, then we might already have some of the answers," Jeff says.

"I have notes," I say.

"So where are you?" Mindy says.

"I'm just explaining what each file does for the fund transfers," Barry says. "Overall, it's not that difficult to decipher. The hardest thing is learning the architecture basics. Once you know how all of the files work together, I don't think there will be any issue in solving whatever may come up."

"And I'd like to add that it even makes sense!" Jeff says.

As Barry continues to organize the edge puzzle pieces and build a border around business process information, I wonder why I'm still here ... not just in this meeting, but with the company. Did I really check the "Yes" box on the agreement? What the hell was I thinking? The work is intriguing, but is it something I want to do for an extended period of time? It doesn't seem as if that's the case. Maybe I should jump out the window. It's only seven floors high.

Then again, who else wants to do the kind of work they are doing right now? It doesn't seem as if too many people here feel that way. I haven't met a lot of gung-ho people, prepared to fight through all of the elements for their job at Northern Lineage. People are indifferent at best, paranoid and fearful at worst. And there are rare anomalies, like Don, who are happy. I came to this juncture on a technicality; there was an open position that Mettle had to fill during a certain time frame. The others have been here for a while, presumably, and haven't been opposed to the company direction. Maybe Mettle was a great place to work, and because of all the great people, many of them stayed.

Man, now I'm talking about Mettle in the past tense. Not only that, but I'm talking about Mettle to myself, which proves either that Barry's training session is boring or that my subconscious has finally started to feel sorry for itself.

"Barry, I didn't quite understand the last thing you said," Mindy says. "Who has the capability to fix the funds, if there is a problem with them?"

"The power resides in a couple of places," Barry says. "Since the scripts update on a nightly basis, it's not just our team that will have to fix it, because the other database is updated as well."

"So we will just need to document this procedure for everyone to know," Mindy says. "This is totally off the subject, but Jeff, I wanted to let you know we talked about Annuity Profit Plus in the meeting I came from."

"Awesome ... I guess?" Jeff says.

"There were murmurs during a Project Giza meeting about potentially holding on that project during the knowledge transfer," Mindy says. "But I told them that you have things under control, and that I feel it's necessary to proceed with it. I think they wanted a different team to start working on it."

"A different team?" I say. "Who would do it then?"

"Probably my team in Cincinnati," Mindy says.

"Then it would have to be rewritten, since you guys use .NET," Jeff says.

"That's what I told them," Mindy says. "I don't think they realized how far you have gotten on it and how much has actually been completed."

"It has been an eternity since someone reviewed it," Jeff says.

"Well, just so you know, I'm going to bat for the team because it's important that you go along with your usual business," Mindy says.

"That's great," Jeff says. "Is it just me, or is it weird to name a big company project after the construction of a predominantly slave-made structure?"

"Huh?" Mindy says.

"Never mind," Jeff says.

"What do you think will happen when the teams merge?" Barry says. "It seems that lately, Northern Lineage has been trying to dictate what will happen, even though at the beginning, it was understood they were going to keep things pretty much the way they are right now."

"It does seem that way," Mindy says. "And I really don't know why, since Mettle has been a successful brand for quite some time. It's almost as if Northern Lineage wants total control of your company."

"That's the impression I get," Jeff says. "I mean, if you look at the moving benefits, everything is in Northern Lineage's favor. They say they will help you sell your house, but they are probably making money off that somehow."

"The company isn't making much off the real estate deals," Mindy says. "But I can see how that looks a little shady. I can tell you this much about my department, though: I like to do things my way, and if the company doesn't like it, then someone will have to tell me."

"Does that count the dress code?" I say. "It seems funny that we have to wear a tie to work every day up at the main office, but now you guys are allowed to dress down when you come here. Why can't we just wear what we have on up there?"

"We talked about that on Friday, during sensitivity training," Mindy says. "It comes down to the fact that Claude Simpson feels comfortable in a suit and tie, so he thinks everyone should feel the same way."

"That's insane!" Barry says. "Comfortable? Does he also feel comfortable if someone is choking him?"

No one answers, but it does beg the question: Under the new Northern Lineage rules, do I have to do everything that the president of the company likes to do? I pray he's not into karaoke.

Thursday, September 8

The process of elimination marches on at Mettle. Today's contestant is Nitya, who finally decided on the job with Waveland Healthcare. Apparently, the other deal never panned out, was going to pay her less money, or eventually burned down in a horrible grease fire.

We have prepared a potluck lunch for Nitya's last day. Everyone brought a dish, so we're setting up in the basement conference room. Diya and Reshmi made Indian dishes; Jeff furnished the chips; Sam, in IT support, picked up the drinks; and the rest of us made sides and desserts.

The spread is a regular Viking feast. Unfortunately, we don't have any mead, and we don't plan to pillage any other tech shops in the area. At least, not yet.

Though we're celebrating Nitya's new life at an even larger corporation, we are also welcoming back Don, who drove down for the event.

"How do you like it up at corporate, Don?" Barry asks.

"It's pretty good so far," Don says. "The food is OK, nothing amazing. I'm just working on the same stuff as always. The people are more polite there than here."

"No way!" Barry says. "They seemed pretty stuffy ... but they are polite?"

"Yeah, but only because they don't talk at all," Don says.

With the food on the table, we probably could have fed 50, but only 15 attend. Mindy said yesterday she was coming to the luncheon, but I haven't even seen her at the office today.

From what I've seen so far, I think Mindy will be a good boss. I get the impression that she trusts her employees to find the right way to do something, and she will stand behind them when needed. Then again, it's tough to tell how someone is as a boss until that person is actually your boss.

In the afternoon, I wait to see if more training sessions are percolating or if APP questions have been answered. Unfortunately, neither comes true. Instead, I visit Diya in her cube. At this stage, confronting her about why she has been despondent lately will probably be a waste of time. Since Tuesday, every time I have attempted to talk with her, she has been busy. Besides wanting to just catch up with her in general, I want to ask her again about going to a friend's wedding. I mentioned it to her a week ago, but she hesitated to give me a response. Earlier this week, I brought it up again in an email, but she responded that she would feel uncomfortable going to the wedding with me. I assumed the "be-my-date-to-a-wedding" invitation was a sure thing with Diya. But if she's hesitant about spending an hour with me at a wedding, that's not a good sign.

Besides, the conversations with Sarina, my sister's friend in New Jersey, have been going pretty well. I've been emailing and talking with her more than Diya lately, and we seem to have more in common than I expected. I may book a flight this weekend to visit her and forget about the disorder here in Louisville.

But I have to give Diya one last chance. She's right in front of me — at least for the time being.

"Hey there ... how are you?" I say as I back into her workspace.

"Not good," Diya says. "Chris dumped more work on me. And I have talked with HR every day this week regarding my visa. There might be an issue where I have to return to India sooner than I had planned. I was going back around Christmastime, but I may have to go before that."

"When will you find out?"

"I have no idea. I can handle the move and all of this at the same time. But I don't want to dump all of this on you as well ... you have other things going on."

"You can always talk to me about it."

"I don't want you to think that I'm always depressed and in a bad mood all of the time, that's all. The last few months — well, ever since you have been here — it has been a stressful time in my life."

"I understand. When are you leaving tonight?"

"I need to leave soon for dance."

"I'll walk out with you."

This is not the most optimal time to interrogate Diya about my friend's wedding. But if she completely blows me off about going, then I can stop considering a relationship. I'm not going to get a direct answer about it, mostly because I'm not going to ask for one, even after we arrive at her TrailBlazer.

"So have you decided about going to my friend's wedding with me?" I say. "I won't know that many people there, and it would be nice to sit with someone I know."

"Jason, I understand what you are saying," Diya says. "I am sorry, but I don't think I can go. I just don't think it will be right."

"Why? What's the issue?"

"It would be different if we were married or engaged."

"Why would that be different?"

"Because ... it just would be. There is conflict about the perception of us being together at an event like that."

"What perception? People go to weddings all of the time. Maybe things are handled another way in India, but ... "

"I don't think so. We have weddings just the same, where everyone invites family and friends. It would also be different if I knew your friend, if I had met her before."

"So if we go over to her house right now, and you meet her, you would go to the wedding?"

"No, not like that. But if I had known her for a while, and we had been together for long ... maybe then."

"Diya, I sort of see your rationale behind this, but it just seems you don't want to go. If you don't want to go, you can just say so."

"But I wouldn't mind going, it's just ... "

"Then you should go!"

"Jason, I can't. It just doesn't feel right to go, and with everything else going on."

"So you don't have time?"

"It's not that I don't have time. It's that ... our friendship is something that is hard to explain."

"I'll agree with you on that one."

"I don't completely know how I feel about it, primarily because you are the first guy who is not Indian who I've been good friends with. It's hard for me to interpret what that means. I care about you and I don't want to lose your friendship."

"So where do we go from here? We're sort of at a stale-mate. We're more than just friends."

"That is true."

"What do you want to do?"

Diya slumps in her seat a bit and takes a deep breath. I await her answer, without the faintest idea of how she will respond.

"I think we should talk about this more," Diya says. "But I can't tonight ... I have to get to dance class. I hope you do understand how much I enjoy your company. But dear, I need to leave."

As I stand there in the parking lot watching Diya pull away, my mind spins. Do I move for a job I'll hate, for the chance to be with Diya, whom may or may not stay in America ... and even if she does, whom may or may not want to be with me?

Do I stay in Louisville for a job I'm pretty sure I'll enjoy much more than my current one but may or may not land, and the chance to be in an even longer-distance relationship with Sarina, who I like but don't really know?

Why does Diya feel this way? Is it chemistry? Is she scared? Did she ever "like me" like me? Is her culture in con-flict with her personal desires? I think back to the movie about the forbidden love between the Hindu woman and the Muslim photographer. What's the big deal? Why does everything have to be so complicated? Why do I have to wear a damn tie to work in Cincinnati? Why the hell can't we just say and do the things we want for our career and love lives, the things that make us happy?

Does she love me, or does she love me not? Does she love me, or does she love me not? I stand in the parking lot, trying to decide if there's a petal left on the dandelion.

And the more I think, the more I begin to wonder if that flower even still exists.

24
An Opening

Friday, September 9

This is the first time in my short career that I've ever been summoned back for a second interview. Every other place has been either "Great, you're hired!" or "Go away, you freak!" But this isn't the only reason my second trip to TurtleWeb is special. This is also the first time I've ever gone to a job interview without wearing a tie. If I do secure the job, maybe I'll donate my trove of ties to Jeff or, better yet, create some sort of wall hanging out of them. I should keep one handy, though, in case I need to pretend later in life that I'm somewhat important.

I walk into the office and see Vic Carmen, the guy with whom I met last time, walking nearby.

"You received my coding test, right" I say.

"Yep, I got it last night," Vic says. "I haven't had a chance to look at it yet. I wanted you to meet the guys in charge here, but I don't know if they are available. Let me call."

He summons "the guys in charge," and I scan the room while I wait. There are rather interesting items in the office, including turtles. Not real ones, but plastic ones, glass ones, rubber ones, and even a metal one.

"It looks like Denny is busy, but Alex wants to meet you in his office," Vic says.

We walk down two offices and sit in Alex's office. There are more turtles in this office, but there's another thing I notice: awards. I don't see any Emmys or Oscars, but the trophies must be for something decent. I can't make out the print on every single one, but I see the words "TurtleWeb" and "first" often.

"I'm Alex Garrison. It's good to meet you. So why are you looking for a job?"

I repeat the same, ridiculous story that I told Vic on my initial visit. Man relocates to new city. Man buys house. Man finds job. Job decides to relocate. Et cetera.

"We are not a big company, but some of our clients include the largest corporations here in Louisville. We obviously want to grow, but I don't think we ever want to get to the point where nothing gets done because there are too many layers of management."

"That's what happens at my current job. I like the people at my current job, but one of the biggest downfalls in moving is that we will be under more control by the parent company."

"So when are you looking to start? Will you be able to give two weeks' notice?"

"Something like that. I have been doing some contract work for JobImp. The manager said he may offer me something permanent, but I haven't heard anything yet."

"That's cool. I hate to cut this short, but I have a meeting in a few minutes that I need to get ready for."

I don't want to leave without mentioning Jeff.

"One more thing: I do know a guy who might be interested in the R&D position. He's actually a guy I work with now."

"Tell him to send his résumé over, and maybe I can meet with him. We already have a few good candidates, and I want to hire someone pretty fast."

Vic heads down the hallway, and I retreat to the entrance. Before I leave, I see the guy who was wearing shorts the last time I was here. Even if the job were awful, wearing shorts to work would definitely be my bag.

Back at Mettle, it's Friday, which means we have the normal skeleton crew. I walk past the cubicles and take a quick count: besides Debbie and Reshmi, I can't find anyone else in our area. Debbie mentions she found a house in Cincinnati but will probably need to build a garage. Reshmi has another job interview, but she's not really keen on finding something right now anyway. In December, she will be returning to India with her husband and son for a visit.

As we are talking, I hear my work phone ring, so I run over to answer it.

"Hello, is this Jason Harris?"

"Yes ... who is this?"

"Hi, my name is George Winston from Cardinal Realty. How are you today?"

"OK."

"I'm calling because you are on the list of people who are moving to Cincinnati from Mettle. We are calling all individuals who are coming up here so that we can get the relocation process in order. You may be getting a call from an appraiser to set up an appointment at your house, assuming you have one."

"I do, but I haven't even decided if I'm going to sell it."

"That's all right. It doesn't hurt to get some of these things done. After all, Northern Lineage is paying for it, so no need to worry."

"I understand that, but ... "

"Have you found a house up here yet?"

"No, and I'm not looking. If I come up there, I'll probably get an apartment or something."

"Very well, then. If you need our services, you can contact our office. Thank you, and have a great day."

I suppose one call about the relocation isn't too big of a deal. Northern Lineage wants to start the conveyor belt of new employees, and the housing thing is a pretty big deal. I attempt to enjoy a quiet lunch at my desk, but my work phone rings again.

"Hello, Jason? This is Steve Whitfield calling about a house appraisal."

"You have to be kidding me."

"Oh ... have you already had your house appraised?"

"No, but I have no clue if I will even need an appraisal."

"But I have your name on this list of people who are moving to Cincinnati."

"That might be true, but that doesn't mean I'm selling my house right now."

"I see. Well, we were given the list of people, and your name is on it."

"If I need your assistance, I'll give you a call back. Goodbye."

Previously, Northern Lineage sent us a letter explaining that we would need to get our real estate matters in order, and if we needed reinforcement, we could ask. I do not recollect anyone saying Realtors and appraisers would start contacting us without consent.

The remainder of the day creeps by, mainly because hardly anyone is here. I call Jeff at home to see what he's doing.

"Hey hey!" says Jeff, sounding as if he's in a car.

"Hey man," I say. "Where are you going?"

"Lowe's! I have to get more supplies for the basement."

"The basement? I thought you were working on your résumé!"

"I did that for a while, but now I'm back to the basement. Too much stuff to do."

"Oh, I see. I had my second interview with TurtleWeb."

"How did it go?"

"The guy said he would let me know something early next week. Also, I talked to one of the owners, and I mentioned you for the other position. So now you have to send in your résumé!"

"OK, OK ... I'll send it in. But you're going to have to talk to Laura if you think I'm staying. She's already set on going to Cincy."

"I suppose that means I just need to find her a job, too."

Jeff hangs up, so I return to my computer and my email. I

notice a message from Vic at TurtleWeb.

Thanks for coming in today. I'd like to offer you
the position with TurtleWeb. Just let me know ASAP
if you want to accept it. Look forward to working
with you!

Vic

My usual response to this type of email would be "awesome!" But something feels different this time. Maybe it's because the decision-making process is almost over, unless JobImp has an amazing position planned for me. Or possibly I feel weird because I'm leaving my new family here at Mettle.

But maybe most importantly, I know that by leaving Northern Lineage, there is scarcely any way that Diya and I will ever be together. Judging from the last few weeks, though, working for the same business would not change anything.

Perhaps I will feel better about the TurtleWeb job in a few days. Until that time, though, I really need to make sure I'm finally making the right selection.

My cellphone rings. I do not recognize the number.

"Good afternoon! My name is Sarah Parsons. I'm with A+ Moving. Your name was passed to me by Cardinal Realty. I hear you are moving to Cincinnati!"

"No."

"Oh, is this not Jason Harris?"

"Yes it is, but I'm not moving."

"You're not?"

"Well ... I'm almost certain that I'm not."

"Why are you on this list?"

"Does it matter?"

"We are supposed to set up moving dates for new Northern Lineage employees ... "

"Let me help you out. When I decide the date I want to move, I'll let you know."

"But we need to know in advance."

"OK sure, no problem. Thanks for the call."

I need to let someone at corporate know sooner, rather than later, that I'm off the bus. If not, they may sell my house and move my stuff one day while I'm at work.

25
The Real
Decision

Monday, September 12

In the morning, there are spiders everywhere. Web spinners are outside the windows. Arachnids are crawling along the desks near the windows. I even notice one climbing between cubicles. I wonder if Northern Lineage brought down the eight-legged creatures with the hope of transferring knowledge to them. Spiders have a decent shot at surviving a nuclear war, and on top of that, they could wear a tie on each leg. If I do my calculations correctly, eight ties mean eight times more fashionable, which obviously translates to eight times more productive.

But there are more important things to consider than spiders ruling the seventh floor. However, no one I see right now — Diya, Ken, and Barry, when he rolls his chair outside of his work area — wants to ponder their circumstances.

I'm outraged at Northern Lineage. I suspect that someone at the corporate office decided to see how much excitement he could get out of having a house inspector call my cellphone twice during the weekend. The first time, I did not answer the phone in time, and the man left a voice mail. Not an hour later, about noon Saturday, he called again. He wanted to set up the inspection sometime this week.

I should have asked for his fax number so I could send him a couple of blank pages. The title page would read: "Here's the new list. No one is going. Inspect your own home."

Sometime today, I would like to accept the job at Tur-tleWeb. But I can't until I meet with JobImp Lloyd this evening. The other burden is turning in my letter of resignation. Who gets the letter? Chris is technically my boss, but he's not here. He's still out because his wife just gave birth, but it's possible he's in Cincinnati. Chris is like the guy in the office who switches floors and is never seen again. I'm sure Don sees him in Cincinnati, but besides the occasional email to Diya, he's pretty much incognito at the Louisville office.

Mindy is the most likely candidate to receive my letter, but I don't know when she'll be here. We're again planning to have more training meetings this week, but I will do my best to avoid them, especially after I officially jump off the bus. Until the deal has been finalized, I will continue to maximize my options here at work.

As a last resort, I could give the resignation to Sally, who is Chris's boss. However, if she waited until after I was hired to tell me about the relocation, then isn't it feasible she could prolong my attempt at leaving Mettle?

Other choices include anyone on the eighth floor (where human resources is); Ryan Bender, Mettle's president (might as well go all the way to the top); Wilfred, the janitor (at least he'll spread the word); and Sean Connery (can't find his desk).

Another thing I need to do before accepting a new position: find others to go along with me.

Ken is in a trance at his desk. I can't tell whether he's reading his email or whether he's somehow looking through the computer monitor, trying to determine if he can jump into it and leave this world for bytes and pieces of virtual reality.

"Ken. Ken!" I say. He jumps a little, moves his mouse briefly and closes an email.

"Oh ... hey," Ken says. "Sorry about that."

"How is the job searching going?"

"You would have to bring that up, wouldn't you? I applied for a bunch of jobs recently, and I was pretty confident about two of them. But I'm still waiting."

"So your plan is still to move?"

"I guess so. There's just a lot of uncertainty with my position. I'm training Grant on what I spend most of my time on. And I'm supposed to be on Mindy's team, but I'm not a web developer. I have no freakin' idea what I'll be doing. Then there's the housing situation ... "

"I may have some news for you. I had my second interview at TurtleWeb, and things look pretty good there. They might be hiring two new developers. Jeff is sending in his résumé ... maybe you should as well. They might not be able to afford you, considering the amount of experience you have."

"I think that's what happened with these other jobs. That really pisses me off. I don't want to take a huge pay cut. However, I might consider one if the position is something that I want to do."

"Do you know now what you want to do?"

"Ha, not particularly."

"Maybe you should try the music business again!"

"No, I don't think so. Music is a great hobby, but it's nothing more than that."

"But if that's what you want to do ... "

"Well, I do have one lead I could follow up on. You know what? You are right! Screw all of this moving stuff!"

Ken immediately picks up the phone, and I walk away. It's good to see Ken not completely dismayed, as he has appeared the last few weeks. Even though it doesn't appear he has a resolution yet, he has not completely given up.

I leave Ken and pass Diya, Debbie, Barry, and Jeff, all of whom are contently focused on work at their computers. Either that, or they are all playing Second Life or some other group video game. Maybe they built Northern Lineage in Second Life, and they are selling second life insurance. What a great idea! If we move Annuity Profit Plus to that virtual world, we'll need to add the second death benefit as well.

***

After a relatively quiet day, I go to JobImp headquarters in Jeffersonville. There's still a faint chance that JobImp Lloyd has a better deal for me than TurtleWeb. Then again, having me appear in the company's Super Bowl ad and selecting neckties for the referees is probably just as likely.

There's no reason to waste any time. I explain to Lloyd that I've been offered a full-time position, and if he has something for me, I would definitely consider it.

"Jason, that's great to hear you found something already," Lloyd says. "At the present time, I can't guarantee you anything except hours as a contractor. I can pretty much assure you 30 hours a week, but I have no idea how long it would last. If something doesn't work out at TurtleWeb, you have my email address. Keep in touch."

That pretty much seals it — with Mettle, with moving, with everything.

I leave and head home for the last piece of business for tonight. I send an email to Vic to accept the job. The bus driver pushed the metal handle to open the door awhile ago. I've finally maneuvered around the other individuals and made my way out the door.

Tuesday, September 13

"Mindy told me she knew you would leave," says Jeff as he deletes meaningless email.

"What do you mean?" I say. "I was up front with her the entire time. I told her I was trying to find something here in town. It really doesn't take a genius to figure out I might stay."

"Yeah, I guess she just wanted to prove that she was paying attention."

Before we began training this morning, I told Mindy the news. This gave me a free pass to miss training, the best news of the week. Jeff, Debbie, and Barry stuck around with Mindy for the next few hours.

"So does she know yet that you're going to leave, too?" I say.

"I don't think I'm leaving," Jeff says.

"I thought you were working on your résumé for Turtle Web?"

"Yeah, I did, but ... I've pretty much committed."

"No way, man. You can always get off the bus. Just send it in. It can't hurt."

"I don't know. I'll think about it."

"Give it to me, and I'll take care of it!"

Why is he trying to fight emailing his résumé to a prospective employer? Does he not have time to do it? Or is he afraid he might like the job better than moving to Cincinnati? Or is he worried that if he has to change work email addresses, he won't receive as much meaningless email from coworkers, which will mean that he's just not that important anymore? Does he secretly want to wear a necktie?

"Mindy hired another programmer already," Jeff says. "Apparently, she was going to hire him regardless of what you did, to replace Barry and Reshmi. But now she is going to have him come down for training."

"She's already hired him?" I say.

"I don't know that for certain. And I don't know when he'll start, if he has been hired. His name is Mac Almanak."

I almost fall upon hearing the news. Nearly my entire tenure at Mettle has been spent working on date functions in both Java and JavaScript. Now I'm being replaced by an Almanak?

"That's remarkable," I say. "Maybe he will become Northern Lineage's mascot."

"Don't forget the tie," says Jeff, drawing a caricature that looks like a cross between a wall calendar and Mickey Mouse.

I'm glad to hear that Mindy is actively making certain that she has enough people on her team. With the way most corporations act, there's no guarantee that losing a body means adding a new one, especially during a restructuring.

"Seriously, though ... you're going to have a lot of responsibility at Northern Lineage now," I say. "It's just you and Debbie."

"It will be monumental if we can get Almanak down here for the training sessions," Jeff says. "With everything I'm learning, and the APP project, there's no way I have time to answer questions."

"I'll try to do as much on Annuity Profit Plus as I can."

"Thanks, but you don't have to worry about it ... you're leaving! If Debbie left, I would be totally screwed. I would probably quit."

"Do you think she'll bail?"

"If her husband really is transferring within his company to the office in Cincy, then she'll probably move. But if her house shit isn't in order ... she's pretty particular about that. So who knows?"

"How does it feel to be dependent on a coworker to decide what you do about your job?"

"Haha ... not that great. But it's the choice I've made."

"You still have time!"

Vance peeks into Jeff's cube.

"Congrats Jason, I heard the news," Vance says. "I guess you're officially off the bus now."

"Yeah, I felt like I was playing some sort of game," I say. "Jumping on and off at each stop."

"That reminds me of George Carlin," Vance says. "He said something like, 'Sailing isn't a sport. Sailing is a way to get somewhere. Riding the bus isn't a sport; why should sailing be a sport?' Maybe he should have changed his act to incorporate the sport of bus hopping."

Wilfred, the maintenance man/mailman/lead gossiper, appears with an armful of letters. It's not payday, so it's strange that he has such a fat stack. He hands a letter to everyone nearby. We open them at the same time; they are separation letters.

"Did everyone get the same date?" Barry says. "Mine is November 7."

"I have October 31," Jeff says.

"Me too," Debbie says.

"I have October 24," Ken says. "Great ... I get to move before everyone."

Mine is stamped with October 31 as well. Then I remember something Mindy mentioned previously.

"I thought the building wasn't going to be completed until November 14 at the earliest?" I say. "So you're going to have to move up, and then move again?"

"If we do, I might quit on the spot," Debbie says. "I don't see why we can't just stay here until it's ready."

Everyone else reveals his or her separation dates. Reshmi's is the same as Barry's: November 7. Tom Nelson won't be moving until the first week of December, and Vance's is later than that. And Diya's is still February! I have no clue how much leeway people will receive on these dates, because if some people are still going to be at the Louisville office, why can't everyone stay?

Wednesday, September 14

Vance wasn't completely accurate. My leap off the bus isn't official until I hand in my notice. And because I still haven't figured out who should receive it, I guess that in a warped world, I might be stuck with Northern Lineage forever. I've already told Mindy, so it's just a formality now. I slip a copy underneath Chris's door, hoping that's enough. If not, I can print out and sign another copy for Mindy. Or, maybe I can just shove individual copies into the company's monthly newsletter. That way, if other people need to do something similar, they can cross out my name and add theirs.

While the rest of the gang is busy with training, I manage to hammer out more work on Annuity Profit Plus. Vance has a demo this afternoon with the head honchos, so we are all curious to see if they approve of our modifications. Not that I care a great deal, but it would be nice to have accomplished something during my short time at Mettle.

I had considered trying to find Diya for lunch, but the guys are eating outside today, so I go with them. The weather is too nice to pass up, and unfortunately, there won't be many days left eating with Ken, Barry, and Jeff. There's no way I can find jobs for all three of them at TurtleWeb, unless I can find a way to execute current employees without anyone knowing.

Bright sun and warm temperatures bring out the best Louisville has to offer — at least with regard to females traversing near the little park next to our building.

"What about her?" Ken says. Barry, Jeff, and I all take a gander.

"Not bad," Jeff says. "But she still ranks below that one girl you pointed out yesterday."

"I don't know," Ken says. "I think she might be hotter."

"You guys are crazy," Barry says. "She's OK, but nothing to stare at. Now check her out!"

Barry points out a girl who is reasonably attractive but apparently can't tell the difference between makeup and plaster.

"Yeah ... she's all right," I say. "I'm not really into glamour girls anyway. What about that one?"

"I can see where you're coming from," Ken says. "But she's not my type."

"I'm just not into blondes that much," I say.

"Well, we know that, since you ogle Diya all of the time," Barry says.

"So do you!" Jeff says to Barry.

Barry directs a retort at Jeff, but I ignore it and talk with Ken.

"Do you know what's up with Diya?" I say. "She hasn't been talking to me much lately."

"I know she has been really busy," Ken says.

"Anything else?" I say. "She went to a wedding last

weekend, but I ... just normally talk to her more than this."

"I did hear her mention that she met a guy at the wedding," Ken says. "I think they might even be going on a date this weekend."

Barry and Jeff return their attention to the table.

"Diya found a date?" Barry says. "It's about time! How long has it been?"

The rest of us do not say a word. I haven't talked about Diya to any of them in great detail. However, Jeff knows from the little I've told him that something might be going on. And Ken sits right next to Diya, not to mention that he picks up on relationship stuff fast. He probably avoided telling me about this fact because he assumed that either she had told me or we had stopped seeing each other.

"That's cool she found someone," I say. "Is he from around here? Is he Indian?"

"I don't know anything about him," Ken says.

"I can't believe she hasn't said anything to me about this," I say.

"Why would she talk to you about who she's dating?" Barry says. "Are you guys that good of friends?"

"I thought so," I say.

Assuming what Ken says is true, I suppose this means my question about how she feels about me has been answered. Maybe Diya came to the conclusion that there was nothing more to say to me, and that we had both moved on already. I don't know, but it sucks to put a damper on such a beautiful day. I tell myself that I shouldn't let it affect me. Regardless, I wasn't going to be with Diya.

At least there's no possibility of a face-to-face confrontation with Diya in the afternoon: She's not here. Instead, we wait for the results of the APP demo. We had anticipated that Vance would venture down to our cubes to give the reactions from above. There's no sign of him when Barry strolls into Jeff's cube.

"Only a week and a half until the party!" Barry says. "You will be there, right?"

"Sure, I'll be there," Jeff says.

"I will be unveiling my first set of cornhole boards," Barry says. "You're really going to like them. And you'll like these, too!"

Barry unleashes a red beanbag that was hidden behind his back. The bag zips through the air and crashes right into Jeff's abdomen.

"What the hell was that?" Jeff says.

"It's the beanbag for cornhole," Barry says.

"I realize that, but why did you throw it?" Jeff says. "That hurt!"

"Come on, you big baby, it's just some cloth and dried corn!" Barry says. "I made it myself!"

Jeff leans out of his chair and picks up the bag off the floor. He spins and crunches the bag to examine in greater detail.

"Did you grow the corn in the bag?" I say.

"Ha ha, very funny," Barry says. "It was easy to make, but the stitching took longer than I had anticipated."

"So you still think you can make money off this venture?" Jeff says.

"Yeah, but I'll have to get faster at it," Barry says.

"I think that's why they have machines to make the bags and the boards," I say.

IT Sam peeks into Jeff's cube. Jeff throws the beanbag to him. Sam tosses it straight up a few times before setting it down on Jeff's desk.

"Not bad," Sam says. "Maybe you should make the boards out of plastic."

"Plastic?" Barry says. "Are you crazy?"

"It will be cheaper than all wood," Sam says. "And faster ... no finishing needed."

"Yeah, but that would kill the whole objective!" Barry says.

"What's that, to spend a million hours making something to

save a few bucks?" Jeff says.

"Not just that, but the boards I will make will be the finest cornhole boards assembled!" Barry says. "People will buy them because they are handcrafted."

"You sound like an infomercial!" Jeff says.

"Sam, are you coming to my party? It's on September 25. We will be testing out the cornhole boards."

"I'll be there," Sam says. "Gotta run now, though."

Barry doesn't give up easily, whether it's work, his personal relationships, or his newfangled way to make millions.

As the day progresses, Jeff and I still don't hear anything from Vance. Meanwhile, everyone else has gone home by the time the fire alarm sounds.

"Do we have to go outside?" I say. "I'm almost finished with what I'm doing."

"I have no idea," Jeff says. "In the five years I've been here, I don't think it has ever gone off."

The siren stops. But then it starts again. And stops shortly thereafter. Then it's back on.

"What the hell?" Jeff says.

Sam walks back past our cubes.

"They are doing some testing," Sam says. "No big deal."

Jeff and I sit back down at our desks. Maybe they just need to hose down the non-relocation talk before it boils over again.

Thursday, September 15

The latest integration meeting is supposedly geared toward discussing separation dates. Because I'm setting my own separation date (I decided on September 28, a little less than two weeks, but I'll also get two days off before I start at TurtleWeb), I probably don't need to attend.

But what the hell? Everyone else is doing it.

Northern Lineage must have sent a new clone, er, human resources employee to go over this information. But the information is still in everyone's favorite program, PowerPoint, and it's just lines and lines of text that are barely readable, even from the second row of seats. Jeff, Barry, Ken, Diya, Reshmi, Debbie, Nelson, Vance, myself ... nearly everyone on the seventh floor is here, looking bewilderedly at some of the separation dates listed.

"Excuse me," says Vance after the Northern Lineage man motions in his directions. "Are all of those dates accurate?"

"As far as I know," the man says.

"In the letter I received, I'm supposed to move a different time."

"Yeah, our team is scheduled to leave at a different time as well," Debbie says.

"My team's date is wrong," Tom Nelson says.

"Well, this is interesting," the man says. "I guess you should just go by your letters then. I'll have to check and see why these dates are wrong."

The meeting provides no resourceful material ... and no, it's not just because I couldn't care less.

Afterward, back upstairs in Jeff's cube, we receive valuable and exciting news.

"Annuity Profit Plus is a hit!" says Vance while snapping his fingers to a little ditty.

"A big hit like 'This is great!' or a big hit like 'Let's take a bat and kill this thing'?" Jeff says.

"Oh, they liked it well enough," Vance says. "I even performed a tap dance at the end. I was pretty happy."

Vance opens his notebook.

"However, they did have a few things that we need to address ... "

"Of course!" Jeff says. "They're going to love it because we can magically turn it into anything they want, whenever they decide they want something new!"

"Luckily, this doesn't look too bad," Vance says. "But they are extremely interested in tying in existing contracts."

"It won't be easy," Jeff says. "But it should be possible."

"I knew you would say that!" says Vance as he slaps Jeff on the back. "Oh, and they want to add in the new logo, but it's not completed yet."

"New logo?" Jeff says.

"Yes … it's 'Northern Lineage' on top of either a lizard or toad; they can't decide," Vance says. "And they're trying to pick colors as well … amphibians come in a variety of flavors."

"I'm not sure I even know what you're talking about anymore, "Jeff says.

"At least we're finally making some progress!" Vance says.

Vance leaves, and Jeff and I laugh.

"I guess you won't have to worry about this any longer, huh?" Jeff says.

"Yeah, I guess not," I say. "I still have a few more days, so I'm sure I'll get some things taken care of."

I return to my desk and review the email Vance sent with more APP feedback. I also hear a conversation Mindy is having with someone on the phone. I'm not sure what she's talking about, but I hear her say, "There's a lot of crap on the server!" That's funny on multiple levels, but especially the level dealing with Northern Lineage organization. I'm estimating that for every file that contains code, there needs to be five files containing documentation for how that code works. I'd rate some of those files lower than just crap.

Friday, September 16

Wilfred is up to his antics again, delivering nonsensical mail. I open the letter he hands me to reveal a "friendly" message from Northern Lineage, reminding me to take care of all my housing issues before the move. I'm tempted to call HR directly and bitch at them, but surely it can't happen for too much longer.

"Hello, this is Steve Whitfield, calling for Jason Harris."

"Aren't you the house appraiser?" I say.

"Yes, I'm calling to see when will be a convenient time … "

"Look man, I told you that if I needed an appraisal, I would call you."

"Yes, but Northern Lineage is telling me ... "

"Well, someone should probably tell you that I'm not moving."

"Oh."

I wait for him to say something, but he doesn't, so I just hang up.

I spend most of the day collaborating with Jeff on APP changes, but he leaves early. By the end of the day, Barry's the only remaining soldier, other than me.

"Hey man, why are you still here?" I say.

"I have to finish this documentation, so you can read it before you leave," Barry says.

"So where are you in the job search?"

"I'm supposed to have a second interview with Excelsior Computing. But it hasn't been scheduled yet. I think that's my ticket out of here, though."

"Will you still get the bonus?"

"I will try to work that out. From the first interview, they seemed willing to work with me from that aspect of things."

"That's cool."

"It is, but I will miss everyone here, and I'll miss Mettle. I've been here a really long time. I've never worked at a place like this, where everyone works well together plus everyone hangs out together. That's just not something you find every day."

I leave Barry to his documentation, and I can't help considering Barry's fate. Mettle is a surrogate family in every way to him. How will he cope? Will he find a situation even remotely close to that at Excelsior Computing or wherever he lands? Honestly, I'm not sure it matters. Barry is the type of guy who will adopt anyone into his family. And big families are OK, especially when you don't have to live with any of them.

***

In the evening, I drive to a nearby amphitheater, where Diya is performing Bharatanatyam, a classical dance that originated in Southern India. As I attempt to find a parking spot, I see her TrailBlazer. I assume she's already inside, so I start walking toward the location of the performance. However, I turn around to see Diya and a tall Indian man exiting her vehicle. I consider waving, but feeling awkward, I wait until they are out of range before walking toward the entrance.

I find a seat in the middle of the auditorium. I look around to find someone I know, but I'm unsuccessful. Up front, I see Diya's parents. Not that I've met them, but I've seen their picture on her work desk.

Incidentally, I realize that I'm one of three non-Indian people in attendance. I somewhat revel in that, anticipating a true cultural experience. And I'm not disappointed. The program is made up of a number of small parts, telling different stories. Most of the dancers are preteens, and the teachers participate in many of the separate acts. Each dancer is ornately dressed, and I attempt to decipher the meaning of the stories through the interpretative performances. I catch the name of a god or two, but otherwise I'm completely in the dark.

Nitya and her family appear midway through the dance, and Reshmi, her husband, and her son arrive a little after that. When the show ends, I move toward the stage to greet Diya. It's not immediate, though, as she talks to the other dancers, her teacher, her parents, her guy friend, Nitya and her kids, and other random audience members. Finally, I see a break in activity.

"Hey Diya," I say. "You sure are a *porlu ponnu* tonight."

Diya smiles.

"Hi Jason!" she says. "Come up here and get in our picture."

This seems rather awkward, but I'm getting used to being

in situations where I really have no choice.

I oblige and find myself between Diya and her friend. Diya's mom snaps the photo. She then introduces me to the man, who is from Boston, and her parents. I speak briefly with Nitya, Reshmi, and their husbands. Without much more to say, I decide to head home.

It's evident that Diya and the guy are a couple; I can see they are essentially connected at the hip, with her parents not far behind. How did this happen so quickly? Was I really sleep-walking through this entire chance at a relationship?

She's completely out of my picture. But at least for the evening, I plan to dream that she's still dancing through my mind.

26
I'm Out

Tuesday, September 20

We have a date with the Almanak.

Yes, I realize how ridiculous that sounds. It's not my fault, though ... Jeff is the one who keeps saying it.

"Mac can just sit with me, and I'll show him the intranet and the code repository," I say. "I could even show him the APP program if you want, since you'll probably be busy with other things."

"That's a good idea," Jeff says. "I'm sure Mindy will want him in our training sessions, though. I wonder where he's supposed to sit?"

Mindy introduces us to Mac Almanak. He looks nothing like a cross between a wall calendar and Mickey Mouse. I assumed at the very least he would wear a striped button-down or spread collar shirt to appear mildly grid-like.

Jeff and Mindy leave, and I summarize what little I know about how Mettle and Northern Lineage work.

"When you were hired, did you know you'd have to commute down to Louisville?" I say.

"No," Mac says. "They mentioned something about whether or not I would be interested in travel, but I didn't realize that meant every day."

"How did you get down here?"

"Yesterday I came down for orientation, and I rode the bus. I did the same today, but I might drive tomorrow. They said they might be able to put me up in a hotel, so at least I don't have to drive two hours each way every day."

"Sweet!"

"It's not bad, but my wife isn't too crazy about it. Besides, this really isn't what I signed up for."

"Did they tell you how long you'd have to work down here?"

"They weren't too precise about a time frame, although they did mention everyone down here was moving up there in October."

"Well, not everyone ... and the new building in Cincy won't be ready until November."

Mac and I go over a few things regarding the server setup, and I start to talk about Annuity Profit Plus when the rest of the team returns.

"It's time to eat!" Barry says. "Who's up for Indian?"

We head to an Indian restaurant in the east end, and it's apparently a favorite by many people in the office. Jeff drives Barry, Mac, and me, while two other carloads meet there as well.

I see Diya in the buffet line; I smile, and she smiles back We say "hey" to each other and carry on. I watch Mac for a few seconds as he blankly stares at the slapstick comedy featuring Ken, Barry, and Jeff.

As we leave the restaurant, I walk past the attendant's area and attempt to make small talk with Diya.

"Hey, what's that?" I say, pointing to a golden dish that's filled with small colored pellets. "Are those mints?"

"Sort of ... it's fennel seed," Diya says.

"What does it taste like?"

"It's OK, but I don't know if you'll like it."

I scoop a spoonful into my hand, and toss it into my mouth. As I swish them around in my mouth a bit, I realize I have made a mistake. I'm not sure how to attribute the taste precisely, but it's something between cardboard and Ajax — the cleaner, not the pseudo-programming language.

We walk out of the restaurant, and the taste in my mouth is starting to worsen. I try to swallow, but the seeds are stuck to my cheeks and throat. I don't have any water, which leaves just one other option. We reach the car, and I motion to Jeff. He reaches into the glove compartment and pulls out a tissue. I spit out the seeds, as many as I can, and throw them away in the nearest garbage container.

"Why did you try to eat those things?" Jeff says. "I could have told you they were bad."

"But Diya said ... " I say.

"Diya, Diya, Diya!" Barry says. "If you like her so much, why don't you ask her out?"

Jeff shrugs. Mac is already in the car, and Barry is shaking his head at me. At this point, there's nothing left to do but laugh.

At the office, I'm determined to help Jeff finish Annuity Profit Plus. I stamp out a decent amount of code before I run into an issue I can't seem to solve. I contemplate it so long that I realize Jeff and Debbie have already left for the day, and Barry is nowhere to be found. My only other hope is Reshmi, as she may have insight into why it's not working.

We discuss the problem in laconic fashion, but I'm barely paying attention. I really want to find out more about why I never met Diya's parents.

"Do you have any idea why Diya never introduced me to her mom and dad?" I say. "Is it a cultural thing?"

"I don't think so," Reshmi says. "You haven't met them?"

"Yes, but only for the first time at the dance. I talked to her mom on the phone once, because I thought it was Diya. There have even been a few times when she asked to meet me near her apartment, when her parents were at her place, but she never invited me over."

"That's really strange."

"Was she embarrassed of me?"

"No, no, that wasn't it at all. But I really haven't talked to her about it much, either."

"I know she's dating someone now, and I want to be happy for her. But she never even told me she was dating someone."

"I think the relocation has really taken a toll on her. That's the only thing I can think of."

"OK, thanks for talking with me about it ... you're not going to tell her that we talked, are you?"

"No, I won't tell."

"If you can find out anything else, I would appreciate it. I just wish I understood what happened."

I return to my cube and nearly forget how to solve the Java issue we had just discussed. I probably should not have brought up anything to Reshmi. Does it matter at all now anyway?

Friday, September 23

I start to clean out my cube. However, I have almost nothing here. I notice my midyear review, which I never completed and never turned in. I add it to the recycling bin.

We're working with a skeleton crew. Jeff was off both yesterday and today. Mac the Almanak didn't come down to Louisville today, and neither did Mindy nor any of the Cincy crew. Ken is here but busy with job hunting. Diya is in California; she left to visit her brother and his family this morning. Barry is surely putting the finishing touches on his documentation ... that thing must be 100 pages by now. Debbie and Reshmi appear to be collaborating on a project.

I feel more at peace today than I have in quite some time, and I have to attribute a lot of that to Diya not being here. She was in crisis mode earlier this week, for good reason. Last weekend, someone stole her purse, so she has been trying to follow proper procedures to recover her ID, credit cards, etc. Because she still doesn't have a green card, the ID process has been much more of a burden; however, yesterday she finally received a new driver's license.

In general, I'm not good with ending relationships, but this situation is different. First off, we were never officially a couple. Second, it was evident early on that there could be relationship issues that would always be insurmountable. Third, and perhaps most important, is that the entire time, I had been talking to my sister's college friend, Sarina. During the last few weeks, we have conversed more often, and we finally settled on a date for a visit: October 7, which is be my first Friday at TurtleWeb. I actually purchased an airline ticket before accepting the new job, so I emailed Vic, my new boss, to ask him for the day off.

I guess that's that. The book on Diya is closed.

Ken steps into my cube.

"I may have found a way out!" Ken says. "I just got off the phone with the lead I mentioned the other day."

"Sweet!" I say. "Will you be doing DBA stuff? Are you using Oracle?"

Ken shakes his head, smiles, and leans toward me.

"No … none of that. It's with a huge Korean karaoke company. I will be helping them put together the music, background imagery … all that stuff."

"That's what you want to do?"

"It's the music industry, baby! That could be just the break I've been waiting for. Oh, my lead is calling me back. I have to take this."

Ken leaves, and I wonder if he's making the right decision. I don't know at what level, or at what pay, this new job will be. Can he afford to do something like this, even with his huge house and family?

I guess it's not my place to stop someone from finding happiness through karaoke.

Wednesday, September 28

Today is my final full day at Mettle Life Insurance. There hasn't been much to make the news the past few days, besides

Jeff and me constantly working on APP. I went out to lunch earlier in the day with a few coworkers. Most everyone has been extremely cordial to me, and why not? Either they didn't know me, or they knew me as the new guy.

In the afternoon, I try to talk to Diya, but she doesn't have much to say. I tell her that I will return on Friday because a few folks on the floor have put together a mega Happy Hour down at Fourth Street Live. We will be celebrating (you guessed it) a number of people's last days, including mine.

As time winds toward 5, I start to feel a little nostalgic about the place, which is a weird feeling, considering I've been here essentially one summer. I wave goodbye to Jeff, and he motions that he is also leaving. We ride the building and parking garage elevators one last time and commiserate.

"I'm really going to miss this place," I say. "This wasn't like any of my other jobs."

"Why is that ... because you had to deal with Barry?" Jeff says.

"It's too bad that it's over. I never considered working at a job for a very long time, but I think I could have been happy here."

"I know what you mean. This was basically my first job out of college ... and I'm still here."

"Is that a good or a bad thing?"

"I always thought it was a good thing to show loyalty plus be in a position to learn about the industry. Coming out of college, there's no way I was qualified for this. But I've worked my ass off to get to where I am."

"So this is where you want to be?"

"Hell no!" Jeff laughs. "No, seriously, I don't mind it. But there's an entirely different world out there in the graphic design industry. I want to get more into 3-D modeling, and I need to do it sooner than later."

"So why don't you just do it?"

"There's a lot of work involved that I haven't been able to

do. Once I get moved and get up to Cincinnati, it will be easier. I won't have to worry about working on the basement and getting the house ready to sell, that's for sure."

"If you don't devote time to it now, you won't ever get anywhere on it."

"I am devoting time to it now."

"I mean dedicated time ... the amount you want to spend. That's what you want to do, right?"

"Well, yeah, but ... "

"Then do it! I mean come on. Northern Lineage is a nice cushion and all. Yeah, you can learn a bunch. But is it even stuff you want to learn?"

"Sure."

"But wouldn't you rather make progress in the industry you prefer?"

"It's just not that easy to break into."

"No shit it's not easy. Especially when you continue to avoid it."

We're now huddled over Jeff's vehicle. After my last comment, I realize I'm being terser than I really need to be. But then I realize the paradox staring at Jeff. He thinks that to get where he wants, he needs to invest his time first, even if that time isn't toward his long-term goal. I disagree.

"Look man," I say, trying to tone down a bit. "You have unlimited options. Yeah, you can go to Northern Lineage, but where does that get you? Mindy may or may not be an OK boss. You're just going to be working with Debbie and possibly some new people. They're going to expect you to do all sorts of stuff since Barry isn't there. And Ken ... well, who knows with him?"

"You make it sound so grim," Jeff says.

"It's just reality. You might be content there, or maybe you won't be. But it's not what you want to do. Why go through the persecution? You can find a job here and worry about your next move instead."

"Laura and I have talked about it, and she knows I have reservations about staying with Northern Lineage, especially with the added management and the tie B.S."

"And her family is from Louisville, right? So it seems as if it would be easy to convince her to stay."

"Yeah, but she's ready for a job change, too. I wouldn't mind staying, but right now, she's calling the shots."

"Maybe you should stay, let her move, and then commute home to Louisville every day."

What seems to make so much sense to me still eludes Jeff. Then again, maybe after all this time, I still don't understand his logic and situation.

"Here's the deal," I say as Jeff puts the key into the ignition. "You have a choice. Northern Lineage didn't give it to you, though. You have a life choice. You can proceed in this business world, which you yourself agree that you don't fit into. Or you can make the jump to the graphic design field and see if it's to your liking. Yeah, you have a long way to go, but the sooner you start, the better opportunity you'll have to get what you want out of it. If that means you have to move to California for a couple of years and go to school, go as quickly as you can. Waiting will only prolong uneasiness, and possibly unhappiness, if you are always wishing you had done it. And in the interim, there's TurtleWeb, and I'm almost certain they would consider you for a job."

Jeff stares at me as if he's not sure I'm finished.

"OK, fine," Jeff says. "I'll talk to Laura tonight. You're right; it can't hurt to change my mind. I'll keep you posted."

Jeff shuts the door, waves, sticks his tongue out at me, and finally leaves the premises. I walk over to my car, still a bit discontent with Jeff throwing away his potential to follow in line with the others to Northern Lineage. It's his life, though. It's like having a friend who is going to make a mistake, no matter how hard you try to warn him. And maybe this isn't a mistake. Maybe Northern Lineage will provide exactly what Jeff needs at this time. But why chance it when your heart is elsewhere?

**

My diatribe with Jeff makes me four minutes late to volley-ball. But the games are running behind, so our team has to wait another full match.

"Did you guys really date?" Barry says.

"What guys?" I say.

"You and Diya?"

"I'm not sure what you would call it."

"I thought there was something up between you two. You were always over in her cube."

"It doesn't really matter now, though ... I'm moving on, and she is as well."

"Was she upset when she found out you weren't going to Cincinnati?"

"She said all along that I wasn't going!"

"Well, I don't know if you know this or not, but she has a lot of baggage, so you're probably better off."

"Baggage? I know what happened before. I don't consider that much baggage."

"It's hard to find a woman these days without baggage."

"No doubt. People have all sorts of different experiences, and the older you get, the more you have."

"Yeah, that's the truth. I still think about my ex, but every time ... something just goes wrong."

"Like what?"

"Well, she has two kids, and they are cool, but they just don't listen to me."

"What did you say?"

"They don't listen to me."

"What, I didn't quite get that."

"They don't ... hey! That's not funny!"

"I thought it was."

"They are good kids for the most part. And I'm not their dad, so it is somewhat awkward. It's just an emotional strain sometimes."

"You just have to do what's best for everyone involved, and consider everyone's feelings ... hopefully you'll do the right thing."

"Yeah, I hope so."

"It's interesting that you have had the easiest time with the move, when the others are really burdened by it. But on the flip side, like you're saying, there's this relationship dilemma you have."

"The relocation situation was easy. I couldn't move and leave my mom here. And I have too many good friends here to give up. If I weren't in my 40s, I could see giving it a chance. But I already have enough going for me here. Besides, I don't have anything to lose ... Northern Lineage needs me a lot more than I need them."

The other volleyball match is over, which means it's our turn to play. Without possibly realizing it, Barry has summarized perfectly why he has won the moving battle. Then again, I guess it's not much of a war if you don't put up a fight.

Friday, September 30

Diya calls me from her work phone.

"Hello, Jason? Are you busy?"

"I wouldn't say that I'm busy. I'm having some work done on my car. Why, what's up?"

"Oh nothing really. I just missed you, so I wanted to say hi."

"Missed me? I've missed only one day of work, and I'll be there later today!"

"Yes, I know this, but I went over to your desk today to speak with you, and you weren't there. Mac Almanak is using your computer, and it just made me wonder what you were doing, and it made me sad."

"I will be in the office in a few hours, so I'll come over to your cube and talk, OK?"

"That is great. Actually, I have to go to a meeting now, so I'd better run. Talk to you later, sweetie."

I'm not sure if the pet name is supposed to make me feel better, but it doesn't. I do miss her in a certain way, but I also know that the feeling will fade quickly. It's a moment like this that really makes you wonder how you are supposed to react to other individuals who make requests of you. If someone says "jump," do you jump? If you like the person, and you don't do it, will that be detrimental to your relationship? If you are compliant, does that make you a pushover? And if you disobey, will you be thrown into an abyss to be tormented by demons for all eternity?

The only way not to be damned is to just not think about it.

Yesterday afternoon, Diya apologized to me for not introducing her parents. It didn't surprise me that Reshmi mentioned this to her. Diya really didn't have an excuse; she said that it just never came up. The reason seemed strange, but I'm past the point of analytically thinking about our relationship, so I shrugged and told her that it was OK.

Then last night, Diya called me at home to again say that she was sorry for not bringing me over to meet her parents. I again assured her that it is no longer a big deal.

"But if it wasn't a big deal, then why did you talk to Reshmi about it?" Diya said.

"I thought it was a cultural issue," I said.

"No, that's not it at all. I just never really thought about it, and there never seemed to be a good time."

"But I met you right across the street from your complex, and your parents were at your apartment!"

"Jason, I see your point, and all that I can say is that I'm sorry."

"I accept your apology, and it's OK. Our relationship changed over time, for whatever reason, and I understand that's how it is. I'm not going to be mad at you or disappointed because of what happened."

"OK."

"Are you mad?"

She didn't say anything, so I attempted to rephrase the question.

"Is everything all right?"

"I guess so, Jason. It just makes me sad to hear you talking like this."

"Talking like what?"

"You know, just talking about our friendship."

"We are still friends, right? I want to be your friend."

"I want to be yours as well. All right, I must get some rest. Goodbye."

After leaving the car dealership, I run home and take care of a few things before heading to Mettle. I return to the seventh floor, and already, everyone looks different. Part of that, however, is due to the weather. A cold front hit Louisville last night, so everyone is wearing long-sleeved shirts and sweaters. In Cincy, they'd probably have to pull out the worsted wool gabardine pants and cotton ties to stay warm.

I walk around unnoticed for a bit until I pop into Diya's cube. She doesn't realize I'm there until I tap her on the shoulder. She smiles and we chat briefly. She is going to the happy hour tonight, which is shocking, considering she usually passes on after-hour functions. I maneuver to my workspace, where Mac the Almanak is reviewing code. Then I hear a voice behind me.

"Well, well, couldn't stay away long, could you?" Barry says.

"I had to come back for the happy hour, right?" I say. "I mean, it's in my honor."

"Right ... and the other 10 people leaving this week, too." says Jeff, stepping outside his cubicle.

Around 4:30, the majority of the seventh floor heads down

to Fourth Street Live for the group outing. Rumor has it that free food will be available, and that's a good enough reason to get there early.

Jeff, Barry, Ken, Diya, and I walk through the entranceway as the maître d' points us to the back of the bar. We stroll back to find a dimly lit buffet area, where Tom Nelson is already making the rounds. The five of us follow in line and fill our plates with wings, chips, and vegetables. Jeff and I find a four-person table near the backstage, and while Barry disappears to converse with other attendees, Ken and Diya join us.

"So Diya, what made you decide to come to this happy hour?" Ken says. "I don't remember ever seeing you at one of these."

"Since it is Jason's last day, and since so many other people are leaving, I thought it would be good to come out," Diya says. "But I can't stay too long, as I need to finish my home-work still."

We devour our food and order drinks from the waitress, who is a cute brunette with tight-fitting black pants that make her impossible to ignore. I watch her leave our table the first time, then Jeff and Ken notice her at the table next to us. Even Diya seems to be unable to take her eyes off the girl.

"Are you looking at our waitress?" Ken says.

"Yes, she is pretty," Diya says.

"It looks to me like you are staring at her," I say.

"I'm just trying to figure out how she got into those pants," Diya says. "She is an attractive girl."

"Yessshh, there are a lot of hot bodies in these parts, lass," Jeff says in a perfect Connery imitation.

The room starts to fill quite nicely, with both Mettle employees and other typical bar attendees. Then the real action begins: dueling pianists. The men tap out a host of Top 40 hits on the ivories.

Before long, Diya motions that she's leaving. Ken also plans to depart, so Jeff and I walk them back to the parking garage and wish them a good evening.

On the return trip, I decide it's time to explain my relationship with Diya (at least, to the best of my knowledge) to Jeff. It's a six-block walk, so I cover the majority of the details.

"So what happened?" Jeff says. "I mean, if she's going out with someone else now, then why did you guys stop talking?"

"That's a good question," I say. "I'd put most of the problems on cultural differences, but I wanted to give it a shot. Or maybe that wasn't it. Anyway, it doesn't matter now."

"Do you think it would have been different if you had moved to Cincinnati?"

"Eh ... I don't think so. We may have been together longer, but who really knows. I guess it's good to get something over with sooner than wasting more time."

"That's a shame ... Diya is a really cool girl, smart and hot as well."

"Yep ... but what can you do?"

We return to the bar and the dueling piano players. The room is packed now, so we stand closer to the bar area and have another drink. I attempt to talk to Nelson, but I can't understand what he's saying because the acoustics in the room apparently bounce every miniscule noise off the ceiling. After 30 to 40 minutes, Jeff and I decide to leave and grab something to eat.

As we reach the parking garage, Jeff selects Taco Bell. We head over to the drive-through, and because we can't find a suitable place to eat in the parking lot, we return to Mettle's seventh-floor break room. Inside, we feast on tacos and burritos, and for dessert, we pull out the tub of ice cream still in the refrigerator from Chris's baby shower.

"Is anyone else eating this ice cream besides us?" I say. "Not that I care that much. It's like we're stuck in an episode of *The Golden Girls*."

"As long as there is ice cream to be eaten, it shall be eaten!" Jeff says.

"I guess I won't be eating anymore, since today was my last day. How is Ken holding up? He didn't seem to be his usual giddy self at the happy hour."

"He's really struggling now, I think. Maybe it's a midlife crisis. He decided against the karaoke thing … I guess he told you about that. He just doesn't have a good handle on anything right now."

"I can definitely understand that, with a family and all."

"Not only that, but his housing situation is crazy because he has a pretty expensive house here. He can't really sink more money into one up there. Looks like he'll be hanging out with me and Laura until he can move his crew up there."

"But what if you don't move? There's always a shot."

"He can live at the Northern Lineage housing. But the chances of that happening are about as good as us finding the hole in the wall in the bathroom."

"The hole in the wall?"

"Yeah, there's a hole in the maintenance closet where you can see into the girls' bathroom."

"Are you serious?"

"Of course I am!"

"We should go find it!"

Jeff shrugs, and we enter the men's restroom. For whatever reason, the closet is actually open, so we continue. On the left, there's a metal shelf with metal pipes, toilet bowl cleaner, and a few other paper supplies. The corridor goes a few feet forward and then veers right, presumably between the two restrooms. We walk along the passageway and look for any sort of crack in the cement-covered walls. After a few minutes of not finding anything, we retreat from the restroom and head back down the elevator.

"Who told you about this hole anyway?" I say.

"I don't even remember," Jeff says. "I thought I had seen it before, honestly! Maybe the lights have to be on in the other restroom for you to be able to see."

"It sounds to me as if you are trying to pull a Northern Lineage scam. You know, 'We have this great fitness center, but hold on, it's open only 13 minutes a day.' Or 'Our cafeteria is the finest in the city of Cincinnati ... and since we feed you, you can stay at work longer.' It's amazing how niceties can turn into control so easily."

"I'm not trying to control anything! I just wanted to see if the rumor about the girls' bathroom was true."

"That's a likely excuse."

27
Last Chance

Monday, October 3

Today is Jeff's birthday. I'm celebrating by starting a new job.

Well, that is, if I ever arrive at TurtleWeb. Little did I know that driving through the traffic in Louisville's east end would be like the grain of sand at the apex of an hourglass, attempting to make it to the bottom before the others.

I arrive wearing typical Mettle attire — a light-blue striped polo, navy blue pants, and dress shoes. I'm a tad overdressed. Nearly everyone is wearing jeans, including Vic, my new boss.

"There's your desk," Vic says. "If you need software, talk to Earl; he's the IT guy. Just download whatever you need. I have a meeting right now, but I can help you set up if necessary."

I've left the cubicle world for the shared workspace world, with the only separators being thin black boards attached to the back of most desks. Bright fluorescent lights have been replaced with dim "mood" lighting. The walls are forest green, a stark contrast from the bright white at Mettle's offices. I'm still nowhere near a window, which means I can't determine the weather or jump out.

Everyone here is asleep, busy, or exceedingly introverted because no one says anything as I start to configure my machine. I have the startup disks, but something doesn't load correctly. I don't know who Earl is, but before I have a chance to ask, the guy next to me yells, "Hey Earl, come over here."

From behind the glass door directly ahead of me steps Earl. He's the guy I saw during my interviews who was wearing shorts, and he is wearing them again today. Strangely enough, he's also wearing a collarless shirt that I'm pretty certain I have at home in my closet.

"What's up, Teddy?" Earl says to the guy next to me.

"Have you had a chance to look at this?" Teddy says. "I'm still getting an error."

"Not yet ... I have some high-priority stuff to do."

"That's what you said last time I asked about it!"

"I'll get to it, sometime today. Don't worry about it."

"You said that last time, too."

"Take it easy, Teddy, there's plenty to do!"

Earl retreats, and I stop him to introduce myself and ask about the operating system disks. He runs into his office and hands me a folder containing a gargantuan number of CDs.

"I'll help you look later, but I have to run to a meeting now," he says.

I thumb through the binder again, and I still don't see the correct disk.

"Hey," I say to the guy that Earl called Teddy. "Do you have any idea where an operating system disk would be?"

"Do you have the binder?" he says.

"Yeah, but it's not in here. By the way, my name is Jason."

"I'm Ted. It's pretty informal around here."

"I've noticed. I've also noticed that it seems like it's every man for himself."

"Yep, you have that right. OK, so that disk ... it could be in Earl's office."

I follow Ted into Earl's office. He rummages around his desk and in his drawers. Finally, he holds up a CD as if it were the winning lottery ticket.

"This should be what you need," Ted says. "Why Earl has it in his top drawer is beyond me. I have to wait for Earl to get anything done today, so I think I'll play a game of pool. Do you want to play?"

"I don't think so right now ... I should at least get some stuff installed on my machine."

Ted heads to the front of the office, and I retreat back to my desk. I would really hate to get fired on my first day for playing pool; at least at Mettle, I had eight days before my job became endangered.

Fortunately, Ted selected the correct disk. Now I'm supposed to register the operating system. I call Microsoft and give the access key to the operator twice, but there seems to be an issue. I explain that I have no clue whether or not the access key is in use. The answer doesn't sit well with the Microsoft guy, so I hang up the phone. I had hoped that Clippy, the paper clip "helper" in Microsoft Office, would assist me with the registration, because as you know, paper clips are much more understanding than humans, especially when it comes to computers.

Instead, I download other programs I will need for work. I also send Jeff a quick birthday message. And then there's an email from Diya.

How does it feel so far ? Do u like it ... Do u miss us ;-) I wished Jeff a happy birthday gave him the cake. I have been busy with some stuff at work. Day by day, things look more frustrating for me. Eventually perhaps, I will be like one of them ...

Diya's still stressed, but I have my own problems here. Getting acclimated to a new job can be interesting, but it's rarely exhilarating. At least in the computer world, it usually involves securing a number of usernames and passwords, as well as determining the locations of both website and working files.

In the afternoon, Alex, the vice president, hands me a manila folder full of papers for a recent project.

"We need to make some changes to this website," Alex says. "We've gone back and forth a bunch of times because the client really didn't know what she was doing. If you can take a look, maybe we can meet about this tomorrow and get the changes out the door."

"Sure, no problem," I say. "I've worked on e-commerce sites like this before, so hopefully I'll be able to make the appropriate changes."

After Alex leaves, I flip through the literature, most of which shows individual product pages that have been printed to show corrections. This won't be glamorous, but it will give me something to do. Everyone here still appears to be concentrating on doing anything but talking to the person next to him or her. Occasionally, Ted will say something to the man who sits behind me. I deduce he's the project manager, especially because he's constantly on the phone. There are seven of us who sit in a semicircle, which reminds me of an orchestra pit. I can't tell if I'm first seat French horn or flute, but with the banging being produced on the keyboards, we must be playing staccato.

As the day closes, no one leaves early; a few start to trickle out at 5, and I take off a few minutes thereafter. I again find myself in traffic. While I wait to move 15 yards to the next light, I realize that Jeff never responded to my email. I'll need to check with Vic first thing tomorrow if there's even a shred of hope Jeff will be joining TurtleWeb.

Wednesday, October 5

"How about a quick game of pool?" Ted says.

"Sure, why not?" I say.

It's midday on my third day, and I accept the fact that I'm now entitled to a game of pool. A match of eight ball is generally healthier than a smoke break.

"So what exactly do you do here?" I say, wondering why Ted not only wears a gray hooded sweatshirt nearly all the time but also always keeps his hood up.

"It depends on the day, honestly," Ted says. "I'm labeled as the maintenance guy, so I do handle a lot of the customer requests. And I also email and call some of the customers, depending on what they need done. I sort of fill in the gaps, but I do other programming, too."

"What about the other people in the office? I never really met any of them."

"Oh ... maybe Vic was going to take you around, but he was too busy. There's a project manager, another programmer, and three designers over here. The sales staff is on the other side of the wall. Did they tell you about the Coke machine?"

Ted leads me to the back of the office, near the sales staff area. We walk into a kitchen area.

"You can get a drink for 25 cents," Ted says. "Also, in the cabinets, there are some snacks and paper plates, bowls, napkins, stuff like that. And we have an old-fashioned popcorn machine, so we make popcorn sometimes. And of course, there's a refrigerator and a microwave."

The tour ends abruptly when Earl enters.

"Hey Teddy!" Earl says. "I finally have time to work on the stuff you need. What was it again?"

"I'll show you," says Ted as he heads back to his desk.

I return to my desk and email Jeff to see if Vic can meet him this week. Jeff sent his résumé to me yesterday, but I haven't seen Vic today. Someone mentioned that he might not return the rest of the week due to a family emergency. I send the résumé to Alex to see if he would like to interview Jeff instead. Just after lunch, Alex writes and recommends setting up lunch with Jeff later in the week.

I have begun interacting with my coworkers a bit more now, although it's not nearly as much talking as I did at Mettle. I feel rather homesick for a place I "lived" for barely more than three months. I hesitate to think that maybe I should have stayed there, at least a little while longer.

But before I get too nostalgic, I remember another aspect of the Northern Lineage work environment: the dress code. I could have relocated, and every time I went to work, I could

BEN WOODS

BEN WOODS

have pretended that we were in the middle of a big Halloween bash, where everyone was required to dress like a businessperson from the '50s. I could have fooled myself for roughly three weeks, or until the cafeteria ran out of candy corns.

Thursday, October 6

My time is running short with Jeff. If he doesn't act soon on the TurtleWeb position, it will be gone. Vic is still not here, and I am going to New Jersey to visit Sarina tomorrow. Alex wants to meet with Jeff about the developer position. I arrange to have lunch with Jeff at our favorite Thai restaurant, which is around the corner from my new office. Assuming Jeff is interested, I can bring him back to work for pool, popcorn, and a drop-in with Alex.

Jeff arrives just minutes after I enter the restaurant. We are seated in a booth, and I hand him a piece of paper that contains the job description. He studiously scans the paper.

"Damn, dude," Jeff says. "I'm really interested in this."

"That's a good thing, right?" I say.

"I don't know if I'd call it good, only because the chances of me taking this job are slim."

"I thought you were going to talk to Laura about moving?"

"I did, and she's behind me, whatever I decide."

"So ... what's the problem then?"

"It's just that I have already committed, and I don't think I can just change my mind."

"You can change your mind whenever! You just lose the bonus, but other than that ... "

"I could change my mind, true. But I think I should stick with it and see what happens."

"But you're not even planning on being at Northern Lineage long. So why bother moving?"

"I have no idea anymore," Jeff shrugs. "Maybe it is a ridiculous thing to do."

We eat and discuss the week's Mettle events. Everything

seems to be going as planned. The one item of note is that Project Giza is dedicating a day next week for everyone to review documents for the purpose of "record retention." This will be a time when everyone can take file folders and dump out their contents in the middle of the floor. Then, while wearing special snorkel gear that allows you to breathe while submersed in paper, contestants can swim through a pulp-like Caspian Sea, searching for important tax documents, missing invoices, TPS reports, and Al Capone's very own midyear evaluation.

"So training is going OK?" I say.

"As well as it can be," Jeff says. "I'm not sure how much of it Mindy understands, because I can barely follow what Barry is saying! At least she's taking notes so I won't have to document everything."

"Do you think she'll be a good boss?"

"I think she'll be all right. She seems to be on good terms with most of the people at Northern Lineage who can actually get something accomplished. It's all about who you know there."

"Maybe once you get up there, they'll put you in charge of something ... maybe even the cafeteria!"

"I hope they leave us alone for the most part, but I bet in no time they'll be trying to tell us to do everything their way, even if ours is better."

"Well, at least you have something to look forward to."

Jeff has no intention on meeting Alex today. However, I at least convince him to call Alex in the afternoon to find out more about the job. It can't hurt to at least hear Alex out, right?

Tuesday, October 11

The weekend trip to visit Sarina in New Jersey was smashing. It was a pleasant change not to have to worry about work — both current and past — for a couple of days. From what I can tell, Sarina had a good time as well. My next plan is to convince her to visit in the near future.

But before I get ahead of myself, I need to conjure all of my skills of persuasion and use them on Jeff. I just talked to Vic, and he wants interview Jeff. Alex had mentioned that he spoke with Jeff on Thursday afternoon, and the conversation went well. From my desk, I buzz Jeff on his cellphone.

"What? You made an offer on a house, and it has been accepted already?" I say.

"Our move date is November 14 ... it's pretty soon," Jeff says. "I guess I'm sort of locked in now."

"Are you crazy?"

"That's one way to put it," he says, laughing.

"OK, man. I guess there's nothing I can do now. Boy, you had better watch out, or you'll end up in quite a messhhhh."

"I've been in one messsshhh after another all my life ... I can't seem to escape!"

Why I wasted my time trying to persuade that boy not to trek to Cincinnati is beyond me. But I've been conditioned to expect this response from Jeff for a while now. Before I can dwell on it any longer, I receive an IM from Ted.

Ted: Did I hear you imitating Sean Connery over there?
Me: Yesshhh, of coursehhhh you did lad.
Ted: Well that is truly remarkable, if I may say so. I used to trade imitations with the guy you replaced. That was but a wee time ago.

At least the Sean Connery spirit will continue to live.

Thursday, October 13

The shopping cart project is taking nearly all of my time, but luckily, I'm almost finished with it. I'm supposed to have a meeting about a larger project sometime this week. Nevertheless, I'm figuring out who's in charge of certain things, and everyone has been accommodating.

During lunch, I read an email from Ken.

```
Hi,
I had lunch with Nitya today, and we thought it
might be a good idea if we all got together one
evening this month since there are so many birth-
days in October. We also thought it was a good idea
that we give any males over 40 an extra-special
birthday present ... Ok, we didn't think that was a
good idea ... I  did. Anyway, dinner always sounds
good. How about doing something fun afterwards? It
doesn't have to be bowling. Maybe pool or even bad-
minton (Diya). How about binge drinking and then
pedicures? I've always wanted to get a tattoo.
Somebody think of something ... please!

Ken
```

Last month, it would have been easy to organize a simple gathering for the group. But now, with a third of the people at other jobs, and another third not continuing to Cincinnati, things are a little more complicated to plan. It's like college, when you can just knock on as many doors as you would like down the hall and create a large gathering in the cafeteria. Then, when you move off campus, it's not quite as easy to do, but with a little scheduling, you can still manage to gather the same group. But when school ends, you basically have no hope of ever convening with the exact same audience, unless it's a wedding, a funeral, or some other astronomical event.

Mettle school isn't over, but during exam week, there's not a universal dinnertime.

Meanwhile, Diya has responded to my recent email. She mentioned that she goes to school in the building right next to TurtleWeb, so I've been trying to arrange a meeting with her in the evening. I haven't seen her this month, which seems odd. But she has what I assume is a boyfriend, who lives in Boston, and I'm spending quite a bit of time talking to Sarina in New Jersey. Diya and I are being held together only by proximity.

Today is a school day for her, so I wait outside her school building. It's just after 4:30 when I see the blue TrailBlazer.

"Hi Jason!" says Diya as she grabs her schoolbags. "It's so

good to see you!"

"Can you believe it has already been two-and-a-half weeks since I left?" I say.

"Yes, it seems like it has been longer. I miss you at Mettle."

"I miss being there a little ... but I like my new job."

"I'd better go to class, but I really appreciate you meeting with me. I miss talking to you at work. I feel so isolated there."

She leaves, and I walk back to TurtleWeb. I guess it's nice to hear that she hasn't completely forgotten me.

Thursday, October 20

Today is Ken's and Reshmi's birthday. It's rather sad that I know the birthdays of my former coworkers, but even though I've been at TurtleWeb for three weeks now, I barely know their names.

I email Ken about whether or not he's decided to relocate. He responds that he's still planning to move. However, he's still looking in Louisville. Additionally, his house up there won't be completed until the end of December, and his relocation date, like Jeff's and Debbie's, has been moved to November 14. He's going to investigate the temporary housing available, but I bet he'll end up staying at Jeff and Laura's place.

As a continual mind-changer, Ken doesn't want to go, but he seems in better shape now. I thought he might consider jumping out the window and hoping for the best. Out of the entire group, he probably began the job hunt before anyone else. And he's still furiously working on it ... and might be for quite some time into the foreseeable future.

Better news appears in an email from Barry later. Excelsior Computing offered him a job, and he accepted. The best part is that he will be able to finish his time at Mettle, so he'll get the full separation bonus. His job search was by far the smoothest, even after hiccups with a few early interviews.

I don't really feel as if I'm part of the Mettle team anymore. If anything, it's more like watching a TV soap opera, in which most of the main characters stay, but others get killed due to contract disputes. Thankfully, I've been spared any story lines dealing with love polygons and/or the occasional whoops-I-killed-my-long-lost-brother-because-he-was-sleeping-with-my-cousin-and-mistress plot.

It's sad, in a way, because being a part of group of intelligent and witty individuals was just as fulfilling as the work itself. Hell, who am I kidding? That was the best part. The same thing may happen here at TurtleWeb someday, but the atmosphere is different, for whatever reason. It's not just about the workplace environment; it's about the people who surround you that make your job enjoyable or unbearable.

When you say, "I hate my job," do you hate it because of the actual work you do, or do you wish you could replace your coworkers with the leading name brand of cubicle buddy? There's no doubt that it can be some of both, and there are many other variables involved in your enjoyment of work. But if you work with people, and you don't get along with those people, how can you enjoy your job?

Oh, OK, I see. You're a prison guard. Or wait, a professional wrestler? All right, I'll retract my statement for you and a handful of other professions in which it pays to be rude to the people you meet. I'm not sure I'll count the cafeteria lady, though. Especially if she works at Northern Lineage.

Saturday, October 22

Jeff and I are having a guys' night out: a rock concert at a local bar. Yeah, it sounds kind of lame.

The venue provides little space, the ceilings are low, and the amount of air available in the room is apparently being sold on eBay as we listen. We root ourselves in the doorway, giving us equal access to the music, the bar, and of course, the air.

"Back when I was in college, I would have been in the mosh pit out there!" says Jeff, pointing to the kids close to the stage.

"Go for it!" I say.

The band plays its second set. We hang out near the back and enjoy the rest of the concert. As we leave, I have one more request of Jeff.

"Is there any ice cream left?" I say.

"Ice cream?" Jeff says. "Where?"

"At Mettle ... you know, that big tub of ice cream?"

"Possibly. I doubt anyone else is eating any of it."

"Let's check!"

"Are you crazy? We can't go to the office right now. It's 12:30 in the morning!"

"That's an even better reason to go. No one will be there. Come on, we're only a couple of miles away."

"I don't know why you want to go ... but all right."

I still don't understand how I can convince Jeff of some things, like going into work and eating ice cream in the middle of the night, but I can't convince him to find a different job.

We make it to the break room, and sure enough, the ice cream is still there. We fill our bowls and chow down, yet again, on the never-ending ice cream tub.

"Looks like we're almost out of ice cream," I say. "Is someone else having a baby shower soon, so there would be a reason to buy more?"

"I don't think so," Jeff says. "I think this is it. We have only three weeks here anyway."

"Maybe for you, but other people are still going to be here ... Diya isn't leaving until February."

After our snack, we walk into the office area. My work area looks exactly the same, even though Mac the Almanak is working there now. Actually, everything in the office looks pretty much the same since I left.

"Has anyone been working the last few weeks?" I say.

"Hell no!" Jeff says. "Most people are still looking for jobs or surfing the Internet. Of course, I'm still on Annuity Profit Plus. Diya is swamped with all of Nitya's and Don's work."

Diya's cubicle is still fairly messy, although it's not as bad as I've seen it before. I write a little note and place it on her keyboard.

"Do you still talk to her?" Jeff says.

"Occasionally, but mostly via email," I say. "She misses me and says she can't really talk to anyone else."

"That's weird! I thought she was just reclusive and didn't want to talk to people."

"Then why would she want to talk to me?"

"I suppose because she likes you? Do you miss her?"

"Of course ... and I work with all guys now, too."

"Maybe you should talk to her again ... about everything."

"No, it's over, man. I just don't think she wants to be with someone who is not Indian."

"What if she does but doesn't know it?"

"Then she shouldn't have turned her back on me."

"What if she was just scared?"

"If she came to me, I would definitely talk to her about it. Otherwise, there's nothing more to say."

"Nothing more to say? You just left her a love note on her keyboard!"

"Just a friendly note, not a love note."

"OK, then you should leave one on my keyboard, too ... and Ken's and everyone else's who is your friend."

Jeff laughs, and we decide it's time to go. As we drive away separately, I realize that I have no idea when I'll see Jeff again. He'll be moving in three weeks, and before that time, we may not get together. And who knows why he made the comments about Diya? But then again, why did I write that note? I feel sorry about her predicament ... but is that the only reason? Because she's being jerked around by the corporation and the government, in some respects, at the same time? Would I feel the same way about a person who had the same issues but to whom I wasn't both physically and mentally attracted?

Maybe Jeff is on to something. However, the best thing

for me to do, especially at 2 a.m., is to go home and not think another moment about it.

Monday, October 24

OK, so I'm still thinking about it, at least a little. Then I read Diya's morning email.

I want to share good news with you. I got engaged on Saturday :-) It was just a family event and he was here with his parents. He proposed to me. I don't have a ring yet as the ring he ordered is custom designed. But he did bring a temporary one.

How is everything going with u ?

Wow ... she's engaged! At first, I'm speechless, but I have to tell someone. Ted is at his desk, so I get his attention.

"I was dating this girl a month or two ago, and I just found out she is now engaged!" I say.

"Crazy!" Ted says. "When did she meet this guy?"

"I don't know ... maybe a month or so ago."

"Damn, dude ... that's insane. What are you going to do?"

"I'm happy for her because we weren't going to work out."

"That sucks, man."

"No, it's no problem at all. I'm dating a girl now. Really, I'm not that disappointed, amazingly enough."

And just like that, I feel as if a yoke has been removed, and I no longer need to concern myself with why I'm not with Diya. Maybe I'd be disappointed if I didn't like Sarina, but I'm not certain that's it. Sometimes, even when two people care about each other, and two people like each other, and two people think there's something there ... well, sometimes it's more complicated than that.

I re-rank all of the things I like. Ice cream and frozen yogurt have moved back ahead of Diya.

28
Parting Ways

Friday, December 16

Tonight will probably not be the final Mettle happy hour. Regardless, it will be recognized as the end of the Louisville chapter of the company. True, there are still a handful of people working here, but the total is now in single digits. The remaining souls will probably be tasked with turning off the lights, breaking down the movie sets, and burying any computer equipment left behind, to be unearthed years from now as genuine relics from the Partial Information Age.

There's a caravan of people coming from Cincinnati, including Jeff and Ken, who are carpooling. Barry wouldn't miss a party, and neither would Tom Nelson and his band of volleyball-playin' fools.

As I enter the bar, the first person I see is Barry, whom I haven't seen since our volleyball league ended last month.

"Jason Harris is here!" Barry says to the crowd, who is ignoring him.

"Hey buddy," I say. "How's it going?"

"Great! This is what I wear to work on Fridays!"

He gestures toward his apparel and bows, showing off blue jeans and flannel shirt.

"Awesome, man!" I say. "I wear that every day."

"Perfect!" Barry says. "Better than those rejects wearing ties in Cincy. How's the job?"

"It's pretty good. Some things seem a little disorganized,

but I think that comes with the territory. We are adding new people fairly rapidly. What about you?"

"The job is fine, for now. Remember that idea I had with building cornhole boards?"

I roll my eyes.

"Yeah, I remember."

"I've been working on it every night and on the weekends. I found a few enthusiasts online, and we're setting up CornholeWorld.com! The site isn't even live yet, and we have orders streaming in. I hired a kid with a funny-looking hat and a beard to start building immediately. I might have to quit my job to handle all of it!"

"You have to be kidding … "

"I knew you wouldn't believe me, newbie, but believe it!"

"How am I a newbie? We don't even work for the same company … "

Barry is too busy laughing and drinking to hear my question. I scan the room to find others I know. There are a few familiar faces, but I still don't know the names of many. Fortunately, I peer over Barry's shoulder and see Vance throwing back a chilled beverage.

"Hey Vance!" I say. "Did you find a way off the bus yet?"

"Not quite," he says. "But I'm excruciatingly close. I had an interview at Waveland Healthcare two weeks ago, and they're supposed to let me know something next week. If not, I'll be investigating the free room and board at Northern Lineage. I feel pretty good about the job opportunity, though."

"How's Annuity Profit Plus?"

"It's the same as always … nothing new to report. Oh, before I forget, you'll have to stick around for the 'Northern Lineage Blues.' I'll be performing it later this evening."

Vance turns to talk to someone else, and I notice Jeff and Ken entering the bar.

"It's about time you guys got here!" Barry shouts as he strolls to the front. "You didn't even have time to change?"

Both are still wearing their dress clothes, and Ken is still wearing his tie.

"And hello to you, too!" Jeff says.

"Come on, guys; I have a booth over there," Barry says.

We squeeze into the seats that are occupied by a few Mettle employees and castoffs already. Barry goes to the bar to grab drinks for everyone.

"How was the trip?" I say.

"Fine, I suppose," Ken says. "As you can tell, we left right after work."

"But there was no way in hell I was going to wear my tie to the bar," Jeff says.

"And just think ... if you worked elsewhere, you wouldn't ever have to wear a tie!" I say sarcastically.

Jeff and Ken are silent.

"Well, I actually have some news," Jeff says.

"You're going into the cornholing business with Barry?" I say. "The gnomes need your help!"

"I do need someone to sew bags," says Barry as he returns with drinks.

"Thanks, but I'm not touching your bags!" Jeff says. "I was talking to Alex Garrison at TurtleWeb yesterday. I think he's going to offer me an R&D position."

"Whoa!" I say. "Thanks for keeping it a secret from me. But what about the contract on the house in Cincinnati?"

"There might be a way out," Jeff says. "If not, Ken might be buying the house instead of staying there temporarily."

"Let the insanity end!" Ken says.

"So ... how is work?" Barry says.

"Mindy is really trying to take over," Ken says. "We're always fighting about what I should be doing because I'm technically on the wrong team. I try to help the others on the team, but they'll take credit for anything great I do and blame me for anything they do wrong."

"So, there are lying sacks of shit on the team!" I say. "I

guess they kept us away from them until we were trapped."

"With the house stuff here in town and my family, I don't know what I should do," Ken says.

"Have you guys received your bonus money?" Barry says.

"Hell no!" Ken says. "We have to wait until March."

"And I won't get any bonus if I jump off the bus now. Oh Barry, before I forget, Mindy mentioned something about you doing contract work. We're short-handed again because Mac the Almanak left this week to join a trapeze troupe with the Cincinnati circus. I suppose they underestimated your expertise in the systems, because I have no clue about some of them!"

"Contract work? Sure thing!" Barry says as he raises his glass to toast himself. "I'll be pretty busy with Excelsior and the cornhole gig, but why not! I told you guys, they need me!"

Before Barry's ego trip continues, we deviate from the Northern Lineage talk by greeting other friends and discussing our normal topics of food, politics, and girls.

"Has anyone talked to Diya lately?" Barry says.

"Just on email," Ken says. "She's not coming tonight because she's in Boston. Everyone knows she's engaged, right?"

Jeff and I nod, but Barry looks stunned.

"Engaged?" Barry says. "To whom?"

"Some guy in Boston," Ken says.

"Interesting," Barry says. "So Jason, I guess you'll never be able to put the moves on her after all!"

Jeff and Ken chuckle.

"I guess not," I say.

Near the bar, I see Tom Nelson, so I hop out of the booth and head toward him.

"Still no luck finding anything in Louisville?" I say.

"No, not yet," Nelson says. "I have to start working in Cincinnati next week. I'm not too happy about that."

I return to the booth to find Vance in the middle of serenading the others with the "Northern Lineage Blues."

Got the news on Wednesday,
Mettle's leaving town.
My job's gone up the river.
My face it wears a frown.

I got the Western-Southern blues.
They're messing with my mind.
But they know how to party
Like it's nineteen fifty-nine.

We'll all be reunited.
We'll get that big bonus bye and bye.
When we're processing death claims
For that big company in the sky.

After the ditty and rousing applause, some of us head across the street to another bar. However, after paying cover, we realize that few Mettle people actually came along. We stand in a circle in the middle of the main room, and after about 30 minutes, an evacuated booth becomes home.

Unfortunately, it's a pretty dull environment, full of wannabe hipsters and girls with dressed as if they are auditioning for an early '90s music video. Besides, we are really hungry and don't want to pay bar prices for some eats.

The solution, of course, is White Castle. We drive a couple of miles to the nearest location. There, we feast on burgers, onion rings, and a variety of other tasty treats during the optimal time for a White Castle run: 1:30 a.m.

"This is good shit!" mumbles Jeff as he stuffs a good portion of a slider in his mouth.

"I really shouldn't be eating this," Ken says. "But it is definitely delicious."

"You need to blow off some steam, Ken," Barry says. "All the stress up in Cincy isn't good for you."

"Speaking of steam, you should check out the grill now," I

say. "I bet you can't get that in the Northern Lineage cafeteria."

Barry is the only one who laughs. Ken and Jeff are bummed out. I sympathize with them, but for different reasons. There were plenty of times Jeff could have said goodbye to Northern Lineage. He knowingly walked into a trap. In my mind, Jeff is certainly a born leader and can be a manager without a problem. The dilemma, though, is that if he wants to be in charge in Cincinnati, he'll be limited beyond the scope of his projects. Because the company is so large and moves at the speed of molasses, it takes a sizeable effort to accomplish anything, whether it's a text change on the website or inventing an edible business suit. TurtleWeb could be a way out, but the odds of everything working this late in the game seem insurmountable.

Ken, on the other hand, has to take whatever job is available. With a stay-at-home wife and two kids, and nothing concrete in the job hunt, there's no alternative. And that's not considering an imminent house fiasco. Ken is being smart about it and not moving his entire family up just yet. Also, he's still seeking employment in Louisville, and with the experience and contacts he has, surely something will materialize. But when?

So far, he has taken a beating from the relocation turmoil, probably more than anyone I know except Diya. It's easy to sit back and review the options of working at various companies. But ultimately, at least one of the companies has to choose you. And if there's only one, and it's your least favorite choice, and others depend on the goods you bring home, it's tough to avoid.

"So what's ahead for you guys?" says Barry as he finishes his cheese fries.

"Honestly, I really don't know," Ken says. "I guess I'll stick with it."

"Even if I have to stay, at worst it's two years of my life," Jeff says. "And I can work on my own stuff in the meantime."

"That is assuming you won't have to work a bunch of overtime," I say.

"There will probably be some overtime, but hopefully not

any more than what we had at Mettle," Jeff says.

"If that changes, I'll start using more company time to find new jobs," Ken says.

Northern Lineage might be able to take away some of the freedoms enjoyed in Louisville. But the company can't take away the bonds shared between coworkers, and former co-workers at that. As the old saying goes, misery loves company. I seriously doubt, though, that misery ever had to do computer programming while wearing a tie.

Wednesday, December 21

I run down the spiral staircase at TurtleWeb, zip up my jacket, and jet outside into the freezing cold. I sprint across the parking lot and scan the adjacent lot, but her vehicle isn't there. I consider looking in the back parking lot, because it's already 4:30 and Diya's class starts right now. As I turn, I see the blue TrailBlazer pull into the lot. I wave my arms and motion for Diya to pull into a vacant parking spot in the front row. She sees me and swerves past the two rows near the road.

"Hi Jason!" says Diya as she gathers her school material. "I'm so sorry I'm running late. I am not feeling too well, and I had to finish this paper, and ... "

"It's no big deal," I say. "I actually just got out here ... I ran over and thought I missed you!"

"No, you didn't. You are here ... and so am I."

I assume that because she's running late, she will move quickly toward the entrance. I start to head back to TurtleWeb, but Diya hasn't budged. I turn to face her.

"Well, congratulations on the engagement!" I say. "I want-ed to tell you in person, since I haven't seen you in so long."

"Thanks!" Diya says. "It has been awhile ... I guess since last time we met out here. How was the Mettle party?"

"It was great. There were a lot of people there. You should have been there."

"I know, I know. I wanted to go, but I went to visit my

fiancé in Boston. I got to meet his family and friends up there."

"So when is the wedding?"

"I'm not sure yet, but it probably won't be until the spring. We are planning to have a wedding celebration in Louisville. You will be there for it, right?"

"Sure."

"How is your girlfriend, Sarina?"

"She's fine. I'm going to visit her after Christmas."

"When are you getting married?"

"Well ... I don't think anytime soon."

I have nearly forgotten about the harsh wind smacking my face, and it seems that Diya has forgotten about her class, which has already started.

"So when do you move to Cincinnati?" I say.

"It's still February," Diya says. "And I'm still not looking forward to it. Things are worse and worse every day. I have to do everyone's work. It is pretty lonely there."

"I can imagine, especially since everyone is leaving. But now that you are getting married, you can leave, right?"

"Possibly. Maybe I'll move to Boston ... or even India. I'm sure we could find jobs there."

I think back to the time when Diya asked if I wanted to move to India with her.

"I don't want to keep you from your class," I say. "I should get a little more work done before I leave for the evening."

"OK, Jason. Thank you so much for meeting me. I wish we could see each other during the day and talk."

"At least we can still meet here. It's better than nothing."

Diya moves closer, and we embrace for a second.

"Keep in touch, all right?" Diya says.

"Sure, definitely," I say.

I walk briskly back to the next parking lot. As I make it to the separating lawn, I turn and see Diya at the front entrance to the school. She turns and waves to me. I wave back, smile, and return to my new life.

Footnotes

1. *I always thought dress-down days*: Mark Mark and The Van Heusen Creative Group, *Dress Casually for Success ... For Men* (McGraw-Hill, 1996), p. 6.*Of course, this isn't the normal everywhere*: Louis Uchitelle, *The Disposable American – Layoffs and their Consequences* (Knopf, 2006), p. 212.

2. *The history of the modern suit*: Wikipedia, the free encyclopedia, "History of suits," en.wikipedia.org/wiki/Suit_(history) (accessed Sept. 13, 2009).

3. *By the mid-1800s*: Ibid.

4. *Americans continued tradition*: Schorman, Rob, *Selling Style: Clothing and Social Change at the Turn of the Century* (University of Penn Press, 2003), p. 25.

5. *During this time period*: Ibid., p. 7.

6. *Studies have shown*: Human Resources Professional Information Center, "Is Business Casual Becoming a Casualty of Current Conservative Work Climate?" The Bureau of National Affairs, Inc., February 22, 2005, Vol. 56, No. 8.

7. *But wait! Other studies have shown*: *Business Wire*, "Productivity is in the 'Jeans'; Office Survey Reveals that Jeans and Sneakers are Hot While Ties and Pantyhose are Not, and Causal Attire is More Widespread," August 23, 2005.

8. *A pointless meeting was the top answer*: Microsoft Office Personal Productivity Challenge, "Survey Finds Workers Average Only Three Productive Days per Week," Microsoft, March 15, 2005.

9. *In other psychological research*: David R. Butcher, "Let's Have More Meetings!" ThomasNet News, March 14, 2006.

10. *He recommends owning 27 dress shirts*: John T. Malloy, *John T.*

Molloy's New Dress for Success (Grand Central Publishing, 1988), p. 90.

11. *One dressy solid white broadcloth*: Ibid.

12. *It's been a while since*: Wikipedia, the free encyclopedia, "Revolving door," en.wikipedia.org/wiki/Revolving_door (accessed March 29, 2010).

13. *Scholar Tim Hall originally equated*: Douglas T. Hall, *Careers in Organizations* (Goodyear, 1976), p. 200.

14. *Spencer Johnson, the author*: Spencer Johnson, *Who Moved My Cheese? An Amazing Way to Deal with Change in Your Work and in Your Life* (G.P. Putnam's Sons, 1998).

15. *People who do not exercise*: James S. Kouzes and Barry Z. Posner, *Credibility: How Leaders Gain and Lose It, Why People Demand It* (Jossey-Bass, 1995), p. 161.

16. The Opt-Out Revolt *explains how individuals work*: Lisa Mainiero and Sherry Sullivan, *The Opt-Out Revolt: Why People are Leaving Companies to Create Kaleidoscope Careers* (Intercultural Press, 2006), pp. 16-17.

17. *I prefer the term "ranking and spanking"*: The Economist, March 31, 2001, p. 57.

18. *The reason for moving*: Charles Derber, *Corporation Nation: How Corporations are Taking Over Our Lives – and What We Can Do About It* (St. Martin's Press, 1998), p. 222.

19. *As noted in* Credibility: James S. Kouzes and Barry Z. Posner, *Credibility: How Leaders Gain and Lose It, Why People Demand It* (Jossey-Bass, 1995), p. 108.

20. *Sharing information, as* Credibility *suggests*: Ibid, p. 172.

21. *From* The Opt-Out Revolt: Lisa Mainiero and Sherry Sullivan, *The Opt-Out Revolt: Why People are Leaving Companies to Create Kaleidoscope Careers* (Intercultural Press, 2006), p. 82.

22. *Elegant dress ... not only shows*: Thorstein Veblen, *The Theory of the Leisure Class* (The Macmillan Company, 1912), p. 170.

23. *Derber acknowledges that downsizing and even outsourcing*: Charles Derber, *Corporation Nation: How Corporations are Taking Over Our Lives – and What We Can Do About It* (St. Martin's Press, 1998), p. 111.

24. *One analyst dubs it "dumbsizing"*: Ibid.

25. Corporation Nation *mentions a 1996 national poll*: Ibid., p. 181.

Acknowledgments

I'd like to give a shout out to my two editors, Georgette Beatty and Patrick Coyle. Georgette is a college pal who can edit circles around anyone. Patrick is a random editor I found on Craigslist, and he helped sculpt various passages into words that actually make sense.

I also want to thank my compadres at Spumoni Press, Brad Samuelson and Sean O'Connor. Brad designed the cover and the chapter headers, while Sean assisted multiple times with artwork concepts and ideas.

None of the people above forced me to write this story while wearing a sportcoat and tie.

About the Author

Ben Woods is a freelance writer and computer programmer who was born in the Midwest but now lives on the East Coast. His first book, *The Developers*, is a tech-humor fiction novel about government conspiracy, online privacy, and crazy people on the Internet.

During the past two decades, he has held full-time writing and computer programming positions with companies large and small, collected a stack of employee manuals and health insurance cards, and worked with a litany of CEOs, PMPs, BBMs, and A-HOLEs.

Made in United States
North Haven, CT
28 December 2024

63551065R00183